Levi Parsons

History of Rochester Presbytery from the Earliest Settlement of the Country

Levi Parsons

History of Rochester Presbytery from the Earliest Settlement of the Country

ISBN/EAN: 9783337236410

Printed in Europe, USA, Canada, Australia, Japan

Cover: Foto ©ninafisch / pixelio.de

More available books at **www.hansebooks.com**

HISTORY

OF

ROCHESTER ✢ PRESBYTERY

FROM THE

EARLIEST SETTLEMENT OF THE
COUNTRY,

EMBRACING ORIGINAL RECORDS

OF

*ONTARIO ASSOCIATION, AND THE PRESBYTERIES OF
ONTARIO, ROCHESTER (FORMER), GENESEE
RIVER, AND ROCHESTER CITY,*

TO WHICH ARE APPENDED

BIOGRAPHICAL SKETCHES OF DECEASED MINISTERS
AND BRIEF HISTORIES OF INDIVIDUAL CHURCHES.

PUBLISHED BY PRESBYTERY.

DEMOCRAT-CHRONICLE PRESS, ROCHESTER, N. Y.
1889.

ERRATA.

Page 40, line 9: Reuben Nason was received December 23, 1834.

Page 245, line 6: for " George S. Sill," read George G. Sill

Page 246, line 4: for " Amelia," read Aurelia

Page 247, line 31: for " Morris'," read Moore's; line 35: for " Mann," read Brown

Page 250, line 20: for " Mowatt," read Morvatt; line 24: for " George M. Mackie," read George W. Mackie.

Page 251, line 27: for " George S. Sill," read George G. Sill.

Page 255, line 11: for " Manly S. Woodbury," read Manly G. Woodbury; line 29: for " W. G. Squires," read Urr G. Squires

Page 257, line 8: for " Priden," read Biden; line 16: for " John Still, Louisa Still," read John Stitt, Louisa Stitt.

Page 264, line 7: for " T. Coit," read John T. Coit; last line: for " Charles P. Smith," read Charles F. Smith.

History of Rochester Presbytery.

Compiled by Rev. Levi Parsons, D. D.

AS the present Presbytery of Rochester at the time of the reconstruction of the Presbyteries in 1870, was formed, with a few exceptions, by the union of the former Presbyteries of Ontario, Rochester and Rochester City, together with about half of the ministers and churches which had belonged to the Presbytery of Genesee River, its history will properly be introduced by sketches of the aforesaid bodies, together with certain facts pertaining to the early religious history of Western New York.

At the close of the Revolutionary War the settlement of Western New York was retarded by conflicting land claims of the states of Connecticut and Massachusetts, superadded to the original title to the soil by the Indians, which obstacles were not removed until about the year 1790. The county of Ontario was formed in 1789, at which time it included all that part of the state which was west of Seneca Lake. According to the United States census of 1790 the number of inhabitants in this county was 1,081 and the number of families 205, which numbers very rapidly increased during the subsequent decade and consisted mostly of people from New England, with no inconsiderable numbers from New Jersey, Pennsylvania and Europe.

Unlike their Puritan ancestors who had sought the shores of New England for the sake of religious liberty, these pioneers in the wilderness were influenced mainly by motives of gain, which resulted in increased negligence as to their former religious habits, and being thinly scattered over a vast area, the gathering of churches was, for a number of years, a very discouraging work for the few who loved the house of prayer and the fellowship of the gospel. Added to this prevailing worldliness, was the fact that not a few had imbibed the French infidelity which was so prevalent throughout the country during the closing years of the last century.

We can find no trace of any permanent church organization prior to 1795. There is evidence, however, that before this date the General Assembly had sent two or three missionaries who, as explorers, had visited the feeble settlements and preached from place to place, and that similar work had been done by missionaries from the Congregational churches of New England. There is also evidence that after this date, if not before, settled pastors in New England engaged in brief terms of itinerant missionary service upon this field.

The first Congregational minister who came as a permanent resident was Rev. Zadoc Hunn, in the year 1795. He removed from Berkshire county, Mass., and located upon a farm in Canandaigua. Though he had been a pastor in New England he never took a pastoral charge here, but was very useful among the feeble churches up to the time of his death, May 12th, 1801.

The Rev. Daniel Thatcher, a Presbyterian missionary sent out by the General Assembly, organized in 1795 the church at Lima and the First Church of Geneseo, now located at Lakeville, which were the first church organizations in this section.

In 1796 the Congregational churches of East Bloomfield

and South Bristol were organized, and, in 1799 those of West Bloomfield, North Bristol and Victor.

The first installation was that of Rev. John Rolph over the church of South Bristol by a council in January, 1797. The ministers composing the council were Rev. Zadoc Hunn, Rev. Eliphalet Steele of Paris, Oneida county, and Rev. Asahel S. Norton, of Clinton, Oneida county, and it is estimated that the journey of Dr. Norton and Mr. Steele must have required from three to four days in coming and the same length of time in returning, these being the nearest ministers available for the council.

In the year 1799 the churches were so greatly blessed that long afterward it was referred to as the year of the "Great Revival." Prominent among the laborers in promoting the same were Rev. Jedidiah Bushnell and Rev. Seth Williston, of the Missionary Society of Connecticut, and Rev. David Barclay and Rev. Robert Logan, missionaries of the General Assembly.

These references to Congregational ministers and churches in the early religious history of this section have a legitimate place in the history of this Presbytery because some of our strongest Presbyterian churches were originally Congregational.

For a similar reason a brief sketch of the Ontario Association will not be out of place, because of its ultimate union as will subsequently be seen with the Presbytery of Geneva when that Presbytery covered this ground.

ONTARIO ASSOCIATION.

The Ontario Association was the first organization of ministers and churches in Western New York, having been formed at Bristol, N. Y., March 18, 1800, as follows:

"We, ministers of the gospel, viz.—Zadoc Hunn, Joseph

Grover, John Rolph, Reuben Parmerlee and Timothy Field—being met, think proper to form ourselves into a voluntary society for promoting the interest of religion, and as we consider ourselves Congregationalists we agree to call ourselves and be known by the name of the First Association of Ontario County.

"Being met together for the purpose of forming into an association and having united in solemn prayer to God for wisdom, protection and assistance, we think fit in order to promote the interest of religion to come into the following friendly agreements, viz.:

"1. The association shall meet ordinarily twice in a year, and oftener if it appear needful, to consult and agree upon the most expedient measures to promote religion and give the churches opportunity to apply to us for advice and assistance, which it is proper for an association to afford them.

"2. We agree to invite each church to send a delegate to attend this association, and join with them in promoting the Redeemer's kingdom.

"3. As we design to proceed regularly in our meetings, and endeavor to promote religion, we agree that a moderator shall be chosen at each stated meeting and a clerk to minute the most material transactions, and that we will begin and conclude with prayer.

"4. We agree that this association shall never assume or claim any authority over the churches, or authoritatively intermeddle with the affairs of the churches any farther than they shall apply to us and request our advice, or other assistance.

"5. We agree that this association shall make no rules that shall be authoritative, and all agreements shall be alterable as circumstances shall require.

"6. We agree that the semi-annual meetings of the association shall be the second Tuesday in June, and the second Tuesday in January, and in rotation in the churches, and the association will meet the second Tuesday in June next at Mr. Rolph's, number eight.

"The association agree to recommend to the churches in Ontario County the second Thursday in April, to be observed as a day of public fasting and prayer, and that divine service to Almighty God be performed on that day. Concluded with prayer."

These are the records of the first meeting as found in the original book of the association, which has long been preserved in the archives of this Presbytery.

In addition to the five who constituted the association the Rev. Eleazar Fairbanks, Rev. James H. Hotchkin and Rev. Ahijah Warren were received prior to 1804. Subsequent additions were as follows: Rev. Solomon Allen, Rev. Aaron C. Collins and Rev. Ezekiel J. Chapman, Jan. 15, 1806; Rev. John Niles, by ordination, June 11, 1806; Rev. Howell R. Powell, June 10, 1807; Rev. Simeon R. Jones, June 14, 1810; Rev. Silas Hubbard, by ordination, Oct. 10, 1811; Rev. Allen Hollister, May 27, 1812.

The churches connected with the association prior to 1804 were South Bristol, Victor, West Bloomfield, North Bristol, Canandaigua, East Bloomfield, Lima, Rushville, Richmond and Naples.

Those subsequently received were as follows: Pittsford and Prattsburgh, June 10, 1806; Livonia, Jan. 13, 1807; Palmyra, June 14, 1807; Phelps, Williamson and Stonetown, June 13, 1809; Elmira, June 11, 1810; Geneseo 2d, Oct. 11, 1811; Bergen and Riga, May 27, 1812. Whole number of ministers, 16. Whole number of churches, 21.

The Rev. James H. Hotchkin, of Prattsburgh, whose name appears on the aforesaid roll, was subsequently the author of *The History of the Presbyterian Church in Western New York*, to which we are indebted for many important facts.

From the records it appears that on the 21st of April, 1813, the association inquired of the Presbytery of Geneva, both bodies at that time being in session at Honeoye, N. Y., upon what terms they could be received into said Presbytery; and the following answer was returned: "The members of Presbytery are of the opinion that our union with the ministers and churches of the Ontario Association is highly important, as it will combine their influence in promoting the great interests of the Redeemer's kingdom, and they cordially invite the said ministers and churches to unite with the Presbytery by adopting the Confession of Faith and Form of Government of the Presbyterian Church. But should any of the said churches find it most for edification to continue the practice of receiving and rejecting members by a vote of the brethren of the church generally, instead of a session of ruling elders, the Presbytery do not consider that any bar to the contemplated union, and are willing they should continue that practice as long as they shall deem it expedient."

As a result of this answer by the Presbytery, the association at an adjourned meeting held at Pultney, May 25, 1813, adopted the following preamble and resolutions which had been proposed by Mr. Hotchkin:

"WHEREAS, It appears, from the Holy Scriptures, of immense importance that all those who love our Lord Jesus Christ should be united in the strictest bonds of Christian fellowship, that they may with one heart and voice unite in opposing error, and in disseminating the knowledge of divine truth; and, whereas, in the view of this association there is no reason why those denominations of professing Christians usually called Presbyterian and Congregationalist should not receive each other as brethren and be united as one body in the spiritual sense; and, whereas, there exists in this country a Presbytery connected with the General Assembly of the Presbyterian Church, therefore,

"*Resolved*, That it is very desirable that this association become united with the Presbytery of Geneva.

"*Resolved*, That as a means of forming this union aforesaid, it is expedient that this association be dissolved, and the moderator is hereby directed to declare it dissolved at the close of the session."

In accordance with the aforesaid resolution the association after directing its registrar, the Rev. Aaron C. Collins, "to present the records of the association to the Presbytery of Geneva that they may be preserved," was declared by the moderator to be dissolved, the same having existed thirteen years.

HISTORY OF THE PRESBYTERIES HAVING CHURCHES IN THE COUNTIES OF MONROE AND LIVINGSTON PRIOR TO THE REUNION IN 1870.

In the year 1802 the Presbytery of Albany, which at that time contained only fourteen ministers, was divided into the Presbyteries of Albany, Columbia and Oneida, the latter embracing all the territory in the State of New York west of the east line of the counties of Otsego and Herkimer, but no church in this section was connected with that Presbytery.

In 1805 the Presbytery of Oneida was restricted to the western line of the counties of Oneida and Chenango, and all west of that line within the state was assigned to the Presbytery of Geneva, which was then formed, and which consisted of Rev. Jedidiah Chapman, of Geneva, Rev. John Lindsley, of Ovid, Rev. Samuel Leacock, of Hopewell, and Rev. Jabiz Chadwick, of Genoa. Its churches at that time were Ovid, Geneva, Geneseo First now located at Lakeville, Trumansburgh, Ithaca, Seneca, Seneca Falls and Hopewell. The first meeting of this Presbytery was in Geneva, Sept. 17, 1805, and was opened with a sermon by Rev. David Higgins, of Auburn.

In October, 1810, this Presbytery was reduced by the

formation of two Presbyteries east of Cayuga Lake, but continued to hold all the state west of Cayuga Lake up to the year 1817.

We have already noticed that the church at Lakeville belonged to the Presbytery of Geneva at the time of its organization in 1805, and has therefore the honor of being the first church regularly connected with Presbytery west of Canandaigua. Other churches on this field were received by this Presbytery in the following order: Caledonia, 1806; Livonia, July 7, 1813; West Bloomfield and Richmond, Sept. 21, 1813; Penfield, April 19, 1814; Geneseo 2d and Pittsford, April 20, 1814; Ogden, Aug. 9, 1815; Rochester 1st, Jan. 16, 1816; South Bristol, Aug. 13, 1816; and Mount Morris, Feb. 12, 1817.

At Geneva, on the 19th of February, 1817, the Presbytery of Geneva, which then consisted of twenty-nine ministers, forty-five churches and seven licentiates, was, at its own request, divided into four Presbyteries by the synod of Geneva as follows:

1st. The ministers comprised within the counties of Steuben, Allegany and Tioga, together with Rev. Ebenezer Lazell and Rev. Lyman Barrett, and the church of Naples were constituted the Presbytery of Bath. The other ministers and churches in this Presbytery were Rev. David Higgins, Rev. James H. Hotchkin, Rev. Robert Hubbard, Rev. Clement Hickman and Rev. Hezekiah Woodruff. Churches—Bath, Painted Post, Angelica, Almond, Prattsburgh, Wayne and Elmira.

2d. The ministers and churches west of the eastern boundary of the Holland Purchase, which is not far from the present western boundaries of the counties of Livingston and Monroe, together with Rev. David H. Tullar and the church in Le Roy, with Mr. David N. Smith, licentiate, were constituted the Presbytery of Niagara. The other ministers and churches were Rev. Hugh Wallis and Rev.

Miles P. Squire. Churches—Attica, Warsaw, Buffalo, Hamburgh, Lewiston and Pomfret.

3d. The ministers and churches comprised between the eastern boundary of the Presbytery of Niagara and the dividing line between the third and fourth ranges of townships in the County of Ontario, together with Warren Day, Ebenezer Everett and Josiah Pierson, licentiates, were constituted the Presbytery of Ontario.

4th. The remaining ministers and churches, with Daniel S. Butrick and Stephen M. Wheelock, licentiates, remained as the Presbytery of Geneva; being bounded on the east by Cayuga Lake and on the west by the Presbytery of Ontario; and consisting of Rev. Messrs. Benjamin Bell, Charles Mosher, Howell R. Powell, Joseph Merrill, William Clark, Henry Axtell, Frances Pomeroy, Eleazer Fairbanks, Moses Young and Stephen Porter, with the churches of Geneva, Trumansburg, Ovid, Palmyra, Seneca Falls, Hopewell, Romulus, Hector, Lyons, Benton, Sodus, Phelps, Huron, Augusta, Rushville, Junius 2d, Clyde and East Palmyra.

Of these four Presbyteries, that of Ontario covered very nearly the same territory as that occupied by our Presbytery of Rochester at the present time, and subsequently formed a constituent part of the same.

PRESBYTERY OF ONTARIO.

The Presbytery of Ontario held its first meeting at Livonia, March 11, 1817, and was opened with a sermon by Rev. Ebenezer Fitch, D. D., of West Bloomfield, from Malachi III, 3. "And he shall sit as a refiner and purifier of silver; and he shall purify the sons of Levi and purge them as gold and silver, that they may offer unto the Lord an offering in righteousness." Dr. Fitch was chosen moderator and Rev. Andrew Rawson, of Bristol, clerk. In regard to Dr. Fitch, it is proper to remark that before taking the pastoral charge of the church at West Bloomfield, he had been the first president of Williams College, Mass., for about 22 years, in which position he was honored, beloved and very successful. But some of his best work for the Master was done after he was about sixty years of age, in his twelve years' pastorate at West Bloomfield, followed by about five years of retirement on a farm in the same place prior to his death, March 21, 1833. The infant Presbytery and the churches in this region were greatly indebted to him as an efficient leader and a judicious adviser.

At this first meeting there were present beside the moderator and clerk just named, Rev. Aaron C. Collins, of East Bloomfield; Rev. Reuben Parmerlee, of Victor, and Rev. Comfort Williams, of Rochester. Also, as elders, Elisha Parish, of Bristol; Oliver Gibbs, Rochester First; Isaac Chamberlain, Richmond; Justus Brown, Parma; Dan Canfield, West Bloomfield; Zera Blake, Livonia, and Uriah Parker of Pittsford. In addition to the aforesaid ministers and churches, there belonged to the body at the time of its organization, Rev. John Lindsley, of Geneseo; Rev. Ezekiel J. Chapman, of Bristol; Rev. Alexander Denoon, of Caledonia, and Rev. Silas Hubbard, of Moscow, with the churches of Penfield, Mount Morris, Perry Centre, Geneseo 1st, Geneseo 2d, and Caledonia; with the following licentiates: Warren Day, Ebenezer Everett and Josiah Pierson. In all there were nine ministers, thirteen churches and three licentiates. At this first meeting Rev. Alonzo Darwin, of Riga, Rev. Chauncey Cook, of Lima, and Rev. John F. Bliss, of Avon, were received.

Subsequent receptions by ordination were as follows: May 8, 1817, Rev. Silas Pratt; July 2, 1817, Rev. Abraham Forman and Rev. Loring D. Dewey; Feb. 4, 1818, Rev.

Ebenezer Everett; March 2, 1819, Rev. Warren Day; Jan. 19, 1822, Rev. Norris Bull; Feb. 1, 1825, Rev. B. Foster Pratt; April 23, 1828, Rev. Silas C. Brown; Jan. 21, 1829, Rev. Nathaniel W. Fisher and Rev. Benjamin C. Cressey, that they might go on a mission to the State of Indiana. March 10, 1831, Rev. Isaac Crabb; August 24, 1831, Rev. Hiram L. Miller; Feb. 18, 1834, Rev. William P. Jackson; Oct. 1, 1834, Rev. Elam H. Walker; March 17, 1835, Rev. Oliver S. Powel, to labor for the A. B. C. F. M., among the Indians near the Rocky Mountains; August 25, 1835, Rev. John H. Redington; Sept. 10, 1839, Rev. Daniel Gibbs; Sept. 19, 1839, Rev. Daniel B. Woods; Sept. 21, 1842, Rev. John P. Foster; Sept. 25, 1844, Rev. William Hunter; May 25, 1847, Rev. Charles Richards; Sept. 27, 1848, Rev. Edward B. Walsworth; Sept. 25, 1855, Rev. Orson P. Allen, and Rev. Herman N. Barnum; July 10, 1856, Rev. Levi Parsons; March 6, 1861, Rev. Alphonso L. Benton; June 23, 1863, Rev. Ira O. De Long; July 2, 1867, Rev. Isaac N. Lowrie; Oct. 6, 1868, Rev. Willis Clark Gaylord.

Receptions by letter were as follows:

June 17, 1817, Rev. Asa Carpenter, from Coos Association, Vt.

July 2, 1817, Rev. Elihu Mason, from an Association in Connecticut.

Jan. 20, 1818, Rev. Julius Steele, as pastor of the church at East Bloomfield.

July 4, 1819, Rev. John Barnard, from the Oneida Association; and Rev. Elijah Warren, from the Geneva Consociation.

Aug. 23, 1831, Rev. John B. Whittlesey, from the Presbytery of Lancaster.

April 22, 1828, Rev. Jeremiah Stowe.

Aug. 26, 1828, Rev. Horace Galpin, from the Pesbytery of Troy.

Jan. 20, 1829, Rev. Orange Lyman from the Presbytery of Troy.

Sept. 17, 1829, Rev. James W. McMaster, from the Presbytery of Buffalo.

Jan. 20, 1830, Rev. Benjamin B. Smith, from the Presbytery of Geneva; Rev. Daniel Johnson, from the Barnstable Association, Mass., and Rev. Elijah Wallage, from Windham Association, Vt.

Aug. 24, 1830, Rev. John Walker, from the Monadnock Association, N. H.

Sept. 21, 1831, Rev. James B. Wilcox, from the Presbytery of Genesee.

July 3, 1832, Rev. Edward Bronson from the Genesee Consociation.

Aug. 28, 1832, Rev. George W. Elliott, from the Presbytery of Rochester; Rev. James Cahoon, from the Presbytery of Angelica, and Rev. Ludovicus Robbins, from the Presbytery of Huron.

March 5, 1833, Rev. Richard Kay, as pastor of the church at Victor.

March 19, 1833, Rev. Robert Hubbard, from the Presbytery of Angelica.

Jan. 22, 1834, Rev. Justus S. Hough, from the Presbytery of Cayuga.

Feb. 13, 1834, Rev. Stephen Porter, from the Presbytery of Geneva.

Feb. 18, 1834, Rev. Jacob Burbank, from the Presbytery of Rochester.

July 31, 1834, Rev. John C. Lord, from the Presbytery of Buffalo.

Aug. 25, 1835, Rev. John H. Carle, from the Presbytery of Geneva.

Oct. 28, 1835, Rev. Linus W. Billington, from the Presbytery of Geneva.

Nov. 11, 1835, Rev. Samuel Shaffer from the Presbytery of Bath.

Jan. 20, 1836, Rev. Clark H. Goodrich, from the Presbytery of Columbia.

Feb., 1836, Rev. Hezekiah B. Pierpont, and Rev. Wm. C. Wisner, from the Presbytery of Rochester.

Jan. 17, 1837, Rev. Caleb Burge, from the Presbytery of Oswego.

Jan. 18, 1837, Rev. Lyman Thompson, from the Presbytery of Genesee.

July 25, 1837, Rev. Henry Snyder, from the Presbytery of Cayuga.

Oct. 11, 1837, Rev. Abel C. Ward, from the Presbytery of Buffalo.

Oct. 3, 1838, Rev. John N. Lewis, from the Presbytery of Columbia.

Oct. 10, 1838, Rev. Edwards Marsh, from the Presbytery of Onondaga.

Jan. 15, 1839, Rev. E. A. Platt, from the Genesee Consociation.

April 16, 1839, Rev. Ebenezer H. Stratton, from the Presbytery of Genesee; and Rev. Leveret Hull, from the Presbytery of Angelica.

Sept. 11, 1839, Rev. Aaron Garrison, from the Presbytery of Oneida.

Jan. 21, 1840, Rev. Jonathan Leslie, from the Presbytery of Grand River; and Rev. Moses Gillette, from the Presbytery of Oneida.

Aug. 25, 1840, Rev. Cyrus Hudson, from the Berkshire Association.

Nov. 17, 1840, Rev. John G. L. Haskins, from the Baptist Ontario Association.

April 13, 1841, Rev. Loring Brewster, from the Oneida Association.

Aug. 25, 1841, Rev. Chapin Rufus Clarke, from the Presbytery of Portage.

Jan. 18, 1842, Rev. William U. Benedict, from the Presbytery of Rochester.

March 21, 1843, Rev. Lemuel Leonard, and Rev. Abel Caldwell, from the Presbytery of Angelica.

March 22, 1843, Rev. Benjamin G. Riley, from the Presbytery of Otsego.

Oct. 11, 1343, Rev. Benjamin B. Stockton, from the Presbytery of Rochester.

Jan. 21, 1845, Rev. Samuel M. Hopkins, from the Presbytery of Buffalo.

Sept. 22, 1846, Rev. Peter S. Van Nest, from the Presbytery of Detroit.

Sept. 28, 1847, Rev. William Lusk, from the Presbytery of Otsego.

Oct. 20, 1847, Rev. Charles H. A. Bulkley, from the Presbyterian and Congregational Convention of Beloit District, Wisconsin.

May 4, 1848, Rev. W. Fithian, from the Illinois Presbytery.

Sept. 27, 1848, Rev. A. V. H. Powell, from the Presbytery of Steuben.

April 24, 1850, Rev. Joseph R. Page, from the Presbytery of Genesee; and Rev. Henry Kendall, from the Presbytery of Utica.

August 21, 1850, Rev. Ferdinand DeW. Ward, from the Presbytery of Rochester.

April 23, 1851, Rev. Darwin Chichester, from the Presbytery of Montrose.

April 28, 1852, Rev. E. M. Toof, from the Presbytery of Genesee.

April 26, 1853, Rev. J. W. Ray, from the Presbytery of Kalamazoo.

Sept. 21, 1853, Rev. R. L. Hurlburt, from the Presbytery of Niagara, and Rev. C. L. Hequemburg, from the Presbytery of Angelica.

Jan. 12, 1854, Rev. Daniel C. Houghton, from the West Genesee Conference of the M. E. Church.

April 25, 1854, Rev. Pliny F. Sanborne, from the Hartford North Association.

Sept. 20, 1854, Rev. Sabin McKinney, from the Presbytery of Montrose.

Jan 8, 1856, Rev. Anson H. Parmerlee, from the Presbytery of Chemung.

June 3, 1856, Rev. John N. Hubbard, from the Presbytery of Oswego.

July 9, 1856, Rev. Edwin G. Moore, from the Presbytery of Chicago.

June 2, 1857, Rev. Robert R. Kellogg, from the Presbytery of Genesee.

June 22, 1857, Rev. Milton Buttolph, from the Presbytery of Chemung.

Jan. 6, 1858, Rev. Samuel M. Campbell, from the Oneida Association.

June 1, 1858, Rev. Luther Conklin, from the Presbytery of Cayuga.

Sept. 29, 1858, Rev. Nathaniel Elmer, from the Presbytery of Chemung.

Jan. 4, 1859, Rev. Levi G. Marsh, from the Lincoln Association, Maine.

Feb. 2, 1859, Rev. George P. Folsom, from the Presbytery of Genesee.

Sept. 12, 1860, Rev. Samuel Jessup, from the Presbytery of Hudson.

June 3, 1862, Rev. Dwight Scovel, from the Presbytery of Onondaga.

June 29, 1864, Rev. S. Mills Day, from the Presbytery of Chemung.

Sept. 15, 1864, Rev. Claudius B. Lord, from the Presbytery of Buffalo.

Sept. 12, 1866, Rev. Edwin R. Davis, from the Presbytery of Onondaga.

June 9, 1868, Rev. A. Baker, from the Presbytery of Onondaga.

Feb. 1, 1869, Rev. Lucius D. Chapin, from the Presbytery of Washtenaw, Mich., and Rev. Isaac N. Sprague. D.D., from the Presbytery of Newark, N. J., and Rev. Henry M. Hazeltine, from the Western New York Consociation.

June 9, 1869, Rev. Joseph L. Whiting, from the Presbytery of Cayuga.

In addition to the original thirteen churches, others have from time to time been added to the roll as follows:

June 17, 1817, West Poultney and Riga.
Jan'y 20, 1818, North Avon.
Jan'y 19, 1819, Gainesville and Pike.
Jan'y 20, 1819, Groveland.
Jan'y 20, 1820, Nunda.
Feb. 8, 1820, Dansville.
June 20, 1820, Lima.
Jan'y 15, 1822, Avon.
Aug. 20, 1822, East Bloomfield.
Aug. 19, 1823, North Bristol.
Aug. 23, 1825, Sparta second.
Jan'y 16, 1827, Springwater.
Jan'y 15, 1828, Victor.
Aug. 25, 1829, South Richmond.
June 24, 1829, West Bloomfield 2d.
Nov. 17, 1830, York.
Jan'y 18, 1831, Mount Morris 2d and Moscow.
Jan'y 17, 1832, Conesus.
Dec. 26, 1834, South Avon.
Sept. 18, 1839, Cohocton 2d.
June 2, 1846, Tuscarora.
Feb. 13, 1855, Dansville 2d.
Dec. 11, 1866, Avon Springs.
June 10, 1868, Ossian.

The Rev. Comfort Williams, pastor of the First Church of Rochester, was elected the first stated clerk March 11,

1817, which office he held for about two years, when with others he was transferred to form the Presbytery of Rochester. He was succeeded by Rev. Abraham Forman, of Genesco, who held the office less than a year; when, Feb. 8th, 1820, the Rev. John Barnard, of Lima, was elected to the office, which, for fifty years, he continued to hold, greatly to the satisfaction of his co-presbyters, until the Presbytery was merged into that of Rochester at the time of reconstruction.

During the fifty-three years of its existence the interest which Ontario Presbytery took in ministerial education is worthy of notice. At its first meeting, which was years before the founding of Auburn Seminary, it was "Resolved that Rev. Messrs. Fitch, Williams and Collins, and Messrs. Perrin and Parish be a committee to devise some plan for the purpose of educating pious, indigent young men for the gospel ministry, and that they be required to report at the first stated meeting of Presbytery."

In connection with the report of the aforesaid committee the following minute appears: "The subject of forming a society for the education of pious, indigent young men for the gospel ministry was called up, and after mature deliberation it was considered inexpedient to proceed at this meeting of Presbytery to organize the contemplated society. Therefore, resolved that the business be deferred to a meeting to be held at East Bloomfield on the first Wednesday of September next at 10 o'clock A. M.; that Rev. E. Fitch, D.D., be required to notify the public of said meeting through the medium of the newspapers printed in this region; and that the Doctor open the contemplated meeting with a sermon." What action was taken at this meeting does not appear in the records; but we cannot doubt that it all tended toward the ultimate founding of Auburn Seminary; for which we have reason to believe large credit was due to the influence of Dr. Fitch. Under date of Aug. 24, 1821, the following resolutions appear:

"1. *Resolved*, That a contribution be taken up in each of our congregations in the month of February, annually, which may be appropriated to the aid either of the Seminary at Auburn or Princeton, or to both of them, as those who take it may see proper.

"2. *Resolved*, That it be recommended to the ministers and elders of our churches to form associations in their congregations to cultivate small portions of land, the avails of which shall be appropriated annually, for the benefit of the Seminary at Auburn.

"3. *Resolved*, That Dr. Fitch be appointed to receive accounts of the formation of such associations and forward them to the trustees of the Seminary."

That the Presbytery took a very deep interest in the education of the Indians living at Squakie Hill, in the town of Leicester, appears from the following resolutions under date of Aug. 23, 1821:

"1. *Resolved*, That a representation of the situation of the Indians at Squakie Hill, together with a statement of the proceedings of the Presbyteries of Ontario and Genesee in relation to the establishment of a school among them, be made by this Presbytery to the Board of Managers of the United Foreign Missionary Society, with a view to the relinquishment of the school on the part of Presbytery, provided that society will undertake its management.

"2. *Resolved*, That in case the Board of Managers of the U. F. M. Society determine to undertake the management of the school at Squakie Hill it be relinquished by this Presbytery; and that this Presbytery relinquish in favor of said society whatever right this Presbytery has in the house prepared for the accommodation of said school.

"3. *Resolved*, That in case the Board of Managers of the U. F. M. Society do not determine to undertake the management of the school before mentioned, the Presbytery ask of the said Board of Managers a portion of the money appropriated by the President of the United States to the instruction and improvement of the Seneca Indians, to be employed by Presbytery in support of said school.

"4. *Resolved*, That the Committee on Indian Affairs propose the foregoing to the Presbytery of Genesee at their next meeting, for their concurrence; and in case these resolutions or the substance be adopted by said Presbytery, to co-operate with any committee that said Presbytery may appoint for that purpose, in making the contemplated representation to the Board of Managers of the U. F. M. Society.

"5. *Resolved*, that in case the Board of Managers of the U. F. M. Society do not undertake the management of the school of Squakie Hill, the above mentioned committee, in connection with a committee for the same purpose from the Genesee Presbytery, conduct the school according to their discretion, and that they report their proceedings and the results of them, to Presbytery at its next stated meeting."

The interest which the Presbytery took in the care of its feeble churches appears in the following "Constitution of the Voluntary Missionary Society for the Presbytery of Ontario," which was adopted by the Presbytery at its meeting in Lima, Jan. 18, 1820:

"ARTICLE 1. The officers of this Society shall be a President, Vice-President, Treasurer and Clerk, who shall be annually elected by ballot.

"ART. 2. It shall be the duty of the President, or in case of his absence, the Vice-President, to preside in all meetings of this Society.

"ART. 3. The object of this Society shall be to afford occasional supplies of preaching and evangelical instruction to those places in this region which must otherwise remain destitute.

"ART. 4. For the accomplishment of this object it is recommended to each Minister in this Presbytery to spend as much time in missionary labors as his own sense of duty shall direct, and his congregation shall be willing to allow him for that purpose.

"ART. 5. It shall be the duty of the missionary to make collections for the benefit of the Society, wherever practicable, and to transmit the same to the Treasurer.

"Art. 6. It shall be the duty of every missionary to keep a journal of his proceedings and labors, to collect useful information relative to the moral state and religious prospects of the people among whom he shall labor, and to make a report of the same to this Society once a year at their semi-annual meeting in January; and this journal is to be forwarded to the General Assembly, in the same manner as other missionary journals are forwarded.

"Art. 7. This constitution may be altered or amended afterwards, but only by the consent of two-thirds of the members of this Presbytery present."

The Presbytery then proceeded to elect the following officers:—President, Rev. Ebenezer Fitch, D. D.; Vice-President, Rev. Andrew Rawson; Treasurer, Rev. Julius Steele, and Clerk, Rev. John Barnard.

As early as Aug. 24, 1825, "Messrs. Barnard, Bull and Day were appointed a committee to compile a history of the Presbytery and to report it at the next stated meeting." It was also "*Resolved*, that the several churches be directed to prepare histories of their origin, and to forward them to the above committee, on or before the 3d Tuesday of September next." At the next meeting, Jan. 18, 1826, this committee reported in part, which was approved, and they were authorized to conduct the business in that way which they should think proper.

The following report on intemperance was adopted Aug. 29, 1827. "The committee appointed to consider the recommendation of the General Assembly on the subject of Intemperance, report that they have attended to the business assigned them; and that they view the common use of ardent spirits in our country an alarming evil, and would recommend the adoption of the following resolutions, viz.:

" 1. *Resolved*, that the intemperate use of ardent spirits is an evil which the friends of the Redeemer ought to unite in suppressing; and that it is hereby earnestly recommended to the churches in connection with the Presbytery to lend their aid in effecting this object.

"2. *Resolved*, that the intemperate use of ardent spirits grows out of the temperate use of them, and that, in the judgment of this Presbytery, entire abstinence is the only effectual remedy for the evils of intemperance.

"3. Therefore, *Resolved*, that the temperate use of ardent spirits ought, in all ordinary cases, to be conscientiously avoided and discouraged.

"4. *Resolved*, that we consider the address of Mr. Kittridge on the effects of ardent spirits, as well calculated to promote the object of the previous resolutions, and that the members of this body will encourage its circulation.

"*Resolved*, that Messrs. Hastings and Chipman procure the publication of the above resolutions and phamphlet for the benefit of our congregation."

January 19, 1831, " It was resolved that the Rev. Charles G. Finney be invited to come and labor within the bounds of this Presbytery; and that the Rev. Norris Bull be a committee to communicate the resolution to Mr. Finney with such a statement of facts as he may deem expedient."

The following report on the subject of slavery was adopted January 17, 1837:

" The committee on the subject of slavery would respectfully report that they have endeavored carefully to examine the subject, and beg leave to recommend to the Presbytery the following resolution :

" *Resolved*, That we consider the enslaving of one part of the human race by another as a gross violation of the most sacred rights of human nature ; as utterly inconsistent with the law of God, which requires us to love our neighbor as ourselves, and as totally irreconcilable with the spirit and principles of the gospel of Christ, which enjoins that 'All things whatsoever ye would that men should do to you, do ye so to them.'

" That therefore we consider it the duty of all Christians, adopting all wise and prudent measures, to use their honest, earnest and unwearied endeavors, as speedily as possible, to obtain the complete abolition of slavery in our land, and if possible throughout the world."

"Messrs. Goodrich, Brown and Tracy were appointed a committee to procure the publication of the above resolution in the *New York Observer*, *New York Evangelist* and *Buffalo Spectator*."

The Presbytery of Ontario held its semi-centennial celebration at Mount Morris, March 12th, 1867, at which time the Rev. Joseph R. Page preached the Historical Sermon from Ps. 48: 12-13, " Walk about Zion, and go round about her, tell the towers thereof, mark ye well her bulwarks, consider her palaces, that ye may tell it to the generation following." This sermon, together with other important historical papers and speeches, was published, from which the following extracts are taken: "Geographically and ecclesiastically and generally this Presbytery soon came to occupy the middle ground, in some respects unfavorable to its growth, excellent as it is in itself. The attractions of the Great West beyond drew thither thousands and tens of thousands of our population, which is less to-day than it was a quarter of a century ago. * * * * Individuals and churches of extreme views and intolerant spirit disliked our exemplification of the gospel precept, 'Let your moderation be known unto all men,' and separated from us. Ultra abolitionism reveled in its derisive and destructive work. Five of our congregations became connected with the Old School. The 'millstones,' by which we were to be 'ground to powder,' began to revolve, but the predicted result did not follow. Immediately after the division of the church this Presbytery placed on record its 'unqualified disapprobation' of the act by which it was accomplished, and for three years continued to elect commissioners to the General Assembly. Then for twelve years it deemed it inexpedient to be represented therein, though its connection with the Synod of Genesee remained as cordial as ever. In

1852, commissioners were again elected, and the usage has not since been departed from."

"A deep interest has been manifested by it to sustain and carry forward the benevolent and reformatory enterprises of the age, to improve the temporal condition of men. It was among the first to set up the banner of total abstinence from all that can intoxicate, when whiskey was universally regarded as among the first necessities of the settler, and it has continued to the present day to advocate and exemplify the scriptural principles of the beneficent temperance reform. With no uncertain sound has it from time to time proclaimed the inalienable right of all men to 'life, liberty and the pursuit of happiness,' and the wisdom and obligation of at once breaking the chain of the bondman, and restoring manhood to the slave. It has occupied no timid or time serving position during the recent rebellion, and the grand, and blessed be God, successful effort to subdue it, but with unshaken faith in an ultimate triumph of freedom and righteousness, even in the darkest hour, in common with every religious organization about us, it has rallied its sons around the flag, and encouraged its daughters to sustain the nation's brave defenders."

"The Presbytery of Ontario had its origin at an auspicious period. All the vast enterprises of the church, which are the glory of our age, were just beginning to engage the thought and to kindle the zeal of the 'Sacramental host of God's elect.' They were arousing from a long and dreary night of inactivity and slumber, to make resistless onsets upon the strongholds of the kingdom of darkness. Bible and Missionary and Education and Tract and Temperance Societies were springing into life. Sabbath-schools and Bible-classes were a novelty, but rapidly growing in favor and efficiency. The men who organized this body were in full sympathy with these great movements."

"This Presbytery has always shown a special regard for

the pastoral office. Its ministers have remained longer with the churches than any other in the region. Rev. Dr. Barnard was pastor of the church in Lima thirty-eight years. At the present time, nine of its churches, all save one, able without aid to support the institutions of the gospel, have settled pastors; the one of longest standing, twenty-seven years, of least, six years; the whole, united, one hundred and eight years, making the average period of settlement just twelve years. No other Presbytery, it is believed, can exhibit a similar record. In every respect we have derived great advantages from this course. It has increased our power over the public mind. It has strengthened all our interests."

In addition to the historical sermon of Dr. Page, from which these extracts have been taken, this memorial service was rendered intensely interesting by speeches from those representing other Presbyteries, churches and religious institutions: Rev. William C. Wisner, D. D., of the Presbytery of Niagara; Rev. Joel Wakeman, D. D., of the Presbytery of Bath; Rev. M. N. McLaren, D. D., and Rev. J. E. Nassau, D. D., of the Presbytery of Genesee River; Rev. Rev. C. F. Mussey, D. D., of the Presbytery of Genesee; Rev. Timothy Stillman, D. D., of the Presbytery of Buffalo; Rev. S. M. Campbell, D. D., of the Presbytery of Rochester; Rev. Cyrus Hudson, of the Presbytery of St. Lawrence; Rev. Henry Kendall, D. D., Secretary of Home Missions; Rev. C. P. Bush, D. D., Secretary of the A. B. C. F. M.; Rev. Wm. S. McLaren, of the U. P. Church; Rev. E. B. Walsworth, D. D., of California, and Rev. J. M. Fuller, of the M. E. Church. Dr. S. H. Gridley, of the Presbytery of Geneva, contributed an important historical paper.

The following hymn was composed for the occasion by Dr. Thomas Hastings, of New York:

"Smiles and tears full oft are blending
  Mid the scenes of hallowed joy ;
While our sorrows may be tending,
  Bliss that nothing can alloy.
Life, a priceless boon, is given
  To be filled with earnest zeal
In preparing souls for Heaven,
  Where we hope ere long to dwell.

" Where are they, who, strong foundations
  Fifty years ago did lay ?
Gone from human habitations—
  Numbered with the dead are they.
But they live in realms of glory
  Round our blest Redeemer's throne,
And perhaps to-day's glad story
  May to them be fully known.

" What prosperity attends us,
  What enlargement fills our bounds !
Israel's Guardian still defends us
  And his light our path surrounds.
Thousands who have gone before us
  Ran with zeal the Heavenly race ;
Tens of thousands joined in chorus
  Yet shall sing recovering grace."

In the work of Foreign Missions the Presbytery co-operated with the A. B. C. F. M. In the work of Home Missions, in addition to the society formed within the Presbytery, and for the purpose of helping its own feeble churches by such aid as might be afforded by its own pastors, the churches on this ground seem, according to Hotchkin's History, to have co-operated with the Genesee Missionary Society, which was organized in 1810, and maintained a vigorous existence until 1818. This same author is our authority for saying that about one-third of all the funds raised for this Society were contributed by Women's Missionary Societies as connected with the different churches. Honorable mention is made of contributions from these societies at East and West Bloomfield, Victor and Lima; showing that the noble work which Christian women are now prosecuting is only the resumption of work which our mothers commenced in the early settlement of the country.

FORMER PRESBYTERY OF ROCHESTER.

At a meeting of the Synod of Geneva, held Feb. 18, 1819, the Presbyteries of Ontario and Niagara were so divided as to form the new Presbyteries of Rochester and Genesee. The boundaries of Rochester Presbytery were: "On the east by the east line of Penfield and Perinton; on the south by the south line of Perinton, Pittsford, Henrietta, Riga, Bergen and the Tonawanda Swamp; on the west by the west line of Genesee County (which included Shelby, Ridgeway and Gates), and on the north by Lake Ontario."

This Presbytery, in compliance with the order of Synod, held its first meeting at Rochesterville, April 6th, 1819, in a small wooden building on State street, as is supposed, the same being occupied at that time by the First Church as a house of worship, and was opened with a sermon by Rev. John F. Bliss, from 2d Cor., II : 16, "To the one we are the savour of death unto death, and to the other the savour of life unto life. And who is sufficient for these things."

The Rev. Comfort Williams, pastor of the First Church, was elected moderator and also stated clerk and treasurer. All the ministers were present, viz: John F. Bliss, Asa Carpenter, Chauncey Cook, Alanson Darwin, Ebenezer Everett and Comfort Williams; together with Josiah Pierson, a licentiate.

The elders present were Levi Warren, Penfield; Samuel Stone, Pittsford; Hubbard Hall, West Riga; Oliver Gibbs,

Rochester; Pittman Wilcox, Bergen; Moses Fulton, Ogden; John Bosworth, Sweden, and Levi Smith, Clarkson. East Riga or Chili was the only church then belonging to the body not represented.

The ministers subsequently received will be found in the statistical table which accompanies this sketch.

Other churches have been received into the Presbytery at dates as follows:

Carthage, April 6, 1819; Parma, Jan. 25, 1820; Barre and Ridgeway, June 27, 1820; Shelby, April 17, 1821; Sandy Creek, Sept. 11, 1821; Gaines and Wheatland, April 16, 1822; Clarendon, Feb. 4, 1823; Mendon, July 1, 1823; Rush, Feb. 5, 1829; Webster, Sept. 20, 1825; Rochester Brick, Nov. 18, 1825; Rochester Third, Feb 28, 1827; North Bergen, June 24, 1828; Brockport, June 24, 1828; Parma, March 4, 1829; Parma Corners, June 29, 1830; West Mendon, June 28, 1831; Rochester Free, April 19, 1832; Churchville, July 10, 1832; Bushnell's Basin, June 25, 1843; Henrietta, June 27, 1833; Kendall, Feb. 4, 1834; Rochester Central, Aug. 4, 1836; Rochester Fifth, June 26, 1838; Charlotte, June 29, 1852; Victor, April 6, 1858; Rochester Westminster, April 5, 1868.

The aforesaid dates are taken from the Statistical History written by Louis Chapin, Esq., and read by him at the Half Century celebration of this Presbytery, April 7, 1869, and which was published, together with a poem by Rev. Charles E. Furman, D. D., a historical discourse by the Rev. Charles P. Bush, D. D., and speeches by Rev. F. DeW. Ward, D. D., Rev. M. N. McLaren, D. D., and Rev. J. R. Page, D. D.

The following extracts are taken from Mr. Chapin's history:

"This exhibit shows that of the forty churches that have belonged to this Presbytery, eighteen are now in its connection, four have been set off to Niagara Presbytery, six belong to the Rochester City Presbytery, three have returned to Congregational relations and nine have been disbanded. * * * * * The eighteen churches now connected with us had at their formation a total membership of 356. Their present total number is 3,848.

"Of the ministers connected with this Presbytery, twenty-five are still in it, twenty-two have died when members, one hundred and thirty-seven have been dismissed, four have been stricken from the roll, two have been set off, one has been deposed and one suspended. Six are believed to have been dismissed without record being made; one hundred and seven of the whole number are believed to be now living; forty-seven are known to have died after being dismissed; twenty-two have not been heard from lately, but most of them are believed to be dead.

"Lemuel Brooks has been connected with this Presbytery thirty-eight years, five months and eighteen days. James B. Shaw has been pastor while in it, twenty-eight years, two months and eighteen days. The average time that the one hundred and ninety-eight ministers have been in the Presbytery is six years, four months and three days. The present twenty-five members have been connected with it an average of eleven years and nine months.

"At the first meeting of the Presbytery, committees were appointed to draft constitutions for a Voluntary Missionary Society (home, in its character), and for a Religious Tract Society, and the next year an Education Society was organized; an Auxiliary Foreign Missionary Society and a Sabbath School Union were resolved upon.

"Among the duties enjoined on pastors were the assembling of baptized children to instruct them in the catechism, and to visit the district schools, and make efforts for the improvements of scholars.

"At times the Presbytery was not free from disturbing elements. In 1829, an overture on the subject of Free Masonry was introduced. Several churches had become agitated and well-nigh sundered. Pacific counsels prevailed and divisions were prevented. Several of the churches were also disturbed on the doctrine of Christian perfection, to such an extent as led, in some cases, to discipline of pastors and people."

" The act of excision by General Assembly in 1837, caused deep and lasting feeling. Commissioners to General Assembly were appointed in 1838, who went. I cannot say how diligent search they made, but on their return they reported 'they could not find the General Assembly.' Appointments were made again in 1839. In this case the appointees reported better success; they found the new school body. After that this Presbytery stood aloof from connection with either body till 1854. In 1850, they had a committee draft a petition to both General Assemblies to reunite. As it did not effect the desired object, several attempts were made to recognize and send commissioners to the New School Assembly. A vote was taken in 1852, resulting in there being 14 for to 24 against sending. In 1853, a similar vote showed 14 for to 17 against it. After further debate a second vote was a tie, there being 13 on each side. In 1854, the question was disposed of by a vote of 20 for to 12 against sending.

"So far as I have found evidence for it there have been 9,774 added to the churches on profession; and the same evidence reports that there has been collected in our churches for benevolent objects as follows: For Foreign Missions, $107,245; Home Missions, $57,894; Educational Objects, $53,617; Publication, $28,486; General Assembly Commissioners' Fund, $2,111; Ministerial Relief, $681; Miscellaneous objects other than above, $132,660; total, $382,694. If we had full reports to compare from, I believe they would show that the total number of additions to our churches by profession would exceed 11,000; and that the collections to various benevolent objects would appear to have exceeded half a million of dollars. No reports have been asked for or made of sustaining our own churches until in 1865. The footing of this shows the amount for five years to have been $155,570, or an average of $31,570 per year for sixteen churches.

"The early efforts of our Presbytery in behalf of various benevolent objects were not limited in their fruits to the amount of money contributed. The following named persons who have been connected with it, or its churches, have for a longer or shorter period been employed as Foreign Missionaries: To the Sandwich Islands—as ministers, Jonathan Green, T. Dwight Hunt and Soreno W. Bishop; as physician, Seth L. Andrews; as printer, Edwin O. Hall; as assistants, Delia (Stone) Bishop and Fidelia (Church) Coan. To India—as ministers, Alanson C. Hall, Ferdinand DeW. Ward and Henry Cherry; as printer, Elijah A. Webster. To Syria—as minister, Milan II. Hitchcock; as physician, Henry A. De Forest; as assistants, Caroline (Sargeant) De Forest and Maria W. (Chapin) Smith. To Singapore—as minister, Alfred North. To Turkey—as minister, Joseph W. Sutphen; as assistant, Harriet Seymour. To Siam—as assistant, Julia Johnson. To Zulus, Africa—as assistant, Fanny M. (Nelson) McKinney. To Choctaws—as minister, Ebenezer Bliss. To Mackinaw, Mich.—as printer, Elisha Loomis. Quite likely there may be others whose names I have omitted. It is not possible to state the amount of labor that has been performed in the Home Missionary work. Much of the labor of our original members was of that kind; and some has been continued within our bounds to this present time; while scores of our older or younger ministers have been, or now are, in Home Missionary employ in this and other states.

"In the Sabbath School cause, the Union organized in 1821 was followed by a Rochester Union, organized in 1822, which has, with some modification, been continued in existence to this time. A County Union was organized in 1824, which held annual meetings for many years, at which schools from the villages and towns gathered in the Court House yard, or other places, to hold their exercises. Their annual reports were printed in pamphlet form as late as 1834."

The historical discourse of Dr. Bush consisted mainly in biographical sketches of those who had been quite prominent in the history of the Presbytery and in the religious history of the city, from which are gathered the following facts: Rev. Comfort Williams, pastor of the First Church and the first moderator and stated clerk of the Presbytery, " was the acknowledged patriarch of the wilderness." He was a graduate of Yale and Andover. He resigned his charge of the First Church in 1821, and died in Rochester, Aug. 26th, 1825.

Rev. Solomon Allen, a native of Northampton, Mass., had been a Major in the Revolutionary war, and one of those who conducted Andre to West Point. He was not licensed to preach until he was fifty-three years of age, and, while not a great preacher, was great in consecration, courage and benevolence, securing very largely the confidence of the people. He was the father of Solomon Allen, of Philadelphia, and Moses Allen, of New York. He closed his labors in Brighton in 1820, and died Jan. 19, 1821, in New York city.

Rev. Josiah Pierson, pastor of the church in Bergen, where he died March 7th, 1846, is referred to in the minutes of Presbytery, passed at the time of his death, as having " probably done more than any other minister of the gospel in establishing churches and sustaining them in that region. For years when the country was new, he preached to small congregations in school-houses, barns and private dwellings, receiving but a small salary. He counselled and encouraged professors of religion to meet for worship; aided several small churches in their organization; preached for them and administered the ordinances to them occasionally, until they were able to obtain pastors for themselves."

Rev. Joseph Penney, D. D., the second pastor of the First Church, was educated at Trinity College, Dublin, and at Glasgow. He was a man of superior abilities, fine education, with a special interest in the natural sciences, and very successful as an educator, and zealous in the temperance reform. After leaving Rochester, he was pastor of the church in Northampton, Mass., and President of Hamilton College. He died in Rochester in 1860.

Rev. William James, D. D., a native of Albany and educated at Princeton College and Seminary, was the first pastor of the Brick Church. He was a diligent student, vigorous thinker and elegant writer. Having inherited wealth he was noted for his kindness to the poor and generosity among his friends.

Rev. William F. Curry, a native of Kentucky, was installed pastor of the church at Pittsford, July 14, 1825. He was a clear thinker, a thorough Calvinist and an able preacher, helping to turn the wilderness into a fruitful field. He died at Geneva in 1861.

Rev. Norris Bull, D. D., the champion of Orthodoxy as against Unitarianism in Geneseo from 1822 to 1832, was pastor at Clarkson from 1837 to 1847.

Rev. Joel Parker, D. D., when a young man just from the seminary, was instrumental in gathering and organizing the Third Church of Rochester, in 1827, in which his labors were very signally blessed; but after remaining with them a little more than three years, he left, greatly to their grief, to establish the First Free Church of New York City.

Rev. Wm. Wisner, D. D., after a remarkably successful pastorate of fifteen years at Ithaca, N. Y., came to the Brick Church in 1831, and labored with great power for five years.

Honorable mention was made of Dr. J. B. Shaw, Dr. F. F. Ellinwood, Dr. C. P. Wing, of Carlisle, Pa.; Dr. M. J. Hickok, of Scranton, Pa.; Dr. J. H. McIlvane, of Princeton, N. J.; Dr. A. W. Cowles, of Elmira; Dr. Geo. S. Boardman, of Rome; Dr. M. N. McLaren, of Caledonia, and Dr. A. G. Hall, of Rochester.

STATISTICAL TABLE.

PREPARED BY LOUIS CHAPIN, ESQ.

NAMES OF MINISTERS, WHEN AND HOW UNITED TO PRESBYTERY, TIME OF DEATH OR DISMISSION.

WHEN RECEIVED.	NAMES AND WHERE FROM.	WHERE TO	DEATH OR DISMISSION.
June 29, 1819	Solomon Allen, Ontario Association.		Died January 19, 1821.
February 3, 1830	Elisha D. Andrews, Council in Vermont.	Macomb Co. Association.	Dismissed June 29, 1841.
July 13, 1841	Silas H. Ashman, Cayuga.	Wisconsin.	" 1852
February 1, 1853	David C. Ames, licensed.	Niagara.	" June 28, 1853.
June 13, 1860	Horace H. Allen, licensed	Cayuga.	" June 19, 1862.
June 10, 1862	Edwin Allen, Niagara	Kalamazoo.	" June 11, 1867.
April 6, 1819	John F. Bliss	Ontario Consociation.	January 6, 1824.
April 18, 1821	Josiah Bissel, Jr., licensed.	Surrendered license.	March 4, 1828.
November 17, 1824	Stephen V. Barnes, Onondaga.	Huron	September 19, 1823.
October 1, 1828	Abner Benedict, Cayuga.		Died Fall. 1830.
October 1, 1828	Lemuel Brooks, licensed.	Genesee.	Dismissed September 21, 1831.
June 30, 1830	Jacob Burbank, Onondaga	Ontario.	" February 4, 1834
June 25, 1833	Isaac Bliss, Genesee Consociation.	Cayuga.	" February 3, 1835.
June 25, 1833	Joel Byington, Champlain	Niagara.	" July 1, 1835.
October 9, 1833	Lemuel Brooks, Genesee.		
October 28, 1833	John F. Bliss, Geneva.	Genesee.	Dismissed February 3, 1836.
June 24, 1834	Norris Ball, Genesee.	Utica.	Died December 8, 1847.
June 28, 1836	George S. Boardman, Watertown.	Ripley.	Dismissed December 26, 1843.
June 27, 1837	George Beecher, Cincinnati.	Ontario.	" February 1, 1842.
June 26, 1838	William N. Benedict, Cayuga.	Tioga.	" October 13, 1841.
February 4, 1840	Edwin Benedict, Cayuga	Ontario.	" June 25, 1842.
February 2, 1841	Linus W. Billington, Ontario.	Rochester City.	" February 5, 1850.
June 29, 1841	James Ballantine, Cayuga.		" February 7, 1854.
November 14, 1843	Chandler Bates, Niagara.		Died July 2, 1857
June 25, 1844	Jacob Burbank, Ontario.	Niagara.	Dismissed June 27, 1848.

85

36

WHEN RECEIVED.	NAMES AND WHERE FROM.	WHERE TO.	DEATH OR DISMISSION.
February 2, 1847	Obadiah C. Beardsley, Buffalo	Niagara	Dismissed June 6, 1858.
February 6, 1849	Milton Buttolph, Niagara	Chemung	" August 17, 1852.
February 6, 1849	Thomas Bellamy, Black River Association	Buffalo	" February 5, 1850.
June 28, 1853	Linus W. Billington, Ontario	Niagara	" February 4, 1862.
September 19, 1855	Albert Bigelow, Buffalo	Nassau	" January 6, 1857.
April 6, 1858	Nathan Bosworth, Watertown	Onondaga	" June 14, 1864.
January 4, 1859	Charles R. Burdict, licensed	Genesee	" September 10, 1861.
June 11, 1861	Byron Bosworth, Cayuga	Catskill	" April 14, 1868.
September 10, 1862	O. Holmes Barnard, Niagara	Kalamazoo	" " "
June 10, 1863	Charles P. Bush, New York, Third		
July 14, 1863	George S. Bishop, licensed	Brunswick	Dismissed February 23, 1864.
September 12, 1866	Nathan Bosworth, Onondaga		
January 9, 1867	Horatio W. Brown, Lyons		
April 15, 1868	John E. Baker, Troy		
September 8, 1868	Linus W. Billington, Niagara		
April 6, 1819	Asa Carpenter		Died September 10, 1826.
April 6, 1819	Chauncey Cook	Geneva	Dismissed October 9, 1852.
August 1, 1820	Charles James Cook, London		Deposed July 6, 1824.
July 5, 1825	William F. Curray, Philadelphia	Niagara	Dismissed February 5, 1828.
February 7, 1826	James Cahoon, Bangor, Ireland	Angelica	" September 15, 1829
October 10, 1826	George Coan, East New Haven Consociation	Buffalo	" February 2, 1830.
June 25, 1827	Ralph Clap, Hampshire Co. Association	Genesee Consociation	" June 24, 1834.
February 3, 1829	Ebenezer Child, Niagara	Hillsborough Association	" February 2, 1830.
September 21, 1831	Alfred E. Campbell, Geneva	Cayuga	" June 27, 1833.
September 21, 1831	Lewis Cheeseman, Genesee	Caledonia	Joined February 9, 1839.
February 4, 1834	Robert H. Conklin, Angelica	Angelica	Dismissed February 4, 1840.
October 14, 1834	Ward Child, Grand River	Genesee	" June 30, 1835.
February 3, 1836	Henry Cherry, licensed, ordained Aug. 11	Florida	" June 29, 1852.
November 10, 1840	Ralph S. Crampton, Genesee		Died March 25, 1864.
October 24, 1843	Jonathan Copeland, Cayuga	Champlain	Dismissed January 5, 1859.

June 25, 1844	Ralph Clap, Genesee	Methodist Episcopal	Dismissed September 3, 1844.
February 3, 1847	Augustus W. Cowles, New York, Third	Chemung	" June 7, 1857.
March 6, 1850	N. Marcellus Clute, licensed	Niagara	" February 6, 1855.
June 12, 1860	I. Norton Crittenden, Niagara	Geneva	" September 9, 1863.
June 13, 1860	Elisha M. Carpenter, licensed		
June 12, 1866	Samuel M. Campbell, Mohawk	Coldwater	Dismissed April 4, 1868.
January 9, 1867	William W. Collins, Tioga		
January 12, 1867	Hiram W. Congdon, licensed		Died December 15, 1831.
April 6, 1819	Alanson Darwin		Dismissed June 24, 1834.
February 5, 1829	Richard Dunning, licensed	Niagara	" September 9, 1842.
December 23, 1834	Richard De Forest, Black River Association	Monroe Association	" August 15, 1848.
July 19, 1842	Richard Dunning, Niagara	Geneva	" June 24, 1844.
February 21, 1843	George E. Delevan, Chenango	Onondaga	
January 4, 1859	David Dickey, licensed		
June 14, 1864	Richard Dunning, Cayuga	Lyons	Dismissed September 12, 1866.
January 9, 1866	Hiram Dyer, Chenango		
April 6, 1819	Ebenezer Everett	Niagara	Dismissed July 6, 1824.
June 24, 1828	Edward Evans, Independent	Unknown	
September 21, 1831	George W. Elliot, Onondaga	Ontario	Dismissed June 26, 1832.
July 21, 1834	Tyron Edwards, New York	New York	" February 4, 1845.
January 9, 1855	Frank F. Ellinwood, Philadelphia, Fourth		
June 13, 1855	Nathaniel Elmer, Ontario	Ontario	Dismissed September 15, 1829.
October 16, 1822	Abraham Foreman, Ontario	Niagara	" June 30, 1846.
September 21, 1830	Charles E. Furman, Cayuga		Died June 25, 1868.
October 10, 1838	George Freeman, Ontario	Niagara	Dismissed August 15, 1848.
June 28, 1842	Bela Fancher, Dayton	Nassau	" June 11, 1861.
August 15, 1848	James Fenner, Genesee	Rochester City	" February 7, 1854.
August 19, 1851	Archibald Ferguson, Ogdensburgh	Buffalo	" June 13, 1865.
November 6, 1851	William A. Fox, Niagara		
September 17, 1857	Charles E. Furman, Niagara		
June 30, 1840	Abner Goodell, Geneva		Died March 30, 1845.
September 6, 1842	Moses Gillett, Ontario	Utica	Dismissed June 24, 1845.
June 4, 1844	Frederick W. Graves, Alton	New York, Third	" August 12, 1845.

WHEN RECEIVED.	NAMES AND WHERE FROM.	WHERE TO.	DEATH OR DISMISSION.
April 29, 1845	Blackleach B. Gray, Buffalo	Geneva	Dismissed August 21, 1850.
October 14, 1845	Cornelius Willet Gillum, Buffalo		Died October 7, 1853.
June 26, 1849	Rufus S. Goodman, New York	Marshall	Dismissed June 27, 1854
June 27, 1851	Stephen C. Goetschies, Buffalo	Schuyler	" June 9, 1863.
June 12, 1861	Corlis B. Gardner, licensed	Genesee Valley	" June 2, 1865.
September 10, 1861	Ansen Gleason, Buffalo	Utica	Dismissed September 10, 1862.
January 10, 1865	Hugh B. Gardner, Montgomery Classes	Albany	" April 14, 18.8.
June 11, 1867	Willis Clark Gailord, licensed	Ontario	" September 8, 1868.
April 6, 1819	Herman Halsey	Niagara	" February 4, 1831
June 30, 1829	Jacob Hart, Champlain	Ontario	" July 13, 1831.
October 9, 1832	Hiland Hubbard, Cincinnati	Genesee	" October 9, 1833.
February 5, 1834	Alanson C. Hall, licensed, ordained Sep. 4, 1834	Foreign Missionary	Died April 3, 1840.
November 4, 1834	Jacob Hart, Ontario	Caledonia	Dismissed July 19, 1852.
July 1, 1835	Eli S. Hunter, Albany	Wisconsin	" February 4, 1851.
December 23, 1834	Albert G. Hall, licensed	Buffalo, without letter	Stricken off February 5, 1850.
February 4, 1841	Parsons C. Hastings, licensed	Onondaga	Dismissed October 14, 1845.
February 5, 1845	Milo J. Hickox, Marietta Association	Rochester City	" February 7, 1854.
October 14, 1845	Truman C. Hill, Utica	Buffalo	" August 31, 1850.
February 3, 1846	David L. Hunn, Niagara	Genesee Valley	" June 10, 1862
February 6, 1849	Augustus F. Hall, licensed	Buffalo	" June 26, 1852.
February 3, 1852	Robert W. Hill, Ontario		
June 26, 1855	Nathan Hurd, Oneida		Died January 16, 1856.
August 25, 1857	Milan H. Hitchcock, Penobscot Association	Association, Mass.	Dismissed October 23, 1867.
January 7, 1862	Henry M. Hurd, New Brunswick, licensed		" January 6, 1863.
January 7, 1863	Gavin L. Hamilton, licensed	Utica	Died March 2, 1863.
June 9, 1863	Yates Hickey, Chicago	Albany	Dismissed June 14, 1864.
October 20, 1838	Gavin L. Hamilton, Utica		" June 12, 1866.
February 4, 1834	Alvan Ingersoll, licensed	Niagara	" October 14, 1835.
July 4, 1826	William James, Albany	Albany	" February 4, 1831.

39

Date	Name	Place	Status
February 5, 1828	William Jones, Oneida, licenciate		
February 4, 1834	Daniel Johnson, Ontario	Detroit	Dismissed February 4, 1831.
June 30, 1846	William P. Jackson, Buffalo		Died October 11, 1867.
February 4, 1851	Charles Jerome, Chenango	Buffalo, stricken off	Stricken off Feb. 5, 1850.
September 17, 1856	John L. Jones, Cortland	Buffalo	Dismissed January 9, 1855.
July 1, 1829	George P. King, Andover Association	Northern Missouri	January 4, 1860.
October 10, 1838	Richard King, Ontario	Bath	October 24, 1832.
October 14, 1840	William P. Kendrick, Genesee	Caledonia	Stricken off June 26, 1842.
June 27, 1843	Charles Kenmore, Monroe Association	Ottawa	Dismissed February 3. 1847.
February 4, 1845	Elias W. Kellogg, Ontario	Albany	February 1, 1848.
April 8, 1845	Charles Kittridge, Tolland Co. Consociation	Niagara	August 15, 1848.
February 4, 1851	Elias W. Kellogg, Niagara	Rochester City	February 7, 1854.
June 27, 1820	Ebenezer Lazell, Bath	Niagara	February 3, 1852.
September 1, 1821	Archy B. Lawrence, licensed	Genevra	Sept. 17, 1822.
June 24, 1828	Benjamin I. Lane, Oneida	Ontario	October 16, 1822.
July 13, 1831	Luke Lyons, Cayuga	Niagara	February 4, 1831
February 7, 1838	Beaufort Ladd, Ontario	St. Josephs	October 25, 1836.
December 26, 1843	Charles G. Lee, Ithaca	Geneva	July 29, 1841.
September 19, 1828	Joseph Myres, Genesee	Onondaga	February 4, 1845.
June 30, 1829	Ebenezer Mead, Cayuga	Niagara	June 27, 1832.
November 10, 1829	Asa Mahan, Oneida	Niagara	June 25, 1833.
June 27, 1832	Gilbert Morgan, Albany	Cincinnati	Sept. 21, 1831.
June 25, 1833	Roswell G. Murray, Niagara	Albany	October 10, 1838.
June 25, 1833	Samuel Marsh, Champlain	Niagara	July 1, 1835.
February 3, 1835	William Mack, New York	N. W. Association, Vt.	February 3, 1846.
October 9, 1839	Samuel S. McCullough, Cortland	West Tennesee	February 6, 1814.
June 24, 1844	Ebenezer Mead, Genesee	Chenango	June 28, 1842.
June 24, 1845	Hugh Mair, Albany	Wyoming	Died December 28, 1848
June 24, 1845	Malcom N. McLaren, Albany	Long Island Classes	Dismissed February 2, 1847.
February 16, 1847	Charles N. McHarg, Hartford Association	Otsego	" "
June 27, 1848	Joshua H. McIlvaine, Albany	Rochester City	February 6, 1849.
June 27, 1848	Charles Merwin, Geneva	Cayuga	February 7, 1854.
June 26, 1855	Sabin McKinney, Ontario	Tioga	June 27, 1852.
			Sept. 29 1863.

WHEN RECEIVED.	NAMES AND WHERE FROM.	WHERE TO.	DEATH OR DISMISSION.
February 19, 1856.	Henry G. Miles, New York, Third.	Bath.	Joined by letter June 29, 1859.
September 17, 1861.	George D. B. Miller, licensed.	Episcopal.	Struck off January 7, 1863.
January 7, 1862.	Robert McMath, Geneva.		
January 8, 1862.	Royal Mann, Ithaca.		
February 23, 1864.	Enoch K. Miller, licensed.	Philadelphia Fourth.	Dismissed April 10, 1864.
July 10, 1866.	Henry M. Morey, Albany.		
February 19, 1823.	Nahum Nixon, Hopewell, Geo.		Unknown.
December 23, 18—.	Reuben Nason, Cumberland, Maine Association.		
April 6, 1858.	Alfred North, Otsego.	Geneva.	Died January 18, 1835.
October 14, 1834.	Moses Ordway, Genesee.	Madison District.	Dismissed January 7, 1862.
April 8, 1845.	Franklin W. Olmsted, licensed.	Addison Co. Association.	Stricken off June 27, 1851.
April 6, 1819.	Josiah Pierson, licensed.		Dismissed June 27, 1848.
June 27, 1820.	David Pratt, Oneida Association.		Died March 7, 1846.
April 2, 1822.	Joseph Penny, New York Association, ref'd.		Set off Sept. 16, 1823.
July 4, 1826.	David Page, Geneva.	Niagara.	Dismissed July 22, 1834.
June 14, 1827.	Joel Parker, Ontario.	New York, First.	February 4, 1831.
June 24, 1828.	Abial Parmele, Genesee.	Niagara.	June 17, 1830.
February 3, 1829.	Silas Pratt, Ontario.	New York.	July 14, 1829.
November 3, 1831.	Hezekiah B. Pierpont, licensed.	Buffalo.	February 5, 1839.
February 7, 1832.	Simeon Peck, Oneida.	Caledonia.	February 5, 1833.
October 12, 1836.	Oliver H. Powell, Ontario.	Geneva.	March 14, 1833.
August 18, 1847.	Hamilton W. Pierson, licensed.	Bath.	October 11, 1837.
June 25, 1850.	William K. Platt, Genesee.	Genesee.	February 1, 1848.
February 4, 1851.	Job Pierson, Chenango.	New York, Fourth.	January 7, 1857.
February 4, 1851.	Robert Proctor, licensed.	New York, Third.	September 29, '63.
February 24, 1852.	James S. Pierpont, Cayuga.	Kalamazoo.	January 6, 1857.
January 6, 1857.	James H. Phelps, licensed.	Rochester City.	February 1, 1853.
January 6, 1857.	David Powell, Niagara.	San Francisco.	January 10, 1865.
September 12, 1860.	Hezekiah B. Pierpont, Ontario.	Grand River Valley.	Died June 15, 1867.

41

Date	Name	Location	Status
June 11, 1862	D. Henry Palmer, licensed	Buffalo	
June 12, 1866	Hamilton W. Pierson, Paducah		Dismissed June 9, 1863.
September 11, 1821	Andrew Rawson, Ontario	Niagara	Set off Sept. 16, 1823.
December 5, 1834	John B. Richardson, New Haven, West Ass'n	Geneva	Dismissed June 16, 1855.
April 18, 1821	George G. Sill, licensed	Albany	February 4, 1835.
November 17, 1824	Avelyn Sedgwick, Berkshire Association	Ontario	" October 9, 1833.
June 14, 1827	Jeremiah Stow, Congregational Association	Ontario	" February 6, 1828.
February 2, 1830	Solomon Stevens, Cayuga	Cayuga	" February 4, 1831.
February 7, 1832	Ezra Scoville, Deerfield Association	Genesee	" February 5, 1833.
October 19, 1833	Charles Sparry, Baptist	Baltimore	" February 6, 1834.
August 30, 1838	Benjamin B. Stockton, Hudson	Ontario	" October 10, 1843.
April 16, 1839	Avelyn Sedgwick, Genesee		Disc'ntin'd from roll Sep. 6, '42.
October 14, 1840	Henry Snyder, Ontario	Angelica	Dismissed October 14, 1843.
December 8, 1840	James M. Sherwood, North River	Brooklyn	" September 4, 1845.
February 2, 1841	James B. Shaw, Buffalo		
February 2, 1841	Ephraim Strong, St. Louis		Died November 6, 1843.
October 13, 1841	Stephen Stanley, Genesee		Suspended July 19, 1842.
June 25, 1844	Avelyn Sedgwick, reinstated	Oneida Association	Dismissed February 4, 1851.
February 4, 1845	William B. Stow, Oswego	Bath	" June 30, 1846.
February 3, 1846	Norman B. Sherwood, Cayuga	Ontario	" June 27, 1845.
November 6, 1851	Joseph W. Sutphen, New York, Third		" October 9, 1852.
February 19, 1856	Frederick Starr, Jr., Lexington	Cayuga	" January 7, 1862.
January 7, 1863	Alexander C. Stewart, Toronto	Utica	Dismissed January 9, 1866.
December 15, 1863	Augustus C. Shaw, licensed		
September 11, 1867	Dwight Scovell, Ontario	Niagara	" October 14, 1835.
October 20, 1868	William B. Stewart, Philadelphia	Champlain	" December 18, 1865.
June 28, 1831	John Thaliner, Cayuga	Buffalo	" November 20, 1865.
June 26, 1855	Ebenezer M. Toof		
January 8, 1862	John C. Taylor, Ontario Association		
November 21, 1865	Alexander McA. Thorburn, Troy		
February 5, 1839	Aaron Van Wormer, Genesee	Genesee	Dismissed October 14, 1840.
June 9, 1863	Edwin B. Van Aucken, Rochester City		
April 6, 1819	Comfort Williams		Died August 26, 1825.

WHEN RECEIVED.	NAMES AND WHERE FROM.	WHERE TO.	DEATH OR DISMISSION.
October 2, 1821	Jonathan Winchester, Champlain	Grand River	Dismissed July 5, 1825.
July 13, 1831	William Wisner, Cayuga	General Letter	" October 14, 1835.
February 7, 1832	William C. Wisner, licensed	Ontario	" February 3, 1836.
October 9, 1832	Worthington Wright, Genesee	Albany	" October 14, 1834.
June 6, 1834	Ferdinand D. W. Ward, licensed	Ontario	" June 25, 1850.
February 3, 1835	Conway P. Wing, Geneva	Monroe	" November 5, 1838.
March 24, 1835	Jairus Wilcox, West New Haven Association	Ottawa	" February 6, 1838.
June 30, 1835	Alfred Wright, Genesee Consociation		Unknown.
October 25, 1836	Elijah D. Wells, Bath	Chemung	Dismissed September 12, 1837.
October 9, 1839	Hugh Wallis, Genesee		Died September 7, 1848.
October 29, 1839	James W. Wood, licensed	Geneva	Dismissed October 14, 1840.
February 6, 1849	George G. Wickson, C. W. Consociation		
February 3, 1852	Calvin Waterbury, Cayuga	Peoria and Knox	Dismissed September 17, 1857.
January 8, 1861	Jeremiah Woodruff, Bath	Dubuque	Dismissed September 12, 1866.
January 7, 1863	Coles K. Wilkins, from Methodist Episcopal	Niagara	" January 9, 1866.
September 14, 1864	William H. Webb, Ontario Association	Monroe	" November 12, 1865.
June 11, 1867	Austin G. Wilcox, Lyons		
June 11, 1867	Calvin Waterbury, Holston, Tenn		
February 16, 1847	John R. Young, New York, Third	Geneva	Dismissed October 22, 1847.

STATED CLERKS.

April 6, 1819, Comfort Williams, September 17, 1822.
September 17, 1822, Joseph Penny, June 30, 1829.
June 30, 1829, Joseph Myers, June 27, 1832.
June 27, 1832, George G. Sill, May 27, 1834.
June 6, 1834, Luke Lyons, October 25, 1836.

January 3, 1837, William Mack, February 6, 1839.
June 25, 1839, John B. Richardson, February 7, 1854.
February 7, 1854, Jonathan Copeland, January 5, 1859.
January 5, 1859, Charles E. Furman.

PRESBYTERY OF ROCHESTER CITY.

The Presbytery of Rochester City was organized in connection with the old school branch of the Church at Phelps, N. Y., Oct. 7th, 1851, in accordance with the action of the Synod of Buffalo, by taking from the Presbytery of Steuben the following five churches with their ministers, viz: First of Vienna, Seneca Falls, First of Mentz, East Williamson and Conquest; also the following four churches with their ministers from the Presbytery of Buffalo City, viz.: Rochester 2d, Rochester 3d, Penfield and Webster.

The ministers who were present at the organization of this Presbytery were Rev. Benjamin B. Stockton, Rev. Albert G. Hall, D. D., Rev. Thomas Bellamy and Rev. George C. Heckman. Those who were absent were Rev. A. B. Vanhanizan, Rev. Alexander McColl and Rev. John Fisher.

The elders present were D. Sherrell, from Vienna First, and H. S. Wier, from Seneca Falls. The other churches above named were not represented.

The Rev. Albert G. Hall, D. D., preached the opening sermon from 1st John, V: 13: " These things have I written unto you that believe on the name of the Son of God, that ye may know that ye have eternal life and that ye may believe on the name of the Son of God."

The Rev. Benjamin B. Stockton was chosen moderator and the Rev. George C. Heckman stated clerk. Of the seven ministers who formed the Presbytery, Dr. Hall alone remained a member to its close.

The Rev. B. B. Stockton was dismissed to the Presbytery of New York, April 7th, 1858, after the pastoral relation between himself and the First Church of Vienna had been dissolved.

Rev. Thomas Bellamy died at Charlotte, N. Y., April 31st, 1867.

Rev. Geo. C. Heckman was dismissed to the Presbytery of Winnebago, Nov. 27, 1856, after his pastoral relation to the church at Port Byron had been dissolved.

Rev. A. B. Vanhanizan was dismissed to the Classis of Geneva, Oct. 8, 1862, together with the church at East Williamson, of which he was the pastor.

The Rev. Alexander McColl was dismissed to the Presbytery of Niagara, April 25, 1855.

Rev. John Fisher having united with the Baptist denomination, his name was stricken from the roll, April 29, 1852.

Additions by ordination were as follows: Oct. 7, 1851, Edward Hall, as evangelist; April, 27, 1853, Alexander McFarland, and installed at Penfield; whose pastoral relation was dissolved Oct. 12th, 1854, and he dismissed to the Presbytery of Whitewater.

June 21st, 1853, Dugald D. McColl, and installed at Wheatland; which relation was dissolved March 8, 1870, and on the 17th of the same month he was installed at Phelps.

March 22, 1866, E. Maurice Wines, and installed at Rochester First; which relation was dissolved July 14, 1868.

Aug. 1, 1866, Daniel R. Foster, and installed at Phelps; which relation was dissolved Sept. 22, 1869.

April 31, 1867, Gideon P. Nichols as an evangelist.

Nov. 6, 1867, Charles W. Wood as an evangelist, who was dismissed to the Presbytery of Genesee, Sept. 22, 1869.

Additions by letter were as follows: April 29, 1852, Rev. L. Genstiniani, D. D., from the Lutheran body; and dismissed April 27, 1853, to the Presbytery of Cincinnati.

Oct. 4, 1853, Rev. A. T. Young, from the Presbytery of Wyoming; and dismissed to the Presbytery of Watertown, April 25, 1860.

April 26, 1854, Rev. Charles Kittridge, Rev. James Ballentine, Rev. Archibald Furgerson and Rev. Joshua H. McIlvane, D. D., from the Presbytery of Rochester; the two former came into this Presbytery at the time of reunion; Rev. A. Furgerson died as pastor of the church at Charlotte, Dec. 20, 1856; and Dr. J. H. McIlvane was released as pastor of Rochester First, Aug. 8, 1860, and dismissed to the Presbytery of New Brunswick, Sept. 19, 1860.

Oct. 4, 1854, Rev. Jacob Hart, from the Presbytery of Genesee River, who died at Fergus, C. W., Nov. 26, 1864.

Sept. 19, 1855, Rev. Geo. W. Burroughs, from the Classis of Geneva; and was dismissed to the Presbytery of Baltimore, April 29, 1857.

Oct. 11, 1855, Rev. Charles Ray, from the Presbytery of Genesee River, who was installed first pastor of Rochester Calvary, Sept. 17, 1856, and dismissed to the Genesee River Presbytery, Oct. 14, 1858.

April 23, 1856, Rev. James Harkness, from the Presbytery of North River; installed pastor of North State St. Church, Rochester, June 11th, 1856, from which he was released June 29, 1858, and soon after removed to Yonkers, but never took a letter.

June 10, 1856, Rev. R. H. Richardson, from the Presbytery of Chicago, and on the same day installed pastor of Rochester St. Peters, from which, Dec. 11, 1857, he was released and dismissed to the Presbytery of Chicago.

July 16, 1857, Rev. A. P. Botsford, from the Presbytery of North River, and July 24, 1857, installed pastor at Port Byron, from which he was released April 1, 1861, and dismissed to the Presbytery of New York, April 23, 1861.

Sept. 16, 1857, Rev. Joseph Kimball, from the Associated Reform Presbytery of Washington, N. Y., who was dismissed to the Classis of Poughkeepsie, Feb. 21, 1863.

Oct. 18, 1858, Rev. Joseph H. Towne, from Fairfield Association, Connecticut, and Oct. 28, 1858, installed pastor of St. Peters, from which he was released April 25, 1860, and dismissed to the Presbytery of Buffalo.

Oct. 28, 1858, Rev. James Nichols from the Presbytery

of Genesee River. He died January 31, 1864; to whom in the minute which was adopted in view of his death, Presbytery refers, as having "been peculiarly useful in the organization of three new churches in Oneida, in the teaching of youth in the Genesee Academy, and his own school in Rochester, and as chaplain of the Western House of Refuge in Rochester."

March, 1859, Rev. George Patton, from the Associate Reformed Body, together with the church at Seneca, of which he was pastor and which had belonged to the Associate Reformed Body. He remained pastor of the same to the time of reunion.

April 27, 1859, Rev. E. C. Prichett, from the Presbytery of Geneva; installed pastor of the Westminster Church, Geneva, May 3, 1859, from which he was released April 25, 1860, and dismissed to the Presbytery of Utica, April 25, 1866.

April 27, 1859, Rev. W. S. Parsons, from Luzerne Presbytery, who was dismissed to the Presbytery of Lewis, Pa., Oct. 2, 1861.

Aug. 16, 1859, Rev. Isaiah Faries, from Associate Reformed Presbytery of Big Spring, Pa., and installed pastor of the church at Phelps, from which he was released April 26, 1865, and dismissed to the Presbytery of Albany.

Oct. 15, 1859, Rev. Lemuel Leonard, from the Presbytery of Genesee River, who was dismissed to the Presbytery of Michigan, August 17, 1860.

August 8, 1860, Rev. J. T. Coit, from the Presbytery of Niagara, and installed pastor of Rochester St. Peters, who suddenly died Feb. –, 1863, greatly beloved and sincerely lamented both by his church and the Presbytery.

June 18, 1861, Rev. Edwin B. Van Auken, from the Presbytery of Cayuga, who was dismissed to the Presbytery of Rochester, April 29, 1863.

June 18, 1861, Rev. Belville Roberts from the Presbytery

of Troy; installed pastor of Rochester Calvary, Oct. 2, 1861, from which he was released June 31, 1865, and dismissed to the Presbytery of Rock River.

July 31, 1861, Rev. Timothy H. Quigley, from the Presbytery of Genesee, who was dismissed to the Presbytery of Genesee Valley, April 28, 1869.

Feb. 11, 1862, Rev. Franklin D. Harris, from the Presbytery of Philadelphia, and installed pastor at Port Byron; from which he was released April 25, 1866, and dismissed to the Second Presbytery of Philadelphia, Sept. 19, 1866.

May 13, 1862, Rev. Calvin Pease, D. D., from the Winooskie Association, and installed pastor of Rochester First. He died Sept. -, 1863, respecting which, Presbytery passed appropriate resolutions.

April 29, 1863, Rev. Hiram Harris, from the Presbytery of Cayuga, who was dismissed to the Presbytery of Geneva, March 22, 1866.

Aug. 22, 1863, Rev. Edwin D. Yeomans, D. D., from the Presbytery of New Brunswick; installed pastor of Rochester St. Peters, Nov. 9, 1863, from which he was released April 31, 1867, and dismissed to the Presbytery of Passaic.

April 27, 1864, Rev. George McCartney, from the Classis of Saratoga, and installed at Webster, June 7, 1864.

Dec. 6, 1864, Rev. Silas R. Beadle, D. D., from the Presbytery of Connecticut, and dismissed to the Central Presbytery of Philadelphia, Oct. 5, 1865.

Dec. 6, 1864, Rev. John W. Major, from the Classis of Saratoga.

Sept. 20, 1865, Rev. Alfred Yeomans, from the Presbytery of Raritan, and dismissed to the Presbytery of Huntington, January 2, 1867.

April 31, 1867, Rev. Herbert W. Morris, from the Presbytery of Albany, and installed pastor of Rochester Calvary, June 9, 1867.

April 29, 1868, Rev. Wm. D. Woodruff, from the Baptist denomination.

April 28, 1869, Rev. Oliver P. Conklin, from the Presbytery of Cortland.

Sept. 22, 1869, Rev. James M. Crowell, D. D., from the Presbytery of Philadelphia, who soon after was installed pastor of Rochester St. Peters.

From the previous list it appears that this Presbytery consisted of seven original members, seven added by ordination and thirty-six by letter, making a total of fifty during the nineteen years of its existence, of whom six died, twenty-seven were dismissed, and one was stricken from the roll.

The original nine churches have already been named, to which the following ten, from time to time, were added, making a total of nineteen.

April 27, 1853, the church at Wheatland, from the Presbytery of Rochester.

Oct. 4, 1853, East Bethany, from the Presbytery of Wyoming.

December 13, 1853, Rochester St. Peters was organized.

April 26, 1854, the First Church of Rochester and the church of Parma and Greece were received from the Presbytery of Rochester.

October 4, 1854, the North State St. Church of Rochester, which had been organized by a committee of Presbytery.

April 25, 1855, the church at Charlotte from the Presbytery of Rochester.

June 15, 1856, Rochester Calvary organized by a committee of Presbytery.

March –, 1859, the church at Seneca, from the Associate Reformed Church.

April 27, 1859, Westminster Church, Geneva, organized by a committee of Presbytery.

Of these nineteen churches, four transferred their relations to other bodies and three were dissolved as follows:

April 26, 1854, Rochester Second was reported as having placed itself under the care of the Classis of Geneva, and was stricken from the roll.

April 29, 1857, Penfield asked leave to withdraw, in order to unite with the Rochester Presbytery, which was granted. Also, at the same date, Seneca Falls informed Presbytery that they had taken measures to connect themselves with the Presbytery of Geneva (N. S.), and the name was stricken from the roll.

Oct. 8, 1862, the church at East Williamson asked leave to withdraw, in order to place themselves under the care of the Classis of Geneva, which was granted.

April 23, 1861, the church at West Greece, which had been received from the Presbytery of Rochester, April 26, 1854, as the church of " Parma and Greece," was stricken from the roll, "the church organization having been dissolved."

The name of the North State St. Church, of Rochester, which was organized in 1854, appears for the last time on the Statistical Report of the year 1860, with no members; but no record was made of its dissolution.

The church at Conquest is reported in 1859, for the last time, as vacant, and having eighteen members, but no action is found in regard to its dissolution.

There have been eight licensures, as follows:

April 28, 1852, Charles Ray; April 7, 1858, Robert Proctor; Feb. 8, 1859, George Dutton and Charles Russell Clarke; April 25, 1860, Matthew L. R. P. Hill; May 31, 1865, Gavin Longmuir; April 25, 1866, Charles W. Wood.

Six stated clerks were elected at the following successive dates:

Oct. 7, 1851, Rev. George C. Heckman; Nov. 27, 1856, Rev. Charles Ray; April 27, 1859, Rev. A. P. Bottsford;

April 23, 1861, Rev. Dugald D. McColl; April 27, 1864, Rev. Edwin D. Yeomans, D. D.; April 31, 1867, Rev. Albert G. Hall, D. D.

According to the records, the Presbytery, at the close of its existence, consisted of sixteen ministers and twelve churches.

GENESEE RIVER PRESBYTERY.

[The subjoined sketch has been furnished by Rev. J. E. Nassau, D. D., of Warsaw, N. Y., who, as stated clerk of the Presbytery of Genesee, has in his possession the records of the Presbytery of Genesee River.]

The Synod of New Jersey, in session at Morristown, N.J., October, 1838, in response to overture, erected the Presbytery of Caledonia in Western New York, in connection with the (O. S.) General Assembly.

The Presbytery of Caledonia, having grown to very wide bounds, was, by their own request, divided by the Synod of New Jersey, in session at Elizabethtown, Oct. 19, 1842, into the two Presbyteries of Steuben and Wyoming; the Genesee River to be the dividing line between them, and the Presbytery of Steuben to retain the records and other papers of the Presbytery of Caledonia.

In August, 1844, the (O. S.) Synod of Buffalo, created by the General Assembly out of the three Presbyteries of Steuben, Wyoming and Ogdensburg, met in Buffalo. Soon after the new Presbytery of Buffalo City was erected by Synod, taking those ministers and churches in and around Buffalo, that had belonged to the Presbytery of Wyoming.

All these Presbyteries grew and changed in ministers and churches until 1851, when the Synod of Buffalo, having met August 21st, in Vienna, made some further Presbyterial changes, which weakened the Presbyteries of Wyoming and Steuben, so that in response to overture from these two Presbyteries, the Synod, in its session in Bath, N. Y., August, 1853, "*Resolved*, that the request of the petitioners be granted; that the new Presbytery extend over the ground occupied by the two above named Presbyteries; that the new Presbytery hold its first annual meeting on the last Tuesday of September next, at two o'clock P. M., at Warsaw, and be opened with a sermon by the oldest clergyman present, and that the Presbytery assume the name of the Presbytery of Genesee River."

The Presbytery thus organized met according to appointment in the Presbyterian church of Warsaw, N. Y., September 27th, 1853, at two o'clock P. M., and was opened with a sermon by Rev. Thomas Aitken, (text not given).

Rev. Thomas Aitken presided at the organization and was then chosen moderator, with the Rev. George D. Stewart, stated clerk.

The roll of ministers and churches, including those present and the absentees, shows:

MINISTERS.

Isaac Oakes,	Stewart Mitchell,
Thomas Aitken,	Jacob Hunt,
Lemuel Leonard,	Daniel Harrower,
Jesse Edwards,	Moses Miller,
H. L. Doolittle,	J. W. McDonald,
J. Edwin Miller,	Smith Sturges,
George D. Stewart,	L. R. Lockwood,
Charles Ray,	James Nichols,
J. K. Correnger.	

CHURCHES.

Bath, Peter Halsey, Elder.	Lindley, unrepresented.
Groveland, Peter Titsworth.	Cameron, "
Oakland, George Arnold.	Second Sparta, "
Caledonia, Alexander Frazer.	Portageville, "
Warsaw, Luther Foster.	Wyoming, "
First Sparta, Wm. W. McNair.	Moscow, "
Tuscarora, James Conklin.	Scottsville, "

Rev. George D. Stewart remained stated clerk until his removal west in 1859. At the meeting in Second Sparta Church, April 26, 1859, Rev. Joseph E. Nassau was chosen Mr. Stewart's successor, and has continued stated clerk of Genesee River Presbytery until the reconstruction of 1870, and since then of Genesee Presbytery, thirty years next month.

The statistical report of Presbytery, May 9, 1854, gives 16 ministers, 13 churches and 2 candidates; the churches being the same as those just given, except that Cameron and Lindley seem to be regarded as one, (extinct in 1855); the ministers the same as above given, except changes made by the death of Rev. Daniel Harrower and the accession of Rev. John J. Carroll, Rev. Pliny Twitchell and Rev. John W. Major.

The number of members given in the statistical report is 1,058. At the reconstruction (in April, 1870,) the total membership was 1,420.

March 7, 1855, licentiate John Jones was ordained and installed at Scottsville.

October 24, 1855, licentiate Joseph E. Nassau was ordained and installed pastor at Warsaw.

October 15, 1856, Rev. F. De W. Ward was received from the Presbytery of Ontario.

April 28, 1857, Rev. W. P. Jackson was received from the Presbytery of Michigan, and Rev. Wm. E. Jones from the Presbytery of Troy.

April 29, 1857, Rev. James M. Harlow from the Presbytery of Buffalo City.

September 23, 1857, Rev. W. N. Hall from the Congregational Association of Hampton East, Mass.

February 16, 1859, Rev. Charles Ray from the Presbytery of Rochester City.

January 5, 1860, (Rev.) licentiate Henry B. Thayer ordained and installed pastor of Presbyterian church of Oakland.

November 13, 1860, Rev. Dr. Malcolm N. McLaren received from the Reformed Dutch Classis of Orange and the same day installed at Caledonia.

August 16th, 1861, Rev. E. W. Kellogg from the Presbytery of Buffalo City, and Rev. B. Coleman Smith from the Presbytery of Bath.

March 11, 1862, Rev. Henry Neill from the Presbytery of Michigan.

June 14, 1864, (Rev.) licentiate J. S. Bingham ordained and installed at Portageville.

April 25, 1865, Rev. Henry L. Doolittle from the Presbytery of Washington.

October 6, 1865, Rev. R. W. McCormick from the Presbytery of Susquehanna.

April 24, 1866, Rev. Ephraim S. Wilson from the Presbytery of Vincennes; he went over to the Episcopal church that autumn and his name was dropped.

October 10, 1866, Rev. Charles W. Maccarthey from the Presbytery of Genesee.

July 22, 1867, (Rev.) licentiate John Butler was ordained as evangelist to the foreign field (China).

October 28, 1868, licentiate Thomas Dobbin ordained to the ministry and installed pastor at Groveland, June 16, 1869.

September 28, 1869, Rev. James M. Platt, received from the Presbytery of Alleghany City, and installed at Bath, November 4, 1869.

From the above sketch of Dr. Nassau we deduce the following summary:

Original members, seventeen; subsequently added by ordination, six; by letter, eighteen; total, forty-one; number of installations, seven; number of churches, fourteen.

This Presbytery existed for seventeen years, and at the time of reconstruction, took its legal succession in the Presbytery of Genesee, although about half of its ministers and churches, those within the bounds of Livingston County, were incorporated with the Presbytery of Rochester.

PRESENT PRESBYTERY OF ROCHESTER.*

The General Assembly of the Presbyterian Church being convened in the City of Philadelphia, Pa., in the month of May, A. D. 1870, the same being the first meeting of the re-united body of what had been known for thirty-two years as the New and Old School branches of the Presbyterian Church, in the reconstruction of its Synods throughout the country, defined the Synod of Genesee as including all that portion of the State of New York west of the eastern boundaries of the Counties of Monroe, Livingston and Alleghany. Said Synod met as directed by the Assembly, in the Central Presbyterian Church of Buffalo, on the 28th day of June following, and immediately changed its name to that of Western New York. At this first meeting the present Presbytery of Rochester was formed, to include all the ministers and churches within the bounds of Livingston and Monroe Counties, and to be the legal successor of the former Presbyteries of Rochester City, Rochester and Ontario.

Said Presbytery immediately met at the call of one of their number who had been appointed by the Synod for that purpose, in the Central Church of Buffalo on the 29th day of May, 1870, and after electing Rev. Levi Parsons as moderator, and Rev. J. Jones as temporary clerk, adjourned to meet in the Central Presbyterian Church of Rochester, on the 13th of September following.

With reference to the three Presbyteries to which this was made the legal successor, inasmuch as it contained a

---

* This part of the history was reported to Presbytery April 10, 1888, and having met the approval of the body, was ordered to be printed. But its publication has been delayed until December, 1889, in order that the histories of the former Presbyteries, and of the individual churches, might accompany it.

very large proportion of their ministers and churches, that of Ontario which was New School, and which, with the exception of the churches at Perry and South Bristol, was entirely within the county of Livingston, was the oldest; having been formed by the Synod of Geneva at its session in the village of Geneva, Feb. 19th, 1817.

The following are the names of the ministers from Ontario Presbytery, who helped to constitute this Presbytery of Rochester:

Justus S. Hough,	John Barnard, D. D.,
Isaac N. Sprague, D. D.,	Milton Buttolph,
William Hunter,	Joseph R. Page,
Luther Conklin,	Herman N. Barnum,
Orson P. Allen,	Lucius D. Chapin,
Levi Parsons,	Henry M. Hazeltine,
Samuel Jessup,	Alphonso L. Benton,
Levi G. Marsh,	Willis Clark Gaylord,
Alvin Baker,	Joseph L. Whiting,
Isaac N. Lowrie,	

Nineteen in all, four of whom, Allen, Barnum, Lowrie and Whiting, were Foreign Missionaries.

Edward G. Bickford was a licentiate.

The following twelve churches, with an aggregate of 1,562 members, were also from the same Presbytery: Avon, Avon Springs, Dansville, Genesco First, Genesco Village First, Lima, Livonia, Mount Morris, Nunda, Ossian, Springwater and Union Corners.

The former Presbytery of Rochester was formed by the Synod of Geneva, Feb. 18, 1819, that is, two years after that of Ontario, by taking a part from Ontario and a part from Niagara. This Presbytery, with the exceptions of Victor and Bergen, had been restricted to the County of Monroe.

The names of the ministers coming into the new Presbytery were:

Hezekiah B. Pierpont,
Charles E. Furman, D. D.,
Robert McMath,
Austin G. Wilcox,
William B. Stewart,
Alexander McA. Thorburn,
Edwin B. Van Auken,
Henry M. Morey,

Lemuel Brooks,
James B. Shaw, D. D.,
Nathaniel Elmer,
Samuel M. Campbell, D. D.,
Dwight Scovel,
Samuel A. Freeman,
Gavin L. Hamilton,
John E. Baker,

Charles P. Bush, D. D.,

Seventeen in all, together with David Dickey and Elisha M. Carpenter as licentiates.

Also, from the same Presbytery, the following fourteen churches: Brockport, Chili, Clarkson, Gates, Mendon, Ogden, Parma Centre, Penfield, Pittsford, Rochester Brick, Rochester Central, Rochester Westminster, Sweden and West Mendon, now Honeoye Falls, with members numbering, in the aggregate, 3,262.

The other Presbytery, that of "Rochester City," which, as already stated, had been organized in connection with the Old School Assembly at Phelps, N. Y., October 7, 1851, contributed seven of its sixteen ministers to form the new Presbytery, whose names are as follows:

Albert G. Hall, D. D., Charles Kittridge, Oliver P. Conklin, George McCartney, James Ballentine, Herbert W. Morris and James M. Crowell, D. D.; also the following seven of its twelve churches with members numbering, in the aggregate, 1,637, viz:

Rochester First, Rochester Third, Rochester St. Peters. Rochester Calvary, Charlotte, Webster and Wheatland.

There was, as has already been stated, a fourth Presbytery, that of "Genesee River," which had been connected with the Old School Assembly and which took the Presbytery of Genesee as its legal successor, which at this time contributed to the new Presbytery the following eight ministers: Isaac Oakes, Malcolm N. McLaren, D. D., Thomas Aitken, Ferdinand De W. Ward, D. D., Washington D. McKinley, William E. Jones, John Jones and Thomas Dobbin; also the following eight churches with an aggregate of members of about 753: Caledonia, Geneseo Central, Groveland, Moscow, Oakland, Sparta First, Sparta Second and Tuscarora. To these may be added the Rev. Geo. W. Lane, of Moscow, who at that time was a member of the Presbytery of Buffalo City.

The new Presbytery at the time of its organization consisted of 52 ministers of whom 17 were pastors, 16 stated supplies, 4 foreign missionaries, 2 secretaries, 2 teachers and 11 without charge; also 3 licentiates, 41 churches and 7,214 communicants.

Since that time the names of 107 ministers have been added to our roll, making a total of 157. Of these 107 seventeen were received by ordination and the remaining ninety by letter from other bodies. Of the seventeen who were ordained eight were installed over churches as follows:

June 4, 1873, Rev. George K. Ward at Dansville.
July 30, 1874, Rev. Fisher Gutelius at Moscow.
October 8, 1874, Rev. George C. Jewel at Parma Centre.
November 10, 1874, Rev. John K. Fowler at Caledonia.
May 25, 1875, Rev. Lewis H. Morey at Pittsford.
October 12, 1885, Rev. Gerard B. F. Hallock at Wheatland.
September 30, 1886, Rev. Robert Kerr Wick at Sparta First and Second.
May 25, 1887, Rev. Bevard D. Sinclair at Fowlerville.

The other nine were ordained " sine titulo," as follows:
June 12, 1878, Rev. Eneas McLean and Rev. James W. White at the Central Church, Rochester.

October 29, 1878. Rev. John P. Campbell at Caledonia.
June 18, 1883, Rev. Theodore S. Day at Rochester First.
October 2, 1883, Rev. Evan R. Evans at North Sparta.
November 15, 1883, Rev. Theodore W. McNair at South Sparta.
September 29, 1855, Rev. Frank P. Gilman at North Sparta.
May 23, 1887, Rev. Albert S. Bacon at Victor.

Three of the aforesaid were ordained with special reference to the foreign work, viz: Rev. Eneas McLean who went to South America, Rev. Theodore W. McNair who went to Japan, and Rev. Frank P. Gilman who went to China. These added to the four already named have made seven of our number who have labored on the foreign field, to which we may add two others, Rev. F. De W. Ward, D. D., and Rev. T. Dwight Hunt, now belonging to this body, who were foreign missionaries prior to the formation of this Presbytery.

In addition to the original 17 pastoral relations and the 8 which have been already named in connection with ordination, there have been 33 others constituted, making 58 in all; of these three have been terminated by the death of the incumbents, thirty-seven by action of Presbytery, while eighteen still remain.

Upon the roll of licentiates 30 names have been added to the original 3, making 33 in all. Of these six have been received by letter from other Presbyteries, the remaining twenty-four have been examined and licensed by this body.

Sixteen of our licentiates have been ordained by this body, fourteen have been dismissed to other Presbyteries, one has died and two still remain upon our list.

Since its organization this Presbytery has received nineteen candidates for the gospel ministry, nine of whom have subsequently been licensed, one has turned to other avocations and nine are still pursuing their preparatory studies.

HISTORY OF ROCHESTER PRESBYTERY. 59

In making the statement that at the time of its organization this Presbytery consisted of 41 churches, there was a slight chronological inaccuracy made for the purpose of crediting the church at Tuscarora to the Presbytery of Genesee River and that at Union Corners to that of Ontario, but as matter of fact these churches after the re-union of the two assemblies at Pittsburgh and prior to the formation of this Presbytery had effected a union and thus came into this body as one church, making the number 40. This union, however, proved to be unhappy and the same was dissolved by act of Presbytery in the fall of 1873, since which time the two churches have appeared separately upon our roll.

On the 19th of October, 1870, the church of Brighton, which before had been Congregational, was received by this Presbytery, it appearing that said church had perfected its organization by the election of a board of ruling elders.

On the 13th of September, 1871, in accordance with the united request of the churches of Nunda and Oakland, the church at Oakland was declared by Presbytery to be extinct and its members were added to the church of Nunda.

On the 19th of October, 1871, the Memorial Church in the city of Rochester was organized by a commission of Presbytery appointed for that purpose and its name was added to our roll, said church being formed from a mission Sabbath-school established years before that time by the Brick Church.

The church at Victor prior to the reunion had belonged to the Presbytery of Rochester and the synod of Genesee, but by the general reorganization at the time of reunion it was assigned to the Presbytery and Synod of Geneva. By the request of the church, which was sustained by both synods, the General Assembly of 1874 transferred the church to this body.

The church of Avon Springs, which at the time of

reunion was virtually extinct, having no minister and never having had a church edifice, and reporting only 35 members, was subsequently resuscitated and by a commission of Presbytery reorganized as a new church in the year 1876, taking the name of the Central Church of Avon, which has subsequently built one of our most attractive church edifices, and for years has been prosperous and self-sustaining.

In compliance with an overture from the church at Fowlerville, which had been Congregational, a commission was appointed by this body to reorganize the same as a Presbyterian church which was accomplished on the 22d of April, 1878, and the name of the church was added to our roll.

As the result of the labors of two missionaries in South America then belonging to this body, Rev. Robert McLean and his brother Rev. Eneas McLean, a Presbyterian church which was organized by them in Concepcion, Chili, was at the request of said church received by this Presbytery on the 21st of September, 1880; the name of said church was retained upon our roll until September 18th, 1883, when, the Presbytery of Chili having been formed, the request of the church to be transferred to said Presbytery was granted.

In the year 1858 the church at Geneseo village, known as Geneseo Second, was divided; the new church being organized by the Genesee River Presbytery, which belonged to the Old School Assembly, was called the "Central Presbyterian Church of Geneseo," the original church still retaining its connection as heretofore with the Presbytery of Ontario. After maintaining a separate existence for twenty-one years, these two churches, at their own request, were consolidated by act of Presbytery, March 30th, 1880, with very happy results up to the present time.

Nor can we fail to recall in this connection the rare self-denial which was manifested by the Rev. Charles S. Durfee, pastor of the Central Church, in relinquishing his beloved flock, to which he had ministered for almost six years, in order to facilitate the union which his judgment approved. The united church took the name of "Geneseo Village."

The church at Penfield which was organized in 1806, and therefore among the oldest in all this section of the state, had by removals and deaths become very feeble at the time of reunion, reporting that year only 40 members, with its pulpit vacant, which with a few exceptions remained vacant with a decreasing number of members, until Presbytery, on the 18th of June, 1883, declared the church extinct. The trustees of the Presbytery subsequently sold the property and appropriated the proceeds of the sale to benevolent causes.

In response to a petition of 68 persons asking to be constituted the North Presbyterian Church of Rochester, a commission was appointed by Presbytery, which organized the same on the 12th day of February, 1884, said church being formed from a mission school which had been sustained in that part of the city by the Central Church, which also had provided the building, first occupied as a school, and afterwards as a church.

In the village of Piffard, a church of twenty individuals was organized by a commission of Presbytery, on the 24th of November, 1886. The building in which this church now worship was erected as a Dutch Reformed Church many years ago, and after that church became extinct, religious services were for years sustained by the church at Geneseo, which church contributed the most of the members to form the new church.

Emmanuel Church, of Rochester, is the result of a mission school established by the First Church of that city, which also provided the edifice first occupied as a school and now as a church. This church was organized by Presbytery on the 2nd day of May, 1887, consisting of sixty-eight members.

With these losses and gains, which we have here indicated, our roll of churches has been increased from forty-one to forty-five.

During these years there have been 10,400 communicants added to these churches, of whom, 6,618 were by examination, and 3,782 by certificate. The rite of baptism has been administered to 5,265 persons, of whom 2,856 were adults, and 2,409 were infants. There has been a commendable promptness on the part of the churches, in furnishing their annual reports for the Assembly's minutes, so that we have yet to have the first star affixed to any of our churches since the time of reunion.

Presbytery at its first meeting, Sept. 14, 1870, appreciating the difficulty of so large a body taking the proper over-sight of all its smaller churches, divided its territory into three districts, as follows:

1st. The County of Monroe, with the exceptions of Mendon, Honeoye Falls and Scottsville.

2d. Springwater, Livonia, Genesco, Lima, Avon, Caledonia, Scottsville, Honeoye Falls and Mendon.

3d. Leicester, Mount Morris, Groveland, Sparta, West Sparta, Dansville, Nunda and Ossian.

Presbytery at this time appointed conveners of these districts, leaving it for each district to perfect its own organization, with a view to promoting the spirituality of the churches and the mutual improvement of the ministers.

The first district never organized, it being thought that the Ministers' Association of the city, which, from that time to the present has been a vigorous body, holding weekly meetings, would quite largely do the work of a more extended association which should include the churches.

The second district was organized at once and adopted

the plan of monthly meetings, going from church to church, each meeting consisting of two services.

This association was, for a time, very prosperous, but the interest was maintained only for a few years, after which the organization was abandoned.

The third, or southern district, which was organized in 1870, has maintained a prosperous existence up to the present time, holding two meetings each year, the one in December occupying two days, and aiming especially to promote a revival spirit, while that in May is for one day, and of a more social character.

Provision has also been made by this association for the annual visitation of all its churches by sending two ministers to each church to hold special services for two days. The second district also provided for similar vistations.

After the abandonment of the second district, Presbytery, on the 21st of September, 1880, enlarged the bounds of the southern district, so as to include the whole of Livingston County, the church at Honeoye Falls being soon after added. The semi-annual meetings of this body have been well attended and the interest well sustained.

Prior to the year 1885, there had been a growing conviction that the stated meetings of Presbytery were too brief and too much restricted to mere business, which resulted in the inauguration of a plan that year for prolonging the meetings and providing for popular services with a view to the promotion of Christian work among the churches, which has been continued up to the present time with the happiest results.

The annual narratives have attested the healthy spiritual condition of the churches, no year passing without the report of some revivals. The labors of the evangelist, Rev. E. E. Davidson, in Rochester, Brockport, Lima, Geneseo, Mount Morris and Honeoye Falls, have been blessed in very large ingatherings, while the powerful revivals wrought of God through the labors of Rev. Charles G. Finney in the years 1830, 1842 and 1856 in the City of Rochester, still retain their impress upon the churches in this section, and are often referred to by those who were then converted, as characterized by very strong conviction of sin, followed by very positive evidence of a change of heart.

The absence of strife is worthy of special mention. Upon the reunion the old party lines were at once obliterated and all seemed desirous of heeding the apostolic injunction, " In honor preferring one another," and this is all the more noticeable when we remember that in connection with the great controversy which had prevailed our territory had been a prominent battle ground, and our ministers and churches had been very earnest—if not sometimes bitter partisans.

The peace of the churches has been attested by the almost entire absence of judicial business, nor have the few exceptions to the rule been traceable to former alienations, so that we may rejoice in the assertion that during all these eighteen years, our body has been as compact and homogeneous as could have been expected had there never been a schism.

In regard to benevolence we are able to give as the aggregate of our statistical reports for the years 1870 to 1887, inclusive, the following amounts:

Home Missions,	$156,811.00
Foreign Missions,	132,186.00
Education,	29,684.00
Publication and Sabbath-Schools,	25,303.00
Church Erection,	34,466.00
Ministerial Relief,	14,237.00
Freedmen,	20,251.00
Sustentation,	5,350.00
Aid for Colleges,	3,032.00
Assembly's Fund,	10,046.81
Congregational,	1,782,235.00
Miscellaneous,	81,710.00
Giving us a grand total of	$2,295,311.81

WOMAN'S MISSIONARY SOCIETY.

Prominent among the agencies for the collection of these funds and for awakening an earnest spirit of missions among our churches, we gratefully recognize the "Woman's Missionary Society of Rochester Presbytery," which was organized in the Central Church of Rochester, April 15, 1873, and which, from that day to this, has been an increasing power for good within our bounds. The officers first chosen were Mrs. H. D. Gregory, of Geneseo, President, and Mrs. D. H. Palmer, of Brockport, Secretary and Treasurer. Twelve churches were represented in this society at its organization, viz.: Brockport, Caledonia, Dansville, Geneseo Central, Geneseo Second, Livonia, Mount Morris, Ogden, Rochester Central, Rochester Memorial, Rochester Third and Sparta Second, and before the close of that year eight others were added, viz.: Groveland, Geneseo First, Ossian, Rochester Brick, Rochester St. Peters, Sweden, Tuscarora, and Union Corners.

Others were added from time to time, as follows:

In 1874, Gates, Lima, Rochester First, Rochester Westminster, Wheatland and Victor.

In 1875, Moscow, Parma Centre and Sparta First.

In 1876, Brighton and Nunda.

In 1877, Avon, Avon Central, Honeoye Falls and Webster.

In 1878, Rochester Calvary.

In 1879, Chili, Fowlerville, Mendon and Pittsford.

In 1883, Clarkson.

In 1885, Rochester North.

In 1887, Rochester Emmanuel.

Making in all, forty-three of our forty-five churches which have had these auxiliary societies.

The Presbyterial Society meets twice each year with a very large attendance. The amounts contributed by this society in 1873 were:

Home Missions,	$ 406.75
Foreign Missions,	1,832.65
Supplies,	745.99
Making a total of	$ 2,985.39

The amounts contributed the present year, 1887–8, are:

Home Missions,	$ 1,938.13
Freedmen,	704.94
Foreign Missions,	4,628.63
Supplies,	3,353.00
Total,	$10,634.70

Being an increase over the first year of $7,649.31. The total of the contributions of this society for the 16 years of its existence is:

Home Missions, including Freedmen,	$28,511.97
Foreign Missions,	44,261.73
Supplies,	30,232.11
Giving a grand total of	$103,005.11

During the last year Women's Auxiliary Societies have been reported from thirty-four churches besides thirty-five young people's societies and bands.

To the list of ministers belonging to this Presbytery, already referred to as laboring on the foreign field, we may add the following as representatives of this Woman's Presbyterial Society: Miss Hattie Seymour and Miss Carrie Bush, formerly of Rochester, now in Kharpoot, Turkey; Mrs. Rev. J. N. B. Smith, of Shanghai, formerly Miss Fannie Strong, of Lima; Mrs. Rev. Charles R. Mills, of Tungchow, formerly of Nunda, and Mrs. Rev. Frank P. Gilman, of Hainan, formerly Miss Marion McNair, of Sparta First.

SABBATH SCHOOLS.

In Sabbath-school work the record of our churches corresponds well with the advance which we have noticed in other departments, some of our schools reporting as high as six, seven and eight hundred members, while all the churches, with very rare exceptions, report schools that are well organized and doing efficient work. The total number of members in the Sabbath-schools reported in 1871, was, 7,655, while that of last year was 9,722, being an increase of 2,067, or more than twenty-five per cent.

TEMPERANCE.

In temperance there has been much accomplished, with alternations of encouragement and discouragement. Early in its history our Presbytery shared in the benefits of the Gospel Temperance movement which secured multitudes of converts throughout the country by means of prayer and moral suasion, which has given place, for the last six or eight years, to a movement more compulsory and political in its character, in which the real friends of total abstinence are quite divided on the question of methods.

The Woman's Christian Temperance Union has had vigorous branches in different parts of our field and in most of our parishes, and through these has furnished very efficient aid to our pulpits and Sabbath-schools in awakening and sustaining a healthy sentiment in favor of total abstinence.

This society traces its origin to what was known as the Woman's Temperance Crusade, which was started in the town of Hillsboro, Ohio, Dec. 23, 1873, by Mrs. Eliza Thompson, and which, after spreading the country over with astonishing rapidity, has subsequently crystallized into this more compact and efficient organization, which in its present form, has grown to be national and indeed world-wide in its extent, numbering already more than 6,000 societies in the United States, which aggregate 236,962 members of all denominations and races, having for its motto " For God and Home and Native Land." Reinforced by numerous recruits in Great Britain, this army has already seized upon strategic points in China, Japan, Australia and New Zealand, and is pushing on to new conquests, thus proving its aggressive and missionary spirit.

YOUNG PEOPLE'S SOCIETIES OF CHRISTIAN ENDEAVOR.

Within the last four or five years there have been springing up among our churches what are known as "Young People's Societies of Christian Endeavor," which are becoming quite common in various parts of our country and in the different religious denominations, and already are recognized as a most efficient agency for the training of young Christians to take part in prayer meetings, and to be helpful in other kinds of church work. Perhaps half of our churches are already blessed with these societies, with the number increasing from year to year.

INCORPORATION.

The Presbytery was incorporated in accordance with an act of the Legislature of the State on the 1st of November, 1875, by nine individuals who had been elected as a board of trustees, and was subsequently reorganized on the 18th of June, 1883. This organization is continued up to the present time by the annual election of three trustees who hold their offices for three years, which board of nine has the power to dispose of the property of extinct churches, and in other ways to care for the temporal interests of the Presbytery.

In comparing the number of communicants reported by our churches in 1871, which was 7,389, with the number reported last year which was 9,531, we find a gain of 2,142, or of about 30 per cent. But with this gain we are confronted with the fact that 14 churches have lost in their members, so that they report 396 less than in 1871. This is attributable in part to a diminished population in many of our rural districts. Indeed, while the city of Rochester has about doubled its population since 1870, the remainder of our territory has barely held its own. But our small churches have come up very nobly in the matter of self-support, very few of them drawing Home Missionary funds, the average being not more than $1,110.00 a year. The whole amount paid into the treasury of the Home Board from April 1, 1870, to April 1, 1889, is $84,360.39, while the amount drawn from that treasury during the same years is $21,075.00, leaving a balance in our favor of $63,285.39.

In noticing the changes which have occurred, we find that fifteen of the 50 original members remain, and that three retain the same pulpits which they then occupied, to which we may add the two foreign missionaries who still labor at Kharpoot. Of the other 35, twenty have been dismissed; while fifteen have died, as follows:

March 16, 1871, Rev. Isaac N. Lowrie at Minneapolis, Minn., aged 28.

August 22, 1871, Rev. Robert McMath at Webster, N. Y., aged 55.

September 10, 1871, Rev. Albert G. Hall, D. D., at Rochester, N. Y., aged 65.

November 9, 1871, Rev. Hezekiah B. Pierpont at Rochester, N. Y., aged 79.

March 24, 1872, Rev. John Barnard, D. D., at Lima, N. Y., aged 82.

December 20, 1872, Rev. Justus S. Hough at Syracuse, N. Y., aged 87.

July 4, 1876, Rev. Isaac Oakes at Nunda, N.Y., aged 81.

June 10, 1880, Rev. Charles E. Furman, D. D., at Rochester, N. Y., aged 79.

September 16, 1880, Rev. Charles Kittridge at Clarkson, N. Y., aged 72.

November 21, 1880, Rev. Milton Buttolph at Lima, N. Y., aged 88.

September 21, 1881, Rev. Lemuel Brooks at Churchville, N. Y., aged 83.

November 6, 1882, Rev. George McCartney at Banks, Mich., aged 69.

December 17, 1884, Rev. Joseph R. Page, D. D., at Rochester, N. Y., aged 67.

March 11, 1884, Rev. Thomas Aitken at North Sparta, N. Y., aged 84.

July 2, 1887, Rev. Malcolm N. McLaren, D. D., at Auburn, N. Y., aged 89.

Of those subsequently received the following eleven have deceased:

March 28, 1873, Rev. Joshua D. Lane at Henrietta, N. Y., aged 61.

August 8, 1873, Rev. Richard Dunning at Rochester, N. Y., aged 74.

September 8, 1875, Rev. John Henry Brodt at Dansville, N. Y., aged 48.

December 4, 1875, Rev. Alexander Douglass at Lima, N. Y., aged 37.

June 26, 1882, Rev. Elijah H. Bonney at Clarkson, N.Y., aged 65.

June 28, 1882, Rev. Thomas A. Weed at Saratoga Springs, N. Y., aged 65.

November 26, 1887, Rev. Benjamin F. McNeil at Adams, Mass., aged 61.

December 9, 1887, Rev. Charles Gillette at Rochester, N. Y., aged 72.

December 24, 1887, Rev. Charles Stoddard Durfee at East Bloomfield, N. Y., aged 43.

January 29, 1888, Rev. David Lathrop Hunn at Buffalo, N. Y., aged 98.

March 25, 1888, Rev. Alexander S. Hoyt at Ogden, N. Y., aged 48.

The average age of these twenty-six is sixty-eight and one-half years.

That both ministers and churches have sought permanency in the pastoral relation, is attested by the fact that we are able to name twenty-one ministers who have retained their pulpits for ten years and upwards. Three of these pastorates have been exceptionally long, viz: That of Rev. Wm. Hunter at Springwater, 44 years, with a promise of more, Rev. Thomas Aitken, 45 years at Sparta, and Rev. J. B. Shaw, D. D., 47 years over the Brick Church of Rochester, where beloved and honored by all he is still retained as pastor emeritus.

Very few churches have we been obliged to mark as vacant from year to year, and even these have seldom been contented to remain long without the permanent ministry.

On our catalogue of 157 ministers different colleges are represented by their graduates, in numbers, as follows: Hamilton 20, Union 20, Amherst 12, College of New Jersey 12, Rochester University 10, Yale 6, Williams 7, University of Pennsylvania 4, Lafayette 3, Middlebury, Westminster, Western Reserve, Washington, New York University, and Genesee, 2 each, and 1 each from Dartmouth, Geneva Hall, Marietta, Carroll, Monmouth, Jefferson, Columbia, Knox, University of Glasgow, Victoria University, Oberlin and Belfast. The remaining thirty-nine are not college graduates.

Theological seminaries have been represented as follows: Auburn 52, Princeton 34, Union 20, Andover 11, Lane,

Bangor, Alleghany U. P. and Alleghany R. P., two each, and one each from Yale, Oberlin, Newburgh, East Windsor, Belfast, Hartford, Edinburgh, Glasgow, Western Reserve, Monmouth, Rochester and Chicago. Twenty have not graduated from seminaries.

Trained as these men have been in so many different colleges and theological seminaries, it has been very noticeable that as a Presbytery we have with so much heartiness maintained our Calvinistic standards, causing us all to rejoice in the fact that our confession of faith and catechism, which were adopted a hundred years ago at the organization of our General Assembly, have remained substantially unchanged to the present, with the probability of successfully withstanding all opposition for the centuries that are to come.

Ours has truly been a favored part of the vineyard in which to labor. As we look about us we can say: "The lines have fallen unto us in pleasant places, yea we have a goodly heritage." He is a favored man to whom the Lord assigns a home in the valley of the Genesee.

And now as we turn from this brief sketch of the more prominent events in the history of the last eighteen years, to anticipate the victories for Christ which our Presbyterian church shall achieve in the years to come, we are confident that our beloved Presbytery will keep step with the others in this great army of conquest; and though one by one our names will be added to the list of those who sleep in Jesus, our covenant God will not fail to raise up from among our youth those who will more than fill our places.

BIOGRAPHICAL SKETCHES.

REV. ISAAC NEWTON LOWRIE.

The following minute, prepared by Rev A. H. Corliss, was adopted by Presbytery, October 19, 1871:

Rev. Isaac Newton Lowrie was born in Mecca, Parke County, Indiana, November 30, 1842, and died at Minneapolis, Minn., March 16, 1871. His parents died, the one in 1850 and the other in 1851. In 1860 he entered Wabash College. On the 26th of May, 1861, he united with the Presbyterian church in Crawfordsville, Ind. He was graduated from Genesee College in 1864, and in the fall of the same year entered the Seminary at Auburn. He was ordained as an evangelist at Lima, July 2d, 1867; married to Miss Mary E. Smith of Auburn, July 23d; sailed from Boston for Syria, October 8th, and arrived at Beyrout the last of November, 1867.

The latter part of the year 1869, his brethren in the mission and the physician advised his return home. He reached his uncle's home in Lima, July, 1870, and after resting a few weeks went to Minneapolis, where he died of consumption.

A modest, earnest, self-sacrificing disciple, the Master made his work day in the vineyard short; yet long enough to win the benediction, "He hath done what he could."

REV. ROBERT McMATH.

The Rev. Robert McMath was born at Romulus, Seneca County, N. Y., February 15, 1815; was graduated from Union College in 1838 and from Lane Seminary in 1841; was licensed by the Presbytery of Cincinnati in 1840, and was ordained by the Presbytery of Detroit, June 1st, 1843. He came into this Presbytery at the time of reunion as a member of the Rochester City Presbytery.

The following minute, as prepared by Rev. Charles E. Furman, D. D., was adopted by Presbytery, October 19, 1871:

"Among the uncommon numbers of fathers and brethren, ministers of the Presbyterian church, who have been called during the passing year, as we believe to the church above, we would not forget to mention and record the name of the Rev. Robert McMath, who died on the 22d day of August last, in Webster, the field of his last professional labors. It is with mournful pleasure we pay our tribute to the modest, but not the less real, worth of our beloved departed brother, in the usefulness of his work wherever called to perform it; the universal esteem in which he was held while living by those who had known him, and the universal sorrow with which his death is mourned."

REV. ALBERT G. HALL, D. D.

Rev. Albert G. Hall, D. D., was born at Whitehall, N.Y., April 12, 1805; was licensed by the Presbytery of Rochester, July 1st, 1835, and was ordained and installed by the same Presbytery as pastor of the church at Penfield, February 24, 1836, where he remained four years; after which he was for thirty-one years the pastor of the Third Church of Rochester; which relation was terminated by his sudden death on the 10th of September, 1871. His pastorate over this important church during those eventful years in the history of this city, is in itself an evidence that he was a man of more than ordinary power. Combined with this strength of character was a very genial disposition which served to attach others to him in strong friendships. In those days of division he was conservative and very pronounced in his preference for the old school branch, and as such was an acknowledged leader in Western New York. Able in debate, he was always at home on the floor of Presbytery and took the most intense interest in all its proceedings. In his death not only the Third Church but the entire Presbytery sustained a great loss.

REV. HEZEKIAH B. PIERPONT.

Rev. Hezekiah B. Pierpont was born in Litchfield, Conn., July 28, 1792; was licensed by the Presbytery of Rochester, Nov. 3d, 1831, was ordained as an evangelist by the same Presbytery, March 14th, 1833, and came into this Presbytery at the time of re-union as a member of the former Presbytery of Rochester.

The following minute, which was prepared by the Rev. Charles E. Furman, D. D., was adopted by Presbytery, April 10th, 1872:

"The Rev. Hezekiah B. Pierpont departed this life in Rochester at the house of his son, J. E. Pierpont, on the 9th day of November last, in the 80th year of his age. He was licensed and ordained to the work of the gospel ministry about forty years ago by the Presbytery of Rochester. He was for many years a successful minister of the gospel, preaching in Avon, Livingston Co., in Hopewell, Ontario Co., and other places. He was a good man and true, a faithful minister and approved of God; many counting themselves Christians as the fruits of his labors.

"Therefore, resolved that while we mourn the loss of a venerable brother as a highly respected and dearly beloved member of Presbytery, we submit to the order of Divine Providence, and rejoice that his last days were his best days and that the testimony of a happy and triumphant death was added to that of a lifelong example of the power of Christian faith."

REV. JOHN BARNARD, D. D.

The Rev. John Barnard, D. D., was born in Bolton, Worcester Co., Mass., Feb. 14th, 1790. He graduated at Union College in this state in the year 1813, and at Princeton Seminary in 1816, and in the same year was licensed by the Oneida Association. He commenced his ministry in Lima in 1818, where he was ordained and installed by a council, Feb. 3d, 1819, the church at that time being Congregational. He was received by letter from the Oneida Association as a member of Ontario Presbytery, July 4th, 1819, and elected its stated clerk, Feb. 9th, 1820, holding the office over fifty years or until the Presbytery was merged into the present Presbytery of Rochester. His pastorate at Lima continued 38 years, after which in the retirement of old age he resided there as the loving and efficient helper of his successors up to the time of his death, which occurred March 24th, 1872. As a writer he was choice in his diction, exact in his statements and classical in his style; as a preacher

REV. JOHN BARNARD, D.D.

he was clear, scriptural, earnest and tender ; as a pastor he was a model which we all loved to study, while as a man his character was remarkable for combining strength with simplicity, dignity with affability, and tenacity of purpose with tenderness of heart. But all his other gifts were secondary to his power in prayer. As his name was John it was not difficult to discover in him the traits of the disciple whom Jesus loved. At our ordination services he of all others was the chosen one to lead us at the mercy seat when by his communion with God he brought blessings to every heart.

REV. JUSTUS S. HOUGH.

Rev. Justus S. Hough was born in Sheffield, Mass., in 1785, was graduated from Middlebury College, Vt., in 1810, pursued his theological course with Rev. J. Bushnell of Vermont, which he concluded in 1814, about which time he was licensed by the Addison County Association, and soon after ordained by the same association.

He was received by the Presbytery of Ontario by letter from the Presbytery of Cayuga, Jan. 22d, 1834, and was installed pastor of the church at Livonia, Feb. 13th, 1834. He continued with that Presbytery until the re-union and thus came into this body.

The following minute, as prepared by Rev. Luther Conklin, was adopted by Presbytery, April 15th, 1873:

"Rev. Justus S. Hough, a member of this Presbytery, died in Syracuse at the residence of his son, in December (20th) last, at the age of 87 years. He * * * preached a number of years in his native state (Vermont). He then removed to this state and labored with great success in Port Byron and Livonia, until the loss of his voice put an end to his preaching thirty years ago. He was still eminently useful in the Bible class, the prayer meeting, and all the relations of private life, in Jordan and East Bloomfield. He was the coadjutor of his pastor in every good word and work. He was a man of strong common sense, vigorous mind and deep piety; and he retained his powers almost to the last. He was an illustration of the truth that a man's usefulness need not end with his labors as a preacher of the gospel."

REV. JOSHUA D. LANE.

The following minute was adopted by Presbytery, April 15th, 1873:

"The committee to prepare a minute in reference to Rev. Joshua D. Lane, a member of this Presbytery who departed this life on the 28th of March, would respectfully report: This beloved and faithful minister of Jesus was blessed with a godly parentage and ancestry. He was a child of the covenant, and devoted to the Lord by his parents with much prayer and careful training in all the doctrines and duties of our holy religion.

"His godly father was an earnest pioneer minister in Central and Western New York, whose great aim was to lengthen the cords and strengthen the stakes of the church. The subject of this brief notice, after a thorough preparation, commenced his work in the ministry in Smithport, Pa., but after several years' labor in the field, and much to the regret of his people, his failing health compelled him to leave. After laboring several years in Western New York till the breaking out of the war, he entered the Union army as chaplain of the 131st Regiment of New York Volunteers, where he was recognized as a true and faithful minister of Christ. Soon after his return from the army he preached for two years at Parma.

"At the beginning of the present year, he was invited to return to Smithport, and had just entered upon his work when he was called to his eternal rest. His end was full of peace, resignation, faith and hope. And we cannot doubt that abundant entrance was ministered unto him into the everlasting kingdom of our Lord. As we remember his many virtues, his noble qualities of head and heart, his love to the church and the truth of God, we hope that his departure may be blessed to the renewed consecration of his surviving friends to the cause of Christ."

REV. RICHARD DUNNING.

The following minute was presented by Rev. Joseph R. Page and adopted by Presbytery, Sept. 9, 1873:

"Presbytery would record the entrance upon his everlasting rest of Rev. Richard Dunning, a beloved member of this body, since our last meeting. He was licensed by this Presbytery forty-five years ago, and soon after by it ordained. Since that time until a year and a half before his decease he continued in the sacred office, ministering chiefly to the feeble churches of the region, to their acceptance and decided advantage. He was a man of a truly Christian spirit, never self-seeking and ambitious, but always ready to enter the most uninviting field, and labor in actual self-denial and comparative obscurity, for the salvation of souls and the extension of the Redeemer's kingdom. His ministry was attended with repeated and powerful revivals, due not only to his faithful and affectionate preaching of the gospel, but also to his habitual illustration of its excellence by a well ordered life and a godly conversation. He died in Rochester, Aug. 8, 1873, in the seventy-fifth year of his age. His last days were cheerful and brightened by the consciousness of his Savior's presence. None entered his sick chamber without feeling that it was just on the verge of heaven, and a blessed privilege to witness the victory which divine grace gave him over the last enemy. Our regret for his departure is swallowed up in gratitude for the worthy example he has left us, the good he was enabled to accomplish, and the reward upon which he has doubtless entered."

REV. JOHN H. BRODT.

Rev. John Henry Brodt was born in Troy, N. Y., June 2, 1827. He pursued his preparatory studies at the school of Mr. Anthony in a neighboring city and at the Polytechnic Institute in his native place. The years 1849 and '50 he spent at Williams College, and graduated at Union Theological Seminary in 1853. He was licensed by the Presbytery of Troy, June 29, 1853, and ordained by the same Presbytery, June 29th, 1854. He commenced his work as a minister of the gospel by accepting an appointment of the Home Mission Board to a field in California. His ministry of twelve years on the Pacific coast was crowned with abundant success. While there Mr. Brodt was for a time an editor of the *Pacific*, a Congregational paper published at San Francisco. This paper in referring to him said: "Mr. Brodt came hither in his youth, full of enthusiasm, fairly running over with good spirits. He had a good presence, fine looks, a bright eye and a clear, full voice, and so was a very pleasing preacher. His abilities were above the average."

Upon his return to the East he was settled for two years over the Presbyterian church in Salem, N. Y., and then over the Park Presbyterian church in New York city, which position he held until the dissolution of that body, when he was called to minister to the large and influential New England Congregational Society of Brooklyn, N. Y., where his labors were blessed with an abundant harvest of souls. About the year 1872, his failing health compelled him to retire from his church in Brooklyn and seek medical relief at Dansville, where, with his wife and six children, he resided for about three years, when his life work was closed.

The following resolutions with reference to his death which were prepared by Rev. G. K. Ward, of Dansville, were adopted by Presbytery, September 21, 1875:

"*Resolved*, That in the death of Rev. John Henry Brodt, which occurred on the 8th of Sept., 1875, [at Dansville, N. Y.,] we as a Presbytery recognize the wisdom and power of our Father in heaven, and bow before His righteous will, humbly acknowledging that He doeth all things well.

"*Resolved*, That we ever cherish with tender regard the memory of one who was at the same time a wise counselor, a true friend and a consistent Christian minister; and that we deeply appreciate the loss which we as a Presbytery, in common with the church and the world, have sustained in his death.

"*Resolved*, That to the bereaved and stricken family, who mourn the loss of a devoted husband and father, we extend our heartiest sympathy and love, while we commend them to the tender mercies of Him who has said, 'Blessed are they that mourn, for they shall be comforted.'

"*Resolved*, That a copy of these resolutions be presented to the family of the deceased, that they be entered upon the records of this body, and that they be published in the religious papers of our church."

REV. ALEXANDER DOUGLASS.

The Rev. Alexander Douglass was born at Cavan, Ontario Co., Canada, August, 1838. He studied three years at Genesee College and Michigan University, and graduated at Auburn Seminary in 1868.

He was received into this Presbytery as a licentiate of the Presbytery of St. Lawrence, and was ordained at Mendon as an evangelist on the 25th of April, 1872. He died at Lima, N. Y., December 4, 1875.

During his last year in the Auburn Seminary he overworked by preaching at Genoa, N. Y., and teaching in the State prison, from which he never fully recovered. In August, 1868, he went to the church in Seneca Castle, N.Y., where he remained more than a year and where his labors were blessed to the quickening of the church. He then, Nov. 4, 1869, took charge of the church at Evans Mills, N. Y., removing from there to East Mendon in 1871, where he was ordained in 1872. But failing health soon compelled him to seek a change of climate, which resulted in his serving the church at Menasha, Wis., for eight or nine months in 1873, when he utterly broke down, but where his labors were blessed with quite a revival Unusual interest also had attended his ministry at Evans Mills.

He was the son of a clergyman who had preached 40 years at Millbrook, Canada.

The following minute in regard to him was adopted by Presbytery, April 11, 1876:

"*Resolved*, That this Presbytery, having heard with sorrow of the death, on the 4th of December, 1875, of Rev. Alexander Douglass, a member of this body, desires to record its appreciation of his earnest and self-denying labors in the ministry of the gospel, to which he had consecrated his life. They rejoice to know that during his long and trying illness, he was sustained and comforted by the grace of that Savior, whom he so longed to commend to others. We deeply sympathize with his bereaved widow and orphans, and assure them of our earnest interest in their future welfare. In attestation of which, our stated clerk is directed to forward to them a copy of this resolution."

REV. ISAAC OAKES.

In regard to the death of Rev. Isaac Oakes, which occured at Nunda, N, Y., July 4, 1876, the Presbytery, under date of September 20, 1876, adopted the following minute, which had been prepared by Rev. F. De W. Ward, D. D.:

"*Whereas*, it has pleased our Heavenly Father in his wise and sovereign providence to remove from us by death Rev. Isaac Oakes, long a member of this Presbytery, at the ripe age of 81 years, therefore resolved, that a brief record of his life is not more our duty than our privilege, viz.: That he was born in Haverly, Franklin Co., Mass., June 10, 1795, graduated at Williams College in 1820 and at Andover Theological Seminary in 1823. He was licensed by the Essex Middle Association, Mass., and ordained by a Congregational council at Salem, Mass., Sept. 25, 1823. He united with the Genesee River Presbytery at the time of its formation. He first had a very useful pastorate of about eight years at Westfield, Chautauqua Co., in this state. Other charges which he served were Lancaster, Riga, East Bethany and Oakland, all in this state.

"*Resolved*, That we recognize in him one who shrank not from the Master's call, when that meant fidelity, amid all the toils and trials of pioneer missionary work in Western

New York. That we hold him in warm remembrance, as one of unwonted firmness in his convictions, tenderness in his family and patience in suffering; and that we see only a renewed pledge of the divine faithfulness, in the abundant grace with which God enabled his servant to endure the accumulated infirmities of his later years, and the perfect peace that attended his departure.

"*Resolved*, That we cordially unite in our expressions of sympathy with his bereaved and now desolate companion, and earnestly commend her to the care of Him, who is the husband of the widow and the father of the fatherless.

"*Resolved*, That these resolutions be entered upon the records of this body, and be sent for publication in the New York *Evangelist* and the Philadelphia *Presbyterian*, and that a copy of the resolutions be sent to the bereaved widow."

DAVID F. STEWART.

The following minute, as prepared by Rev. Charles E. Robinson, D. D., was adopted by Presbytery, June 18, 1883:

"David F. Stewart was born of Scotch parentage in York. Livingston Co , N. Y., July 16, 1848. He was left an orphan at five years of age. He pursued his academic course at Brockport, N. Y., and united with the Presbyterian church in that place about 1864. He pursued his freshman studies by himself while teaching in Buffalo in 1868. He began as sophomore in Rochester University in 1869 and graduated in 1872. He studied in Union Theological Seminary from 1872 to 1874, spending one summer vacation successfully among the New Hampshire hills, and another at Brockport, Me., in sowing the good seed of the word. The following winter, during his last year of study, his health gave way. After a year of rest, mainly spent at Caledonia, N. Y., he resumed his studies and graduated at Union Seminary in 1876. He supplied the pulpit of the Sixth Presbyterian Church at Chicago during the pastor's vacation, but his health again broke down. He retired to his brother's house, D. G. Stewart, Hamilton, Minn. In 1878 he visited California, finding only temporary relief, and returned to his Minnesota home, where he died, October 13, 1879, of pulmonary consumption.

"He was licensed April 13, 1875; he was not ordained. He was a man of a rare spirit."

REV. CHARLES E. FURMAN, D. D.

Rev. Charles E. Furman, D. D., was born in Dutchess County, N. Y., Dec. 13, 1801, graduated at Union College in 1826, and at Auburn Seminary, 1828. He was licensed by Cayuga Presbytery, June, 1828, and ordained by the same Presbytery, June, 1830. He came into this Presbytery at the time of reunion as one who had long been a member of the former Presbytery of Rochester.

The following minute was adopted by Presbytery, Sept. 20, 1880:

"The Rev. Charles E. Furman, D. D., having departed this life, since our last meeting, on the 10th of June, 1880, aged 78 years and 6 months [at Rochester], Presbytery would enter upon its records this minute, to express their sense of his excellencies as a Christian and the value of his long and faithful work as a minister. He preached the gospel fifty-two years, with the exception of a year or two before his death, when he was incapacitated by disease. All this time he was a member of this body, except a little over ten years, while he was a licentiate of the Presbytery of

Cayuga and when he belonged to the Presbytery of Niagara, and most of the time was pastor of the church in Medina. He served as pastor or stated supply, five of the churches of this Presbytery twenty-two years; eight in Clarkson, eight in Victor, three in Gates, two in Chili and one in Brighton. Large accessions were made to most of them, as the fruit of his earnest labors. He was emphatically a peacemaker and a son of consolation, and was beloved by all who knew him.

"In the days of his vigor he was uniform in attendance upon ecclesiastical meetings, where his counsels were highly prized. Ten years he served this Presbytery as its stated clerk [*i. e.* the former Presbytery of Rochester], and over twenty-five he was the permanent clerk of the synod. For some months before his departure he was a great sufferer, but exhibited the same gentle, submissive and trustful spirit that had uniformly characterized him in health. We who knew him long and well can truly say of him, he left the world better for having lived in it."

REV. CHARLES KITTRIDGE.

The following minute, which was prepared by Rev. D. R. Eddy, of Brockport, was adopted by Presbytery, Sept. 21st, 1880:

"Presbytery is called upon to record the death of Rev. Charles Kittridge, an aged and esteemed member, who has been connected with this body since 1870, and who was for twenty-five years previous to that time a member of Rochester City Presbytery. He died in Clarkson, N. Y., Sept. 16, 1880. He was born at Newburyport, Mass., in 1808, graduated at Dartmouth College in 1834, studied at Andover and East Windsor seminaries, and was ordained by the

Tolland Association in 1339. He preached in New England for some years, his labors being more or less interrupted from time to time by ill health. In 1845, he was installed as pastor of the church of West Greece, with which he continued his labors for some eleven years. He then removed to Clarkson, where he supplied the church for about a year. Severe physical sufferings and infirmities greatly interfered with his labors during the entire course of his ministry. For about forty-five years he has been more or less engaged in teaching. His pupils are scattered over the country from Maine to California, and are many of them occupying honorable positions as members of the various learned professions. Bro. Kittridge was a profound student of the word of God. He had read the Greek New Testament through in course some twenty-nine times and was very familiar with every phrase of it.

The latter months of his life were marked by a peculiarly rich and joyful experience. A halo seemed to him to rest upon the summer as it passed, so calm and peaceful and beatific did it prove. Among his latest memorable utterances was the expression, "The victory is won—I have crossed over, and oh what peace!"

REV. MILTON BUTTOLPH.

The following sketch of Mr. Buttolph appeared in the N. Y. *Evangelist* soon after his death:

"He was born in North East, Dutchess Co., in 1792, and consequently was 88 years of age in May last. He commenced active services in the church in early life, but was not ordained until 1827, and at the same time installed over the church in La Grange, Dutchess County, which he assisted in organizing, and with which he remained nearly ten years, leaving it strong and self-sustaining. During these ten years he was called upon to labor in nearly every church in North River Presbytery, holding revival meetings, preaching three times a day, besides holding meetings of inquiry. Hundreds would be the subjects of these meetings, some of whom have since become strong and stable official members of the churches. Upon leaving La Grange he removed to Medina, Orleans County, and while in the Niagara Presbytery in that county he was called upon to labor in many of the churches, as at the East, with great success. After several years in this county, he removed to Scottsville, Monroe County. During his ministry here a very precious revival occurred. The church was greatly revived, and a large accession was made, some of whom to-day are bearing the burdens of the same. He then went to Painted Post and Castile, and after several years of labor in these churches, he removed to Lima, in 1857. During the year he supplied the pulpits in Avon and Richmond. In the spring of 1858 he removed to Richmond, preaching alternately there and at Honeoye for four and one-half years, laboring unceasingly to bring the latter church up to nearly its present independence. In Bristol, Ontario County, he preached four and a half years. In most of these churches additions were made, and during this time very successful work was done in Rochester, Bergen, Knowlesville, Carlton, and many other places which I cannot now mention. In the spring of 1866 he returned to Lima, where he has since resided.

"His wife died nearly ten years since. She was Miss Elizabeth Christie, of Cornwall, Ct. By her he was greatly sustained and aided during his ministerial career, always ready and cheerfully meeting the demands upon her time and strength. Besides his three surviving children, he had an elder son, Edward, a practising lawyer in the city of Poughkeepsie, who died in Castile, in 1854. Mr. Buttolph's prominent traits of character were firmness of purpose, untiring energy, very fearless in defending a cause where a principle was involved. In the early days of the temperance and slavery questions he took decided ground against those evils, regardless of popularity, desiring only to do as the Master would have him. He was not content unless the church which he was serving was advancing, her graces growing, and accessions made to it of such as should be saved. Like David, he served his generation, and now his life work done, he has gone to his reward, to receive that crown of righteousness that was laid up for him. He met death calmly and peacefully, expressing himself as ready to meet his Savior. He was next to the oldest member of Rochester Presbytery."

He died at Lima, N. Y., Nov. 21, 1880.

REV. LEMUEL BROOKS.

The following sketch has been furnished by his daughter, Miss Maria Brooks, of Churchville, N. Y.:

Rev. Lemuel Brooks, was born in Brookfield, Conn., Nov. 27, 1797; united with the 1st Congregational church in Washington, Conn., 1815; and studied at Phillips Academy. He took his theological course at Auburn, N. Y. He married Miss Maria Brown, of Ogden, N. Y., 1827; died at Churchville, N. Y., Sept. 21, 1881; his wife and four daughters survived him.

This sketch of him was published in the *Evangelist*.

" He was born in Brookfield, Fairfield Co., Conn., where his grandfather spent all his life from early manhood to old age, as pastor of the Congregational church. He came to

Rochester when he was twenty-six years old, in the neighborhood of which he thereafter continued to reside. He was licensed to preach by the Presbytery of Rochester, Oct. 1, 1828, at Riga Centre. The following year he was ordained and installed pastor of the church at Penfield by the same Presbytery, Dr. Joseph Penney preaching the sermon. Subsequently he preached in Attica, where his labors were greatly blessed, fifty being added to the church in one year; to the church in Bethany and in Covington a year, where also there was an ingathering into the church. He preached in Chili four years, the same time in Churchville, and was settled seven years over the church in Webster. In consequence of excessive labors, particularly in preaching in the evening and exposing himself in long rides to the night air after the preaching, he lost his voice, and in 1847 ceased his work in the ministry and returned to Churchville, where he lived to the time of his death. He was an earnest, active Christian, in full sympathy with revivals of religion, and never so happy as when engaged in them.

"He made a profession of religion in the nineteenth year of his age, when living in Washington, Conn., where he became one of the converts in a wonderful work of grace, under the labors of Nettleton, the Evangelist. During most of his life he was in quite moderate circumstances. On the death of a brother a few years ago he inherited a large fortune, which he conscientiously used as a steward of the Lord, Hamilton College, Auburn Seminary, Lake Forest University, and all of our Church Boards receiving large sums."

His body was brought to Rochester and interred in Mount Hope.

REV. ELIJAH H. BONNEY.

The following minute, which was prepared by Rev. Henry Wickes, of Rochester, was adopted by Presbytery, Sept. 19, 1882, with reference to the death of Rev. Elijah H. Bonney, who had been received from the Presbytery of Niagara, Oct. 21, 1879.

"Your committee to present a minute concerning the decease of our dear Bro. Bonney, would report his entering into rest on the 26th day of June last, after a life of devoted labor in the work of the Master. He was born in Hadley, Mass., Nov. 4, 1816, was a graduate of Amherst, 1839, and of Union Theological Seminary, 1844, and from 1844 to the time of his death labored successfully in the churches in North Bennington, Pawlet, and Bellows Falls, Vermont, then in Vernon Centre, N.Y., Lenox, Madison Co., afterwards in Somerset, Niagara Co., and last at Clarkson, from whence he has been removed to the church above. In his removal the church meets with the loss of a man with warm sympathies, a wise counselor, quick to see the excellencies of others, and ready to cast the cloak of charity over the defects and errors of others.

"He was genial and warm-hearted as a friend, as a preacher and teacher scholarly, sound, instructive and evangelical, preaching Jesus, whom he loved and trusted as the light and life of the world.

"We tender our warm sympathy to the bereaved family, and to the church which has lost so faithful and excellent an under-shepherd, and pray the Great Head of the church to sanctify to them and to us the sore affliction which has been experienced in his decease."

REV. THOMAS A WEED.

Rev. Thomas A. Weed graduated at Oberlin College, Ohio, in 1843, and at Union Theological Seminary in 1847. He was licensed by the Congregational Association of New York and Brooklyn in 1846, and ordained by the Presbytery of Oswego in 1848. He was received into this Presbytery by letter from the Presbytery of Syracuse, April 11th, 1871, and soon after was installed pastor of the church of Wheatland (Scottsville).

The following minute, which was prepared by Rev. J. R. Page, D. D., was adopted by Presbytery, September 19th, 1882:

"The Rev. T. A. Weed having departed this life since our last meeting, Presbytery enter this record on their minutes, to express their sense of his great excellencies as a Christian man, and of his ability, fidelity and usefulness as a minister of the Word. Our dear brother died, June 28, 1882, at Saratoga Springs, to which place he had gone with the hope of restoring his health, which had become greatly enfeebled. Mr. Weed was born in Stamford, Ct., October 15, 1817. His first pastoral charge was in Mexico, Oswego County, N. Y. Here he labored with great assiduity and success for a period of twenty-three years. He manifested great interest in matters of education, and had a large share in shaping the sentiment of the community in which he so long lived.

"He was called to Scottsville in 1870, where he labored until his death. Genial and kindly qualities were his. Of commanding presence in the pulpit, he was very earnest, able and eloquent in his ministrations. The large attendance of both the brethren of the Presbytery, and of the community in which he lived, at the memorial services held after his death testified to the great esteem in which he was held, and the profound grief felt by all at his death. Above all, none who knew him questioned his earnest, devoted piety. We sympathize with the bereaved family and congregation, and exhort them one and all, ' His faith follow, considering the end of his conversation, Jesus Christ, the same yesterday, to-day and forever.' "

REV. GEORGE McCARTNEY.

The following minute was presented by Rev. Jonathan Copeland, of Webster, and adopted by Presbytery, June 18, 1883:

"Rev. George McCartney, who was for many years an esteemed member of this Presbytery, died in Banks, Mich., November 6, 1882, in the 72d year of his age. He was born and educated in Scotland for the ministry, and came to this country while young, intending only to make a brief visit and return; but finding the ocean passage severe, he concluded to remain, and make this his home. He engaged at first in teaching and editing a paper at Harrisburg, Pa. Afterwards he was ordained and installed pastor of the Dutch Church of Watervliet, N. Y., where he had a very successful pastorate of eleven years. Then he labored for a time at Beacon Hill, and afterwards removed to Webster, and became the pastor of the Presbyterian Church of that place, and continued seven years, when he was obliged to retire on account of feeble health. This was his last work. He was highly esteemed in this relation, both for his piety and able ministry; and his name among the people is still held in affectionate remembrance. He was a diligent student, possessed a clear and logical mind, was very thorough in his investigations of all subjects to which he gave his attention, and when his conclusions were reached was firmly settled in his opinions, was an able preacher and very warmly attached to the work of the ministry and deeply interested in all that related to the church of Christ. The last seven years of his life were years of confinement, and much of the time helplessness, but he gave ample evidence of the sustaining power of divine grace, so long as his mind was clear. He left a wife and two sons, one of whom is a minister of the gospel, and three daughters, to all of whom the brethren of Presbytery extend their cordial sympathy. Resolved, that a copy of this minute be sent to the family."

REV. THOMAS AITKEN.

Rev. Thomas Aitken was born in the town of Falkirk, Sterlingshire, Scotland, November 26, 1799, graduated at the University of Glasgow in 1819, and at the United Secession Seminary of Selkirk and Glasgow in 1823. He was licensed by the Presbytery of Sterling and Falkirk, June 8, 1824, and was ordained by the Presbytery of Cupar of the United Secession Church, June 2, 1829. As early as 1825 he went as a missionary to the Orkney Islands, and after a term of service covering about thirteen years in the old country, came to the United States. Here he first preached a short time at Fall River, Mass., but soon settled in Sparta, where he found a people allied to him by ties both natural and ecclesiastical, with whom he maintained the most tender pastoral relations up to the time of his death, March 11, 1884,—a period of about forty-five years ;—he having been released from the active duties of the ministry less than two

REV. THOMAS AITKEN.

years previous to that date. In him the Scotch clergy had a learned, eloquent and faithful representative. Strongly conservative in his tendencies, and very distrustful of innovations, his advocacy of the old school was so earnest that it seemed impossible that he ever could be reconciled to the union, but when once the two bodies came together there was not a man in all our Presbytery who appeared to enjoy the love feast more than he. In social life he mingled most delightfully with the families of his charge. His love of poetry, coupled with a very retentive memory, enabled him to recite copious extracts from his favorite authors for their entertainment.

Dating from his licensure his entire ministry was a little less than sixty years, during fifty-eight of which he promptly and untiringly met the demands of both pulpit and people.

REV. JOSEPH R. PAGE, D. D.

The Rev. Joseph R. Page, D. D., was born in New Brunswick, N. J., August 1, 1817. He pursued studies preparatory to the ministry with Rev. Alonzo Wilton, and was licensed by the New York City Association in 1838, and ordained by the Oneida Association, February 6, 1839, at Plymouth, N. Y., where he preached for about a year. He commenced his ministry at Perry, N. Y., in 1839, which, with two interruptions, continued until 1868. The first of these was that he might gratify his desire for a more thorough theological course, which he secured at Auburn, graduating with the class of 1844, and second, that he might accept the pastorate of the Congregational Church at Stratford, Conn., for the years 1857–8. After leaving Perry in 1868, he supplied the pulpit at East Avon for five years, and then was settled as pastor at Brighton for ten years. He died of heart disease in Rochester, December 17, 1884. As a member of the former Presbytery of Ontario, he was widely known in this section as very zealous for the New School Assembly, and prominent in the controversies which then prevailed. The merging of Ontario with this Presbytery was largely the result of his influence; and that his whole heart was enlisted in the welfare of this body was attested by the fact that during the fourteen years of his membership he was present at every stated meeting, and at almost all the special and adjourned meetings, giving the strictest attention to business from the commencement to the final correction of the minutes. For fifteen years he was a member of the Board of Commissioners of Auburn Seminary, and for about twenty years was a member of the Board of Trustees of Ingham University. While as a writer he was clear, concise, accurate and forcible, and as a preacher was arugmentative, scriptural, earnest and convincing, it was as a man among men, dealing with living issues and meeting practical questions, that the peculiar force of his character found its expression. On the floor of an ecclesiastical body he was perfectly at home. Ready in debate, ingenious in the arrangement of his points, honest in his convictions and urgent in his pleading, none could fail to recognize in him a successful leader. For fifteen years the correspondent of the New York *Evangelist*, for Western New York, the churches in this section knew not how greatly they were indebted to his vigorous pen, until it was laid down never again to be resumed. His ministry of forty-six years was long, laborious and successful.

REV. J. R. PAGE, D. D.

REV. MALCOLM N. McLAREN, D. D.

The following minute, which was prepared by Rev. F. De W. Ward, D. D of Genesco, was adopted by Presbytery, September 20, 1887:

Malcolm Neil McLaren, D. D., closed his long life at his home in Auburn, N. Y., July 1st, 1887. At the funeral services the city pastors were represented by Rev. C. C. Hemingway; the Theological Seminary by Prof. R. B. Welch; Rochester Presbytery by Rev. Dr. Parsons, of Mount Morris, and Rev. Dr. Ward, of Genesco. The three first named conducted the devotional exercises; the last because of long acquaintance and special intimacy of more than forty years, by request of the family, delivered the address.

His biography, in brief words, is this: Born at Albany, N. Y., July 1st, 1799, educated at Union College, (1824) and at Princeton Theological Seminary (1826); married Miss Patty, who, with two daughters and a son followed his remains to their last resting place. He ministered as stated supply or pastor at Brodalban, Hamptonburgh, Johnstown, Rochester First Church, Newburgh and Caledonia. Gifted and good are terms truthfully applicable to our deceased associate. Gifted with a form tall erect and graceful, specially courteous in manner wherever, seen; endowed with a mind well disciplined by study; having few equals in rhetoric and expressive pulpit delivery. For all these and for goodness of heart, and fidelity as preacher and pastor he will long be remembered in the many places of his abode and labors. His was an active, useful life, a peaceful death, and who can doubt a blessed immortality, in the presence of Him whom he long and faithfully served, and whose name was the last upon his lips. By his own request there was placed upon his coffin a copy of the Bible which was daily read at family worship; and an edition, dating back a half century, of the Westminster Confession of Faith, whose doctrines had so firmly imbedded a place in his intelligent faith, and were defended as occasion required, with a fearlessness worthy of his Scotch ancestry and early Presbyterian training.

Thus lived and labored and fell asleep at the advanced age of eighty-nine years, the next but one of the oldest of our members; leaving a name ever to be mentioned with fraternal esteem; an example worthy of personal imitation. Few of us will reach his age, but be ours the desire and earnest endeavor so to preach from the pulpit, so to counsel from house to house, so to plead with our fellow men, and pray to our God above, that whether called away as many are in mid-life, or with powers exhausted as were those of our venerable father in Christ, we can take up the valedictory utterance of the blessed Jesus: " I have finished O Lord the work thou gavest me to do."

REV. BENJAMIN McNEIL.

The following minute was adopted by Presbytery, April 9, 1889:

The Rev. Benjamin F. McNeil was born April 4, 1826, in the town of Genoa, Cayuga Co., N. Y.

Graduating at Hamilton College in 1852, he for some years after was a successful teacher in Pennsylvania, and was also connected with several newspapers.

In 1868, he graduated at Union Seminary, N. Y., and in May of the same year was licensed by the Presbytery of New York.

Devoting himself to the Home Missionary work, he was ordained as an evangelist in October, 1868, at St. Louis, Mo.

He soon gathered a church at Beatrice, Neb., where he was instrumental in building a church edifice. He organized a number of churches, and endured great hardships until he was prostrated by a sunstroke in the summer of 1874, from the effects of which he never fully recovered. Returning to the East and unable longer to preach, he made vigorous efforts to maintain his usefulness by editing religious newspapers, but his poor health compelled him in a few years to abandon all efforts of the kind and to seek rest in the ministers' home at Perth Amboy.

It was while editing a religious newspaper in the city of Rochester that he united with this Presbytery, April 18, 1879, by letter from the Presbytery of Newark; and though he remained here only about two years, he never transferred his relationship to any other body.

Owing to his poor health, his mind became much impaired. While on a visit to his mother in Adams, Berkshire Co., Mass., he died, November 26, 1887.

REV. CHARLES GILLETTE.

The following sketch was prepared by the Rev. John E. Baker, of Rochester, and was adopted by Presbytery, April 10th, 1889:

Rev. Charles Gillette, a member of this Presbytery, closed his earthly life, and ministerial labors at Rochester, N. Y., December 9, 1887, aged 74.

He was born in Halifax, Vt., Oct. 17, 1813. His parents removed during his early childhood to Ox Bow, Jefferson Co., N. Y. He was fitted for college at Lowville Academy, and Whitesboro, N. Y., graduated at Amherst, Mass., in 1839, and at Union Theological Seminary, N. Y., in 1842

His first ministerial charge was in Granville, Washington Co., N. Y., where he remained from 1844 to 1847. He next supplied the church in Huntington for one year. In 1848, he was installed pastor of the Presbyterian Church in Fort Covington, Franklin Co., N. Y., where he remained until 1858. In December, 1858, he began preaching in Milford, Otsego Co., N. Y., where his pastorate continued twelve years. In 1871, he took charge of the Congregational Church in Mannsville, Jefferson Co., N.Y., remaining with it three years.

His last charge was in Red Creek, Wayne Co., N. Y., which also lasted three years.

Ten years before his death he removed to Rochester, N. Y., for the purpose of educating his children. His subsequent ministerial labors were confined to occasionally preaching in churches near the city.

He left a wife and four children, pecuniarily well provided for.

While in the Theological Seminary, he established a mission on 50th Street that grew ultimately into a large church. While located at Milford, he was stated clerk of the Presbytery for 10 years. He was a genial man—a faithful and successful pastor, and a kind husband and father. His end was peaceful. He sleeps in Jesus.

REV. CHARLES STODDARD DURFEE.

The following minute, which was prepared by the Rev. S. A. Freeman, was adopted by Presbytery April 11, 1888:

Rev. Charles Stoddard Durfee, a member of the Presbytery of Rochester, after a lingering illness of several months duration, died at East Bloomfield, N. Y., Saturday, December 24, 1887. He was born July 22, 1844, at South Dedham, Mass., where his father, Rev. Calvin Durfee, was for fifteen years pastor of the Congregational Church. A graduate of Williams College in 1864, converted to Christ the year before his graduation, his direct preparation for the gospel ministry was made at Hartford Theological Seminary, where he graduated in 1869. Ordained the same year, he was installed as pastor of the First Presbyterian Church, Newburyport, Mass., where he remained until 1872, when he accepted a call to the Oakwood Avenue Presbyterian Church, Troy, N. Y. Thence, in 1874, he was called to the Central Presbyterian Church, Geneseo, of which he remained pastor until 1880. In that year he resigned his pastorate for the purpose of facilitating the reunion of the First and Central Churches of Geneseo, whose separation of more than twenty years duration, was a local relic of the old divisions in the church at large so happily healed in 1870. The successful accomplishment of this reunion, toward which our beloved brother, entirely of his own motion, took the first essential steps, was a consummation whose fruitful results for good are largely due to his self-abnegation, creditable alike to the head and heart of the true disciple of the blessed Master,—a consummation which could probably never have been attained without his entire willingness to sacrifice himself and his apparent interests to what he felt to be the highest welfare of Christ's church and cause in a community which he dearly loved.

After a pastorate of three years with the Presbyterian Church, Liverpool, N. Y., in May, 1884, he accepted a call to the Congregational Church of East Bloomfield, N. Y., in the pastorate of which he continued up to the time of his death. A faithful student of God's word, a clear and forcible preacher of the Gospel, a kind and faithful pastor, courteous and attractive in the intercourse of social and domestic life, thoughtful of the welfare of all about him, of whatever age or outward circumstances, our brother was characterized by the unyielding courage with which he adhered to his convictions of truth and duty at cost of whatever trial to himself. Throughout his useful life he showed a deep interest in the work of Christian missions, Christian temperance, and all that pertain to the welfare of the young. His habitual open-handed, though unobtrusive beneficence ministered to the need of many a sufferer. As a devoted minister of Christ's gospel and as a brother beloved, we would revere his name and honor his memory. May the Lord help us who remain, heirs of a like precious faith, to be true to our high vocation, and to work with redoubled diligence while our day lasts!

To his bereaved widow, Mrs. Ellen R. Durfee, and his five fatherless sons we would express our deep sympathy in what is our common loss,—our joy in the sweet peace given him during his last days by the Master whom he loved and trusted. May such peace be theirs and ours in all the unknown future! In token of our sympathy and kind wishes our stated clerk will forward to Mrs. Durfee a copy of this minute, signed by himself and the moderator of Presbytery.

REV. DAVID L. HUNN.

The following sketch, as prepared by the Rev. George Patton, of Rochester, was adopted by Presbytery, April 9, 1889:

Rev. David L. Hunn was born at Colrain, Mass., on November 5, 1789. His father was a soldier of the Revolutionary war, and suffered and survived the hardships of the infamous "Jersey prison ship." Mr. Hunn was prepared for college at Munson, Mass., under the tuition of the Rev. Levi Collins. He entered Yale College in 1809, and graduated in 1813, with a class of 70 members, under the presidency of Dr. Timothy Dwight. Mr. Hunn studied theology at Andover for three years, and was ordained to preach the gospel on the 17th of February, 1817. His first pastoral charge was at Greenland, Mass. After, he had charge of the churches of Sandwich, Mass., East Windsor, Conn., North Hadley, Mass., Whitesboro, Lenox and Somerset, N. Y.

Mr. Hunn was married to Miss Eunice Saxton, of Wilbraham, Mass., in 1817. They lived together fifty-five years; they had eight children, seven of whom survive them. Mr. Hunn spent most of his active ministry in the Congregational Church, and was quite active in church courts, but for many years he was connected with the Presbyterian Church, and was a member of Rochester Presbytery. He retired from the active duties of the ministry in 1860, but preached occasionally up to 1880. For several years he attended the Third Presbyterian Church of Rochester. In 1881, he went to Buffalo to live with his son, and as long as he was able, attended the North Presbyterian Church in that city. He was very earnest in educational and church work and faithful in his pastoral and religious duties. He voted at every Presidential election since 1812, up to the time of his death, and was greatly interested in public affairs. He could not be called an orator in the pulpit, but he was dignified, earnest, had a well-trained voice and excellent diction. He was a good, faithful minister of the Lord Jesus Christ.

He died at Buffalo, January 29, 1888, at the age of 98 years. He had long been the oldest living graduate of Yale and Andover, and was thought to be the oldest minister in the country. He was buried at Mount Hope, in Rochester, N. Y. He was carried to, and laid in his grave by several of his brother ministers in the full and blessed hope of a glorious resurrection through Christ.

REV. ALEXANDER SYLVESTER HOYT.

The following minute, as prepared by Rev. C. B. Gardner, of Rochester, was adopted by Presbytery April 10, 1889 :

Rev. Alexander Sylvester Hoyt died March 25, 1888. He was stricken with paralysis in the pulpit in the midst of the Sabbath morning service. After lingering several days and experiencing a renewal of the stroke, he passed away in unconsciousness on the following Sabbath. He had expected on that day to receive into the communion of the church a considerable number of the young people of his flock, who had been brought to faith in Christ through his labors. Even after his first stroke he had hoped that he would recover sufficiently to perform that service upon which his heart had been set. But it was ordered otherwise, and the expected communion Sabbath was the day of his death. He had wrought assiduously and effectively in the charge committed to him, and died at his post greatly honored and beloved by his people.

He was born at West Milton, Saratoga Co., N. Y., July 24, 1839. He graduated from Union College in the class of 1864, and from Princeton Theological Seminary in the class of 1868. He was licensed by the Presbytery of Albany, in June, 1867, and was ordained by the Classis of Saratoga, October 20, 1868. His first charge was at Greenwich, Washington County, N. Y., where he remained but a few years. From Greenwich he removed to Ballston Centre, Saratoga County, where he continued in a successful pastorate for a period of twelve years. From Ballston Centre he was called to the pastorate of the church in Ogden, as the successor of Rev. A. McA. Thorburn.

In the beginning of his ministry his physical appearance did not seem to give promise of a long life of service. His first text at Greenwich was—"I shall be satisfied when I awake in thy likeness," and one who was present remarked that the young man himself would soon prove a personal exemplification of the text. But his health seemed to improve in the ministry, and while at Ogden he was apparently possessed of sufficient robustness for a long life.

Brother Hoyt was a close student. He delighted in his books, and his mental tendencies were towards the investigation of metaphysical and theological questions. He had been closely engaged for some time before his death upon a work in criticism of Edwards on The Freedom of the Will, which he intended to publish. He was an instructive, if not an attractive preacher, and an acceptable pastor. He was a staunch defender and upholder of what he regarded as truth and right in all moral and ecclesiastical questions. He was in deed a strict disciplinarian, a thorough reformer, and an earnest and godly man.

He saw that death was near and was ready. Funeral services conducted by ministers of the Presbytery, without funeral drapery or tolling of the bell—as he had desired—were held in the church, filled to overflowing by the bereaved people, on Tuesday following his death, and on the following day the body was removed to Johnstown, N. Y., for burial. The funeral services were conducted by Rev. John E. Baker, assisted by Rev. A. S. Freeman and Rev. C. B. Gardner, also Rev. Mr. Mitchell, of Sweden.

REV. WILLIAM H. MILLHAM.

This sketch was written by Rev. S. A. Freeman, D. D.

William H. Millham, the fifth child of James Millham, a farmer of Charlton, Saratoga Co., was born in 1840. Notwithstanding his lack of early religious training, while yet a lad he began attending a Presbyterian Church at a considerable distance from his home, where he was converted to Christ. Inclined at first to rebel at the loss of a hand at the age of seventeen, he afterwards often said that it was the greatest blessing in disguise of his life. Led to dedicate himself to the ministry of the Gospel, he graduated at Union College in 1864, and at Princeton Theological Seminary in 1867. Beginning his ministry in the Presbyterian Church at Galway, N. Y., in 1867, where he was ordained in 1868, he came to Livonia in 1871. Thoroughly consecrated to his work, full of sympathy for all, especially for the young, studious and prayerful in preparation for the pulpit, diligent in pastoral work, notably consistent in his daily life, from the first he won his way to the hearts of his people for himself, for his Master, and for his message. Their confidence, their respect, and their warm affection were his to the end. This was true, too, among other denominations, his Catholic spirit doing much to encourage Christian union in every good work. His labors were blessed with revival after revival, reaching those of all ages and conditions in life. His conduct of services at such seasons was marked by a happy tact in the choice of the right word, in the use of the right hymn at the fitting moment, delighting as he did in sacred song. The sway of his influence quickening the life of the church along all lines, was firm and forceful as it was gentle. The beneficent agencies of the church at large were heartily supported. He was through life a wise and whole souled friend of the temperance cause. Warm-hearted and sunny-tempered, kind and courteous in his bearing toward his brethren in the ministry, his presence among them was always conducive to the sweetening of Christian fellowship, the deepening and strengthening of their spirituality. The unction with which his carefully prepared sermons were delivered was an inspiration to all who heard them. Pastor for fourteen blessed years of a church strictly rural, the spirit and methods of the ministry of William H. Millham made it a worthy model for young men laboring in similar fields, or, indeed, anywhere. His quiet influence was largely helpful of that harmony in which earnest gospel work has characterized Rochester Presbytery since the re-union. Accepting a call to Hillsdale, Mich., in 1885, he there filled out the measure of his abounding usefulness, almost the last Sabbath of his active ministry bieng gladdened by the reception of thirty young converts. A lingering struggle with disease closed peacefully, April 28, 1888.

He was married in 1867 to Miss Augusta Tracy Barbour, daughter of Rev. Philander Barbour. She survives him, with three sons and one daughter.

REV. LUTHER CONKLIN.

Rev. Luther Conklin was born at Aurora, Erie Co., N.Y. March 29th, 1817, graduated at Hamilton College in 1841, and at Auburn Seminary in 1844; was licensed by the Presbytery of Cayuga, April 18, 1844, and was ordained by the Presbytery of Onondaga in 1845.

From a biographical sketch prepared by his brother, the Rev. Oliver P. Conklin, of Rochester, and adopted by Presbytery April 9, 1889, the following facts respecting his history are gathered:

He was the sixth in descent from Ananias Conklin who with his brother John came from England about 1640 and settled first in Mass., for ten years and then at East Hampton, Long Island. His mother was a Guthrie, whose ancestors were of Scotch descent, and came to this country from the north of Ireland. He was the youngest of eight brothers and sisters, his father dying when he was only six years old. He was converted when he was about sixteen, and two or three years later began to prepare for college with a view to preaching the gospel. He entered college when he was twenty-one, where he was intimately associated with Profs. North and Dwight, and Rev. Drs. Kendall, Nelson and Knox, who were his fellow students.

After graduating at Auburn in 1844, he soon after began his ministry in the Presbyterian Church at Liverpool, N.Y., at the age of 27.

He was married at Leicester, Mass., in November, 1844, to Miss Almira Henshaw with whom he became acquainted while she was principal of the Female Seminary in Fulton, N. Y., who survives him.

After a service of two years at Liverpool, he took charge of the Congregational Church in Moravia, N. Y., where he labored very successfully five years. He then removed to Freeport, Maine, where he spent about six years in a pastorate which seems to have been very satisfactory to all.

He was then called to the pastorate of the Congregational Church of East Bloomfield, N. Y., where he remained ten years, when he resigned, mainly on account of ill health.

With the hope of improving his health by out-door labor he purchased a small farm near Rochester, which he cultivated very successfully, and where he spent the remnant of his days, preaching as he had opportunity, for ten or twelve years after leaving Bloomfield.

From a child his health was frail, and in his later years, he was called to endure very great suffering, often causing him to wish that the end might come. He was confined to his house and to his bed, however, only a few days before his death, which occurred October 2, 1888.

While his contributions to benevolence during his life were very liberal, he may be regarded, though dead, as yet preaching the gospel in the large bequest which he has made to the Presbyterian Board of Foreign Missions.

MINISTERS BELONGING TO ROCHESTER PRESBYTERY

From the Time of its Formation, in 1870, to November, 1889.

NAMES.	WHEN RECEIVED AND WHERE FROM.	DEATHS AND DISMISSIONS.
Justus S. Hough	June 29, 1870, Presb. of Ontario	Died at Syracuse, N. Y., Dec. 20, 1872.
John Barnard, D. D	"	" Lima, N. Y., March 24, 1872.
Isaac Oakes	" Genesee River	" Nunda, N. Y., July 4, 1876.
Isaac N. Sprague, D. D.	" Ontario	Dis. Presb. of Detroit, April 27, 1877.
Malcom N. McLaren, D. D.	" Genesee River	Died at Auburn, N. Y., July 2, 1887.
Thomas Aitkin	"	" North Sparta, N. Y., March 11, 1884.
Milton Buttolph	" Ontario	" Lima, N. Y., Nov. 21, 1880.
Lemuel Brooks	" Rochester	" Churchville, N. Y., Sept. 21, 1881.
Charles E. Furman, D. D	"	" Rochester, N. Y., June 10, 1880.
Hezekiah B. Pierpont	"	" " Nov. 9, 1871.
James B. Shaw, D. D.	" Rochester City	Died at Rochester, Sept. 10, 1871.
Albert G. Hall, D. D.	" Genesee River	
Ferdinand De W. Ward, D. D.	" Buffalo City	
George W. Lane	" Ontario	Died at Rochester, Dec. 17, 1884.
Joseph R. Page, D. D.	" Rochester City	" Clarkson, N. Y., Sept. 16, 1880.
Charles Kittridge	"	" Webster, N. Y., Aug. 22, 1871.
Robert McMath	" Ontario	
William Hunter	" Rochester City	
Oliver P. Conklin	" Rochester	Dis. Presb. Genesee Valley, April 11, 1871.
Nathaniel Elmer	" Ontario	Died at Irondequoit, N. Y., Oct. 2, 1858.
Luther Conklin	" Rochester City	" Banks, Mich., Nov. 6, 1882.
George McCartney	" Rochester	Dis. Presb. of Niagara, April 11, 1876.
Austin G. Wilcox		

NAMES.	WHEN RECEIVED AND WHERE FROM.	DEATHS AND DISMISSIONS.
Samuel M. Campbell, D. D.	June 29, 1870, Presb. Rochester	Dis. Presb. St. Paul, June 7, 1881.
William B. Stewart	" " "	" " Champlain, June 17, 1873.
Washington D. McKinley.	" " Genesee River	" " Genesee, April 14, 1871.
William E. Jones, D. D.	" " "	Dis. North Presb. of Phil., Sept. 9, 1873.
John Jones, D. D.	" " "	" Presb. Louisville, Sept. 10, 1874.
Orson P. Allen	" " Ontario	
Herman N. Barnum, D. D.	" " "	
Levi Parsons, D. D.	" " "	
Lucius D. Chapin.	" " "	Dis. Presb. Genesee, Oct. 22, 1872.
Dwight Scovel	" " Rochester	" " Syracuse, Sept. 13, 1871.
Joseph L. Whiting	" " Ontario	
Samuel Jessup, D. D.	" " "	Dis. Presb. Utica, April 10, 1872.
Henry M. Hazeltine.	" " "	" " Westchester, April 9, 1872.
Levi G. Marsh.	" " "	" " Kalamazoo, Sept. 19, 1876.
Alexander McA. Thorburn	" " Rochester	" " Syracuse, Nov. 6, 1882.
Alphonso L. Benton.	" " Ontario	" " Buffalo, Sept. 14, 1870
Samuel A. Freeman, D. D.	" " Rochester	
Alvin Baker.	" " Ontario	Dis. Presb. Huron, April 9, 1872.
Edwin B. Van Auken	" " Rochester	
Gavin L. Hamilton	" " "	Dis. Presb. Niagara, Dec. 30, 1875
Henry M. Morey.	" " "	" " Logansport, Oct. 20, 1874.
Willis Clark Gaylord	" " Ontario	
Thomas Dobbin.	" " Genesee River.	Dis. Presb. St. Lawrence, Aug. 9, 1875.
James Ballentine.	" " Rochester City	
Herbert W. Morris, D. D.	" " "	Dis. Congl. Ass.,N.Y., and Brooklyn,April 11,1871.
Charles P. Bush, D. D.	" " Rochester	Died at Minneapolis, Minn., March 16, 1871.
Isaac N. Lowrie.	" " Ontario	
John E. Baker.	" " Rochester	Dis. Presb. Philadelphia, Dec. 7, 1870.
James M. Crowell, D. D.	" " Rochester City	" " Buffalo, April 9, 1877.
Henry Wickes.	Sept. 14, 1870, Middlesex Association	

111

Name	Date	Place	Status
J. Lovejoy Robertson	Dec. 7, 1870, Presb. Cincinnati		Dis. Presb. Cleveland, Nov. 12, 1877.
Walter V. Couch	" " " " Buffalo		" Los Angeles. April 12, 1887.
Albert H. Corliss	Dec. 27, 1870, " Utica		" Utica. Dec. 30, 1875.
Joshua D. Lane	April 11, 1871, " Buffalo		Died at Henrietta, N. Y., March 28, 1873.
Thomas A. Weed	April 11, 1871, Presb. Syracuse		Died at Saratoga Springs, June 28, 1882.
William H. Millham	Sept. 12, 1871, " Albany		Dis. Presb. Monroe, Dec. 26, 1885.
Peter Kimball	" " " Buffalo		" Cleveland, Sept. 16, 1879.
David L. Hunn	Oct. 18, 1871, " Genesee Valley		Died at Buffalo, N. Y., Jan. 29, 1888.
George G. Smith	" " " Cayuga		Dis. Presb. Buffalo, July, 21, 1874.
Jerome Allen	" " " Dubuque		" New York, April 10, 1888.
George Patton	Dec. 21, 1871, " Geneva		
Asa S. Fiske	Mch. 3, 1872, Congregational Association		Dis. Presb. San Francisco, Aug. 9, 1875.
T. Dwight Hunt	April 10, 1872, Presb. Kalamazoo		" Lyons, Sept. 21, 1885.
D. Henry Palmer	" " " Steuben		" Geneva, Sept. 21, 1875.
Alexander Douglass	April 25, 1872, Ordained		Died at Lima. N. Y, Dec. 4, 1875.
Richard Dunning	Sept. 10, 1872, Presb. Lyons		Died at Rochester, Aug. 8, 1873.
John Mitchell	Oct. 21, 1872, " Albany		
Ephraim W. Kellogg	April 14, 1873. " Lyons		Dis. Presb. Binghamton, April 13, 1875.
Henry H. Morgan	" " " Kalamazoo		" St. Lawrence, April 11, 1876.
John Henry Brodt	" " Asso. of Brooklyn		Died at Dansville, N. Y., Sept. 8, 1875.
George K. Ward	June 4, 1873, Ordained		
Albert B. King	" 17, " Presb. Lackawanna		Dis. Presb. Elizabeth, April 9, 1878.
George Craig	July 21, 1874, " Albany		" Utica, Sept 18, 1877.
William B. Marsh	" " " Lyons		" Cleveland, Nov. 22, 1875.
Charles S. Durfee	Sept. 10, 1874, " Troy		" Syracuse. April 11, 1881.
George C. Jewell	Oct. 8, 1874, Ordained		D s. Congl. Ass. Western N. Y., Sept. 16, 1878.
Horace P. V. Bogne	" 20, " Presb. Boston		
John K. Fowler	Nov. 10, 1874, Ordained		Dis. Presb. Freeport, Dec. 13, 1877
Corliss B. Gardner	Feb. 4, 1875, Presb. Genesee Valley		
Wm. Tapely Hayward	April 13, 1875, Susquehanna Assoociation		Dis. South Kansas, Ass, April 9, 1877
Lewis H. Morey	May 25, 1875, Ordained		Dis. Presb. Geneva, Feb. 10, 1880.
Charles P. Coit	Dec. 30, 1875, Presb. Binghamton		
Silas McKinney	April 11, 1876, Grand River Con		Dis. Presb. Lyons, Sept. 16, 1879.
Jonathan Copeland	" " " Montpelier Association		

NAME.	WHEN RECEIVED AND WHERE FROM.	DEATHS AND DISMISSIONS.
Bentley S. Foster	April 11, 1876, Presb. Newton	Dis. Presb. Saginaw, April 10, 1882.
Herman C. Riggs, D. D.	May 8, 1876, " Jersey City	" Susquehanna Ass., April 12, 1887.
David R. Eddy	" " " Saginaw	
William G. Hubbard	Oct. 18, 1876, " Niagara	Dis. Presb. Lyons, June 18, 1883.
Bernhard Pick, Ph. D.	" 17, " on examination	" Lutheran Body, April 15, 1884.
Josiah E. Kittredge, D. D.	April 9, 1877, Hartford Central Asso.	
David Conway	" " " Presb. Newton	Dis. Presb. New Castle, Sept 18, 1877.
Henry N. Payne	" " " Syracuse	" Otsego, Feb. 7, 1879.
James Robertson	April 10, 1877, "	
Linus W. Billington	" " " Genesee Valley	
Dugald D. McColl	April 27, 1877, " Geneva	Dis. Presb. Genesee, Sept. 17, 1878.
Charles Gillette	Sept. 18, 1877, " Lyons	Died at Rochester, Dec. 9, 1887.
Charles E. Robinson, D. D.	April 9, 1878, " Troy	Dis. Presb. Lackawanna, March 19, 1888.
Edward Bristol	" " " Buffalo	
Robert McLean	" " " Milwaukee	Dis. Presb. Oregon, Nov. 12, 1883.
Chester P. Murray	May 14, 1878, " Morris and Orange	" Cayuga, Oct 21, 1879.
Thomas E. Babb	June 12, 1578, Central Asso. Worcester	
Eneas McLean	" " Ordained	Dis. Presb. Wisconsin River, March 5, 1883.
James White	" " "	" Milwaukee Con. April 14, 1885.
William F. Millikan	Sept. 17, 1878, Presb. Zanesville	Dis. Presb. Neosho, Sept. 22, 1885.
Eugene G. Cheesman	Oct. 22, 1878, " Otsego	" Lyons, April 15, 1879.
Thomas Stephenson	Oct. 29, 1878, " Winnebago	" Rock River, March 7, 1882.
John P. Campbell	Nov. 18, 1878, Ordained	" Baltimore, Dec. 6, 1878.
Robert J. Beattie	April 15, 1879, Presb. Chemung	" Peterborough, Can., Nov. 18, 1878.
Benjamin F. McNeil	Sept. 16, 1879, " Newark	Died at Adams, Mass., Nov. 26, 2887.
Frederick D. Seward	Oct. 21, 1879, " Steuben	Dis. Presb. Los Angeles, Sept. 20, 1881.
Newton J. Conklin	Oct. 21, 1879, " St. Lawrence	
Elijah H. Bonney	" " " Niagara	Died at Clarkson, N. Y., June 26, 1682.
Alfred A. Graley		
Solon A Whitcomb	April 26, 1880, " Binghamton	Dis. Presb. Niagara, Sept. 18, 1882.

113

Name	Date	Notes
James L. Box	April 13, 1880,	From Free Baptist. Dis. Presb. Lackawanna, Sept. 18, 1888.
John Edward Close	Sept. 21, 1880,	Presb. Syracuse.
James F. Calkins	" "	" Wellsboro.
David M. Rankin	Sept. 21, 1880,	Presb. Utica. Dis. Presb. Niagara, April 11, 1882.
Gavin I. Hamilton	" "	" Niagara. " Buffalo, Sept. 20, 1881.
Robert D. Sproull	Oct. 25, 1880,	" Rochester Reformed. " Boston, Nov. 5, 1883.
William Adams	Jan'y 17, 1881,	Ontario Association. " Louisville, April 13, 1881.
Theodore W. Hopkins	" "	Chicago Association.
Henry Wickes	April 12, 1881,	Presb. Buffalo. Dis. Presb. Genesee, April 10, 1882.
Samuel Bowden	" "	" Niagara.
T. Morey Hodgman	April 13, 1881,	Ontario Association.
Newton H. Bell	May 17, 1881,	Presb. Wooster. Dis. Presb. St. Paul, Sept. 15, 1884.
F. Swartz Crawford	Oct. 27, 1881,	" Detroit. " Pittsburgh, April 10, 1888.
Theodore B. Williams	April 10, 1882,	" Buffalo. " Niagara, June 22, 1885.
John K Kilbourn	" "	" Utica. " Lackawanna, Sept. 4, 1888.
George Craig	Oct. 25, 1882,	Winnebago Con. " Saginaw, Sept. 21, 1886.
John M. Carmichael	" "	Presb. Zanesville.
Alfred K. Bates	" "	" Benecia. Dis. Presb. Council Bluffs, Oct. 2, 1883.
James Pierpont	Nov. 6, 1882,	" Syracuse. " Benecia, April 10, 1883.
Sybrant Nelson	Nov. 23, 1882,	" Bellefontaine. " Lyons, June 14, 1886.
David H. Laverty	March 5, 1883,	" Albany. " Baltimore, April 12, 1887.
Alexander S. Hoyt	April 10, 1883,	" Binghamton. Died at Ogden, N. Y., March 25, 1388.
Nathan B. Knapp	" "	Ordained. Dis. Presb. Otsego, May 12, 1885.
Theodore S. Day	June 18, 1883,	Presb. Lyons. " Pueblo, Sept. 18, 1883.
A. Augustus Wood, D. D.	Sept. 18, 1883,	" Lyons.
Silas McKinney	" "	Dis. Presb. Cayuga, Sept. 22, 1885.
Evan R. Evans	Oct. 2, 1883,	Ordained. " Grand Rapids, April 13, 1886.
Theodore M. McNair	Nov. 15, 1883,	Ontario Association.
Peter Lindsay	Feb. 4, 1884,	Presb. Utica.
Benjamin F. Willoughby	April 15, 1884,	" Syracuse.
Charles S. Durfee	June 16, 1884,	" Albany. Died at East Bloomfield, N. Y., Dec. 24, 1887.
Clarence W. Backus	Sept. 16, 1884,	" St. Lawrence. Dis. Presb. Topeka, Aug. 26, 1889.
James S. Root	April 14, 1885,	

NAME.	WHEN RECEIVED AND WHERE FROM.	DEATHS AND DISMISSIONS.
John V. C. Nellis, Ph. D.	April 14, 1885, Presb. Otsego	Dis. Presb. Binghamton, July 24, 1888.
John M. Wolcott	Sept. 23, 1885, Oneida Association	" Steuben, Sept. 20, 1887.
Frank P. Gilman	Sept. 29, 1885, Ordained	
Gerard B. F. Hallock	Oct. 12, 1885, "	
John C. Henderson	Dec. 26, 1885, Presb. Mankato	
Edward B. Walsworth, D. D.	" " Genesee	
T. Dwight Hunt	April 15, 1886, " Saginaw	Dis. Presb. Utica, June 26, 1888.
Timothy H. Quigley	Sept. 21, 1886, Genesee Association	
Robert Kerr Wick	Sept. 30, 1886, Ordained	
Gavin Hamilton	April 12, 1887, Presb. Genesee	
George W. Davis	" " Free Methodist	
Albert S. Bacon	May 23, 1887, Ordained	Dis. Presb. Utica, May 2
Bevard D Sinclair	May 25, 1887, "	" Boston, April
Theodore B. Williams	Sept. 19, 1887, Presb. Niagara	
Alfred J. Hutton	Oct. 31, 1887, Classis Long Island	
John McColl	April 9, 1888, Presb. Chester	
Henry H. Stebbins, D. D.	" " Syracuse	
Nelson Millard, D D	April 10, 1888, New London Association	
William R. Taylor	" " Classis Philadelphia	
Johnson A. Henderson	May 29, 1888, Ordained	
Lucius F. Badger	Sept. 4, 1888, "	
Glenroie McQueen	March 14, 1889, Presb. Newton	
John Reid	April 10, 1889, " Genesee	
Allen Traver	" " Lyons	Died at Rochester, July 17, 1889
Louis F. Ruf	June 4, 1889, Ordained	
Daniel M. Countermine	Sept. 16, 1889, Presb. Albany	

LICENSURES

BY THE PRESBYTERY OF ROCHESTER.

Henry T. Miller, April 12, 1871.
Theodore B. Williams, April 12, 1871.
George K. Ward, April 10, 1872.
Isaac O. Best, April 10, 1872.
James Robertson, April 10, 1872.
Edward C. Ray, April 15, 1873.
Clark B. Gillette, April 15, 1873.
Theodore W. Hopkins, April 15, 1873.
John K. Fowler, April 14, 1874.
Lewis H. Morey, April 14, 1874.
David F. Stewart, April 13, 1875.
John Q. Adams, April 11, 1876.
Robert McLean, April 11, 1876.
John P. Campbell, April 27, 1877.
Eneas McLean, April 27, 1877.
Simon J. McPherson, April 27, 1877.
James W. White, September 18, 1877.
Frederick Campbell, April 15, 1879.
Theodore S. Day, April 11, 1882.
Theodore M. McNair, May 15, 1882.
Frank G. Weeks, April 15, 1884.
Frank P. Gilman, January 5, 1885.
Albert S. Bacon, April 13, 1886.
Johnson A. Henderson, December 13, 1887.
Robert B. Stevens, April 10, 1889.

CANDIDATES FOR THE MINISTRY

RECEIVED BY THE PRESBYTERY.

David F. Stewart, December 7, 1870.
James Robertson, September 13, 1871.
George K. Ward, October 19, 1871.
Edward C. Ray, April 10, 1872.
Isaac O. Best, April 10, 1872.
Simon J. McPherson, September 19, 1876.
Theodore M. McNair, April 13, 1880.
G. W. Smith, April 12, 1881.
George T. Eddy, April 11, 1882.
George S. Smith, April 11, 1882.
Frank P. Gilman, September 19, 1882.
Rufus F. Hurlburt, April 10, 1883.
Hiram A. Vance, September 16, 1884.
Albert S. Bacon, September 22, 1885.
Frank E. Hoyt, April 13, 1886.
Clay H. Denman, September 21, 1886.
Henry A. Lawrence, October 25, 1886.
Frank A. Ryan, October 31, 1887.
L. E. Tiffany, December 13, 1887.
Frank E. Bancroft, September 18, 1888.
Robert B. Stevens, April 12, 1887.
Van Beshgetoor, September 17, 1889.
William P. Mackenzie, September 17, 1889.

Trustees of the Presbytery.

Since the reorganization of the Board, June 18, 1883, the following persons have served as trustees for the years following their respective names:

Joseph R. Page, 1883 to 1884.
Louis Chapin, 1883 to 1889.
George W. Sill, 1883 to 1885.
Levi Parsons, 1883 to 1889.
Frederick Probst, 1883 to 1889.
Charles N. Leonard, 1883 to 1889.
Charles P. Coit, 1883 to 1889.
John R. Strang, 1883 to 1889.
Alexander H. Campbell, 1883 to 1884.
Charles J. Hayden, 1884 to 1888.
Theodore W. Hopkins, 1885 to 1886.
Marcus K. Woodbury, 1885 to 1888.
David R. Eddy, 1886 to 1889.
Sidney A. Newman, 1888 to 1889.
David M. Hough, 1888 to 1889.

Clerks and Treasurers

of the Presbytery.

The Rev. Levi Parsons was elected Stated Clerk at the first stated meeting, September 14, 1870, and has continued to hold the office to the present time, 1889.

The Permanent Clerks have been:

Rev. John Jones, from 1870 to 1874, followed successively by Elder John R. Strang and Rev. Samuel A. Freeman.

The first Treasurer was Elder Jonathan E. Pierpont, whose successor up to the present time, 1889, is Elder David Cory.

MINISTERS AND CHURCHES

Belonging to Rochester Presbytery, October, 1889.

MINISTERS.	ADDRESS.	CHURCHES.	NUMBER OF MEMBERS.
Linus W. Billington	Scottsville, N. Y.		
James B. Shaw, D. D.	Rochester, "		
Ferdinand DeW Ward, D. D.	Geneseo, "		
George W. Lane	Moscow, "		
A. Augustus Wood, D. D.	Rochester, "		
James Ballentine	Leroy, "		
Jonathan Copeland	Webster, "	Webster	126.
James F. Calkins	East Avon, "		
Oliver P. Conklin	Rochester, "		
William Hunter	Springwater, "	Springwater	26.
Alfred A. Graley	Clarkson, "		
Herbert W. Morris, D. D.	Rochester, "	Gates	99.
Edward B. Walsworth, D. D.	Livonia, "	Livonia	170.
T. Morey Holgman	Rochester, "		
John Mitchell	Lakeville, "	Geneseo First	109.
Henry Wickes	Rochester, "		
John Reid	Clarkson, "	Clarkson	53.
Orson P. Allen	Kharpoot, Turkey		
Herman N. Barnum, D. D.	Kharpoot, Turkey		
George Patton	Rochester, N. Y.	Rochester Third	433.
Levi Parsons, D. D.	Mount Morris, "	Mount Morris	257.
Timothy H. Quigley	Tuscarora, "	Tuscarora	62.

MINISTERS.	ADDRESS.	CHURCHES.	NUMBER OF MEMBERS.
Benjamin F. Willoughby	Lima, N. Y.	Lima	183.
John E. Baker	Rochester, "		
Samuel A. Freeman, D. D	Honeoye Falls, "	Honeoye Falls	117.
David R. Eddy	Brockport, "	Brockport	266.
Nelson Millard, D. D.	Rochester, "	Rochester First	530.
Corliss B. Garluer	Rochester, "	Rochester Westminster	270.
Edwin B. VanAuken	Phelps.		
Gavin L. Hamilton	Rochester, "	Parma Centre	30.
Horace P. V. Bogue	Avon, "	Avon Central	120.
Newton J. Conklin	Rochester, "		
John M Carmichael	Nunda, "	Nunda	121.
Henry H. Stebbins, D. D.	Rochester, "	Rochester Central	988.
Willis Clark Gaylord	Rochester, "		
Josiah E. Kittredge, D. D.	Geneseo, "	Geneseo Village	624.
Thomas E Babb	West Brookfield, Mass		
Charles P. Coit	Rochester, N. Y.	Rochester Memorial	354.
Alfred J. Hutton	Rochester, "	Rochester St. Peter's	492.
James L. Box	Canisteo, "		
Theodore B Williams	Mendon, "	Mendon	107.
George K Ward	Dansville, "	Dansville	357.
James S. Root	Rochester, "	Rochester Emmanuel	135.
John McColl	Brighton, "	Brighton	150.
James Robertson	Pike, "		
Fisher Gutelius	Moscow, "	{ Moscow	94.
		(Piffard	25.
Edward Bristol	Rochester, "	Rochester Calvary	132.
William R. Taylor	Rochester, "	Rochester Brick	1431.
Theodore W. Hopkins	Rochester, "		
Peter Lindsay	Rochester, "	Rochester North	326.
John C. Henderson	Charlotte, "	Charlotte	93.

MINISTERS.	ADDRESS.	CHURCHES.	NUMBER OF MEMBERS.
George W. Davis	Huron, N. Y.		
Theodore M. McNair	Tokio, Japan		
Frank P. Gilman	Hainan, China		
Gerard B. F. Hallock	Scottsville, N. Y.	Wheatland	250.
Daniel M. Counternine	Fowlerville, "	Fowlerville	106.
		Sparta First	85.
Robert K. Wick	North Sparta, "	Sparta Second	63.
		Ogden	202.
Glenroie McQueen	Spencerport, "	Caledonia	170.
Johnson A. Henderson	Caledonia, "	Groveland	170.
Lucius F. Badger	Groveland, "	Pittsford	190.
Louis F. Ruf	Pittsford, "	Victor	243.
		Chili	30.
		Avon	90.
		Sweden	46.
		Ossian	50.
		Union Corners	20.

Ruling Elders Belonging to the Churches of Rochester Presbytery, as Reported in November, 1889.

AVON.
Harvey Bigelow, - - East Avon, N. Y.
Ralph S. Taintor, Jr., - " " "
Solomon Taintor, M. D., - " " "

AVON CENTRAL.
George G. Westfall, Avon, N. Y.
Henry G. Woodruff, West Rush, N. Y.

BRIGHTON.
Elisha Y. Blossom, - Brighton, N. Y.
Harrison A. Lyon, - " " "
Theodore A. Drake, - " " "
Marshfield Parsons, - " " "
Thomas A. Brown, M. D., " " "
Thomas E. Blossom, " " "

BROCKPORT.
Henry W. Gardner, Brockport, N. Y.
Horace A. Metcalf, " "
Joseph A. Tozier, " "
John A. Drake, " "
Edgar Benedict, " "

CALEDONIA.
William E. Masterton, Caledonia, N. Y.
James Fraser, - " "
William S. McKenzie, " "
Archibald A. McColl, " "
Hugh McColl, Le Roy, N. Y.

CHARLOTTE.
Alexander Ferguson, Charlotte, N. Y.
Richard Beniish, " "
William H. Denise, " "

CHILI.
J. Allen Andrews, Chili, N. Y.
Benjamin F. Bowen, Chili Station, N. Y.

CLARKSON.
Chauncey Allan, - Clarkson, N. Y.
William H. Steele, - " "
Thomas Breckenridge, " "
Edward Corlett, - " "

DANSVILLE.

David D. McNair, Dansville, N. Y.
James M. McCurdy, " "
George W. De Long, " "
Alexander Edwards, " "
William T. Spinning, " "
George W. Shepherd, " "

FOWLERVILLE.

Gerritt S. Casey, Fowlerville, N. Y.
Theodore Freeman, " "
Hugh B. Agar, " "

GATES.

Thomas Roe, Gates, N. Y.
Franklin S. Hinchey, Rochester, N. Y.
Thomas M. Joslin, " "
Silas W. Hulbert, Ogden, N. Y.

GENESEO FIRST.

Samuel N. Knight, Lakeville, N. Y.
Daniel Bigelow, " "
Cornelius P. Weeks, " "
David Dinsmore, Livonia Station, N. Y.

GENESEO VILLAGE.

Adoniram J. Abbott, Geneseo, N. Y.
Andrew W. Butterway, " "
William A. Brodie, " "
Thomas Elliot, Moscow, N. Y.
George Fridd, Geneseo, N. Y.
Nelson J. Griswold, " "
Elisha W. Hudnutt, " "
Walter E. Lauderdale, M. D., " "
William J. Milne, LL. D., " "
James S. Orton, " "
John R. Strang, Esq., " "

GROVELAND.

Orimel Bigelow, Groveland, N. Y.
Fort Benway, " "
Samuel Culbertson, East Groveland, N. Y.
John P. Titsworth, Groveland, N. Y.

HONEOYE FALLS.

Albe C. Allen, Honeoye Falls, N. Y.
Seward W. Holdridge, " "
Christopher Eberly, " "

LIMA.

Justin S. Goodrich, Lima, N. Y.
Andrew J. Warner, "
William R. McNair, "
William H. Day, "
Henry Lawrence, "
Edward Salmon, "

MENDON.

Frederick Probst, Mendon, N. Y.
Josiah B. Smith, "
Henry Scribner, "
Curtis M. Gates, Honeoye Falls, N. Y.

MOSCOW.

Daniel T Barnum, Moscow, N. Y.
Newton H. Crosby, "
William Holbrook, "
F. Stuart Gray, Greigsville, N. Y.

MOUNT MORRIS.

Loren J. Ames, M. D., Mount Morris, N. Y.
Wilder Silver, "
Samuel L. Rockfellow, "
Miles B. McNair, "
Robert Crawford, "
Joshua C. Weeks, "
Henry M. Swan, "

NUNDA.

George Arnold, Nunda, N. Y.
James H. McNair, "
Arnold Galley, "

OGDEN.

William B. Nichols, Spencerport, N. Y.
George H. Comstock, "
Horace Rann, "
William B. Lowry, "
John Kincaid, "
James N. Arnold, Ogden, N. Y.

OSSIAN.

David McCurdy, Dansville, N. Y.
Matthias Rolison, Ossian, N. Y.
Jacob Clendening, "

PARMA CENTRE.

Thomas Breeze, Parma, N. Y.
Hugh Johnson, "
Isaac Castle, Parma Centre, N. Y.
Andrew Warren, "

PIFFARD.

T. Nelson Shattuck, Piffard, N. Y.
Zera F. Blakely, "
Willis A. Sackett, Buffalo, N. Y.

PITTSFORD.

George R. Barker,   Pittsford, N. Y.
George W. Canfield,   "
Wesley Van Buskirk,   "
Albert White,   "
Charles F. Thornell,   "

ROCHESTER BRICK.

David Dickey,   Rochester, N. Y.
Louis Chapin,   "
Jesse W. Hatch,   "
Truman A. Newton,   "
Joel G. Davis,   "
Edward Webster,   "
Charles F. Weaver,   "
George N. Storms,   "
Lansing G. Wetmore,   "
Seth J. Arnold,   "
Wm. Henry Gorsline,   "

ROCHESTER CALVARY.

Franklin S. Stebbins, Rochester, N. Y.
Thomas Oliver,   "
Frank T. Skinner,   "

ROCHESTER CENTRAL.

William Alling,   -   Rochester, N. Y.
Henry Churchill,   "
Darius L. Covill,   "
Frank M. Ellery,   "
Heman Glass,   "
John N. Harter,   "
William A. Hubbard,   "
William A. Hubbard, Jr.,   "
William B. Levet,   "
Alonzo L. Mabbett,   "
Samuel Sloan,   "
Henry Wray,   "

ROCHESTER EMMANUEL.

Francis Noye,   Rochester, N. Y.
Edwin E. Shutt,   "
George Lockwood,   "
Frank F. Dow,   "
George A. Tanner,   "
George H. Barons,   "

ROCHESTER FIRST.

George C. Buell, - Rochester, N. Y.
Charles H. Webb, " "
Albert G. Bassett, " "
David M Hough, " "
Henry Goold, - " "
Thomas Chester, " "
Arthur S. Hamilton, " "
Charles F. Pond, " "
George D. Olds, - " "

ROCHESTER MEMORIAL.

Edward W. Warner, Rochester, N. Y.
George H. Rudman, " "
David C Rudman, " "
Wilbur F. Smith, " "
Gottleib W. Hauert, " "

ROCHESTER NORTH.

George W. Davison, Rochester, N. Y.
Frank H. Clement, " "
Frank J. Shields, " "
Hiram T. Jones, " "

ROCHESTER ST. PETERS.

Sidney A. Newman, - Rochester, N. Y.
Jonathan E. Pierpont, " "
Richard K. White, Esq., " "
Ira C. Goodridge, - " "
Hon. John S. Morgan,* " "
Marcus K. Woodbury,* " "
Henry C. Clark, - " "
Harvey W. Brown, " "
Edwin S Hayward, - " "

ROCHESTER THIRD.

Joseph Harris, - Rochester, N. Y.
William F. Cogswell, " "
Edward Harris, - " "
William S. Little, " "
John H. Hill, - " "
Charles R. King, " "
David Cory, " "
David Copeland, " "

*Deceased.

ROCHESTER WESTMINSTER.
Benjamin H. Hill, - Rochester, N. Y.
Jeremiah B. Whitbeck, " "
John M. Cheeseman, " "
James L. Tarrant, - " "
Harvey B. Graves, " "
William F. Parry, - " "

SPARTA FIRST.
James S. Gilman, Mount Morris, N. Y.
Charles B. McNair, Sonyea, N. Y.
Edward L. McFetridge, Scottsburgh, N. Y.

SPARTA SECOND.
Hugh T. McNair, Dansville, N. Y.
David McNair, " "
Samuel Alexander, " "

SPRINGWATER.
Samuel A. Howe, - Springwater, N. Y.
Frank S. Grover, - " "
Timothy D. Connor, M. D., " "

SWEDEN.
George H. Way, - Brockport, N. Y.
James Mershon, - " "
Beman B. Roberts, " "
Charles J. White, " "
Alfred M. White, " "

TUSCARORA.
Garrett C. Conklin, Tuscarora, N. Y.
Andrew Johnson, " "
E. Marsh Petrie, " "

UNION CORNERS.
Jacob Bergen, - Tuscarora, N. Y.
Jacob Knappenberg, " "
Andrew Sedam, - " "

VICTOR.
Albert Simonds, - Victor, N. Y.
D. Henry Osborne, - " "
Stephen J Talmadge, " "
Stafford S. Lusk, - " "
William A. Higinbotham, " "
C. Lewis Simonds, " "

WEBSTER.
Roland W. Warner, Penfield, N. Y.
Alexander McPherson, Webster, N. Y.
George Middleton, West Webster, N. Y.
Andrew M. Holley, Webster, N. Y.

WHEATLAND.
Daniel C. McPherson, Garbutt, N. Y.
Myron Miller, - Scottsville, N. Y.
Wilson R. Ballintine, " "
George V. Hahn, - " "

Histories of the Presbyterian Churches

In the Counties of Monroe and Livingston.

These histories, with few exceptions, have been prepared by the ministers of the several churches, subject to the revision of the committee of Presbytery appointed to publish its history, consisting of Rev. Levi Parsons, D. D., Louis Chapin, Esq., Rev. H. W. Morris, D. D.., and Rev. C. W. Backus.

In the work of revision, the churches of Rochester were assigned to Louis Chapin, Esq.; those of Brockport, Charlotte, Chili, Churchville, Clarkson, Gates, Ogden, Parma Centre, Sweden and Wheatland to Dr. Morris; those of Brighton, Bushnell's Basin, Henrietta, Honeoye Falls, Mendon, Penfield, Pittsford, Rush, Victor and Webster to Rev. C. W. Backus; and those in Livingston county to Dr. Parsons.

AVON.

The town of Avon, which was called Hartford, up to 1808, was settled in 1790 by five families from Farmington, Conn. It is thought that the Rev. Daniel Thatcher organized a Presbyterian church in this town as early as 1795; but this does not appear from Presbyterial Records, nor from any records which the church has handed down.

A Congregational church was organized November 10, 1810, by Rev. Reuben Parmerlee, consisting of the following twenty persons: Samuel Federal, Phoebe Blakeslee, Asa and Jemima Clark, Herman and Mary Ladd, George Crouse,

Martha and Lucy C. Tilden, Elizabeth Strunck, Maria and Catharine Berry, Thankful Bancroft, Lucinda Burfee, Christiana Bishop, Rebecca Scott, Mary Brown and Catharine Miller. The first deacons were Samuel Blakeslee and Asa C. Clark, and the first clerk Federal Blakeslee. The church became a constituent part of the Presbytery of Ontario on the accommodating plan, January 15, 1822; elected ruling elders March 25, 1842, and has continued its connection with the Presbytery up to the present time.

Rev. John F. Bliss was ordained and installed pastor February 25, 1812, and remained until February, 1818. Then followed, for short terms of service, Rev. Chauncey Cook, Rev. Mr. Hyde, Rev. Mr. Knapen, Rev. Mr. Robbins and Rev. Mr. Bird.

January 16, 1822, Rev. John Whittlesey was installed, and was dismissed March 19, 1829. He was succeeded by Rev. H. M. Miller, who was followed by Rev. Jacob Hart for three years from May, 1831. Then followed Rev. William C. Wisner, for two years; Rev. Alfred White, for one year; Rev. Edwards Marsh, two years, and Rev. J. Hubbard, Rev. P. C. Hastings and Rev. E. W. Kellogg for a year each.

In September, 1844, Rev. Samuel M. Hopkins commenced his ministry, which terminated in July, 1847.

September 27, 1848, Rev. Edward B. Walsworth was ordained and installed pastor and continued until October, 1853. He was followed by Rev. Corydon W. Higgins from 1853 to 1855, and by Rev. J. W. Ray, from 1855 to 1857. After Mr. Ray, Rev. William N. Cleveland supplied the church for a short time, and was followed by Rev Nathaniel Elmer from 1858 to 1862. Rev. Archibald M. Shaw, from 1864 to 1865; Dr. E. B. Walsworth, from 1866 to 1867; Rev. J. R. Page, from 1868 to 1872; Rev. Horace P. V. Bogne, from 1874 to 1876; Rev. F. De W. Ward, D. D., from 1876 to 1880, and Rev. James F. Calkins, from from 1880 to 1888.

Services at first were held in a school house.

In 1812 a large brick church was commenced, but was not completed and dedicated until 1827, though services were held in it prior to 1820. In 1841 the building was in part renovated; in 1845 a bell was purchased; in 1850 the park was planted with trees and the parsonage was built.

In 1866 a very strong effort was made to secure the removal of the church to the west village, which resulted in forty or fifty members taking letters to form the church of Avon Springs. The church, however, not only refused to be removed but rallied to new life, and made a very thorough renovation of its church edifice at an expense of $4,000.

During Dr. Page's ministry a study was added to the parsonage, and a pipe organ put in the gallery.

In 1879 a prayer and Sunday School room was added to the church, and in 1888 the platform was lowered and the organ brought from the loft and placed beside the pulpit.

In 1825 the number of members was seventy-one; in 1833, one hundred and two; in 1839, one hundred and fifty, and in 1888, seventy-five.

Two interesting seasons of revival were enjoyed under Mr. Whittlesey's labors which brought an accession to the church of more than fifty members on profession. The labors of Dr. Wisner were greatly blessed in confronting the strong infidelity which had prevailed, resulting in an addition of more than forty members. A similar blessing attended the labors of Mr. Marsh, when seventeen were added.

Much could be said very favorably of the ministrations of Dr. Walsworth, Mr. Elmer, Dr. Page and Dr. Ward.

The eight years ministry of Rev. J. F. Calkins has proved longer than that of any of his predecessors, and very happy in the ingatherings which it has secured. Feeble health compelled him to resign after a very successful ministry of more than forty-four years. The church at this date, 1889, is depending upon transient supplies.

In its entire history, while it has never paid a large salary, owing to the fact that but few of the wealthy men of the place are members, it has always refused to ask for missionary aid.

The elders elected March 25, 1842, when the church first became fully Presbyterian, were Mishael Wilson, Henry L. Young, William Jackson, James Hosmer and David Whitney.

The trustees in 1812 were John Pierson, John Brown, Ezekiel Morly, Jehial Kelsey and Josiah Waterous.

The present officers of the Sunday School are Louis R. Bristol, superintendent; Charles Beckwith, assistant; Charles Lacy, treasurer; Frank Henry, secretary, and Augusta Taintor, librarian.

The young people have a prayer meeting Sunday evening.

A Juvenile Missionary Society was formed five or six years ago.

The Woman's Missionary Society was formed in 1877.

AVON FREE CHURCH.

A special meeting of the Presbytery of Ontario, for the purpose of forming a church in the southern part of the town of Avon, met at the house of Mr. Norman Little, December 16, 1834, and was opened with a sermon by Rev. Justus Hough, from Ps. 97: 1, who also was chosen moderator. It appearing that the church in Avon had not been properly notified of this movement, Presbytery adjourned to the same place on the 26th inst., when the following eighteen members of the church of Avon, viz: Norman Little, William F. Southworth, Solomon Hunt, Jane Ann Little, Lewis G. Howard, Edwin Cook, Lovisa C. Cook,

Sarah Wallage, Harriet Hunt, Isaac Osgood, Jemima B. Osgood, Martha Miller, Rebecca Scott, Ezekiel Scott, Sally Post, Mahitable Fuller, Eunice Weed and Lysander Weed, together with Mr. and Mrs. Thomas B. Lyon of the church at Canandaigua, were constituted a church, known as " The Free Church of Avon," which was located at the village of Littleville. At the time of the organization, Isaac Osgood, Lewis G. Howard and William T. Southworth were duly chosen and ordained to the office of deacon; from which, as no elders were ordained, we infer that the church was Congregational and belonged to Presbytery according to the " Plan of Union."

The Rev. Hezekiah B. Pierpont was the first minister, and on the 18th of February, 1836, was installed pastor by the Presbytery of Ontario, which relation was dissolved August 25, 1841. It is thought that Roderick L. Hurlbert, a licentiate received by Ontario from Cayuga Presbytery August 24, 1842, succeeded Mr. Pierpont, and that after him the church had no other minister. Resolutions respecting his death at Castile were passed by the Presbytery April 26, 1854.

The Committee on Home Missions reported to Presbytery July 9, 1856, in regard to this church, that " Most of the members have died or left the place, or connected themselves with a neighboring church," and that " the committee are told the church is virtually disbanded already."

A house of worship was erected soon after the organization of the church, which remained for about thirty years when it was put to other uses.

Hotchkin's history says: " In 1836 it numbered one hundred and fourteen members. * * * In 1846 a blessed revival and ingathering of souls was granted. Seventy-seven were added to the church on profession."

AVON SPRINGS.

In October, 1865, Rev. Edwin R. Davis commenced preaching in the Academy at Avon, N. Y., with reference to the organization of a church. This resulted in the formation of the Avon Springs Presbyterian Society, November 12, 1866, with the following trustees: R. S. Taintor, Stephen Hosmer, Theodore E. Winans, O. Comstock, D. C. Brayton and D. M Stevens.

On the 11th of December, 1866, a commission of Ontario Presbytery consisting of Rev. John Barnard, D. D., Rev. Pliny F. Sanborne and Rev. George P. Folsom, organized the Avon Springs Presbyterian Church; the Rev. Mr. Folsom preaching the sermon.

Thirty-seven persons, recommended by letter, principally from the First Church of Avon, united with each other in covenant, and were constituted the Presbyterian Church of Avon Springs.

O. Comstock, D. C. Brayton and R. Taintor were duly elected and ordained ruling elders.

Rev. Mr. Davis continued his labors until October, 1867. in all two years, when he retired, and no successor was ever obtained. During these two years an effort was made to erect a church edifice, which for a time was very hopeful, but failed.

In the spring of 1872 an unsuccessful effort was made to revive the church.

In 1876 some of the original members of this organization united with others in constituting the Central Presbyterian Church of Avon. But, though a new church was formed, the old legal organization known as the Avon Springs Presbyterian Society was continued as the legal representative of the new body.

(See History of the Central Presbyterian Church of Avon.)

AVON CENTRAL.

The Central Presbyterian Church, Avon, N. Y., was organized May 9, 1876, by a commission of Rochester Presbytery, consisting of Rev. J. L. Robertson, Rev. S. M. Campbell, D. D., and Mr. Louis Chapin. Forty-two members constituted the organization. The rotary system of eldership was adopted, and two elders were chosen, viz., Edwin I. Stevens and Benj. Long. The trustees of the society, whose legal title is the Avon Springs Presbyterian Society, were Aaron Barber, Stephen Hosmer, Edwin I. Stevens, William P. Low, J. A. Chase and W. S. Curtiss.

On May 22, 1876, the Rev. H. P. V. Bogne was invited to take charge of the church, and began his labors with it June 10. In the fall of the same year the society purchased a parsonage, and a lot adjoining for a church edifice. In July, 1877, the erection of a brick church was begun, which was finished in 1878 at an expense of $12,000. In 1886 the manse was enlarged and improved at a cost of $2,200.

The church has enjoyed two special seasons of revival, though lesser revivals have not been infrequent. In the first thirteen years of its history, exclusive of those who united at the organization, 84 have been received on confession of faith and 67 by letter. It has four missionary societies, and a Society of Christian Endeavor, which was organized in February, 1887. The present pastor is the only one the church has had—Rev. H. P. V. Bogne. The elders are George G. Westfall and Henry G. Woodruff. The trustees, Aaron Barber, Stephen Hosmer, George G. Westfall, James D. Carson, Henry G. Woodruff, John Schanck, David W. Gregg and John March.

BRIGHTON.

The Rev. Solomon Allen of Northampton, Mass., came to Brighton in 1816. Previously acquainted with some of the early settlers of the town from that State, he followed them to care for their religious interests. The church was organized September 18, 1817, by Rev. Messrs. Solomon Allen, Comfort Williams and Aaron C. Collins, with 22 members, and until 1870 was a Congregational church. The first deacons were Daniel West, Daniel Smith and Henry Donley, who were set apart to said office in January, 1818. The regular place of worship was a school house. Mr. Allen was an interesting preacher and a most devoted pastor, and endeared himself to all classes of the community. He paid attention to the children, and started a Sunday school in 1816. The church in the wilderness prospered, and numbered 60 members at his departure for his old home in the fall of 1820. He died in New York City, January 19th, 1821, aged 70 years.

The church has had many stated supplies, but only five regularly installed pastors, the longest time of service by any minister being ten years. Rev. Jonathan Winchester came in January, 1822, and had charge about a year and a half. Rev. Charles Thorpe was installed April 27, 1825; the installation services being combined with those of the dedication of the new church. His pastorate lasted about three years.

Rev. William Jones supplied the pulpit for eight months, and his ministrations were marked by a revival of religion.

Rev. Silas Pratt served the church four months, and was followed, in the summer of 1828 by Rev. Abner Benedict, who remained two years. The church was agitated by the general anti-Masonic excitement, and other troubles, and efforts were made to change it to a Presbyterian church.

Its first report to the "Consociation," on June 1, 1829, credited it with 116 members.

Rev. Linus W. Billington supplied the pulpit two or three months. Rev. Charles G. Finney was in Rochester at the time, and Brighton church enjoyed a revival. In 1831, 79 persons were added to the church. Rev. Worthington Wright supplied the pulpit four or five months.

Rev. Hiram L. Miller came in June, 1831, and remained a little over two years. Fifty-nine were added to the church. Great interest was taken by the people in the cause of temperance. A petition was presented to the Rochester Presbytery for the organization of a Presbyterian church, but in the interest of peace was refused.

Rev. Samuel Griswold served the church for two years, beginning January, 1834. He was well suited to guide in these exciting times, and religious interest increased. Before the year closed 50 confessed Christ.

Rev. Alva Ingersol was installed November 10, 1836, and remained three years. The church was distracted by divisions, which he labored hard to heal.

Rev. Blackleach B. Grey began his ministry here in the beginning of 1840, and served ten years. A general revival attended his labors in 1842. In August of this year the church withdrew from the "Association," and for twenty years was independent. Rev. T. B. Hoyt succeeded Mr. Grey for one year. Rev. Joseph S. Barris came in the spring of 1851 and remained four years and a half. He was a faithful minister, but the church suffered much through loss of members. In 1852 the house of worship was reconstructed and greatly improved.

Rev. John Wickes came April 27, 1856, and remained six years. His pulpit and pastoral labors were appreciated by the people, and a greater harmony prevailed. The Ladies' Aid Society, which has been so useful, came into existence at this time.

Rev. Charles E. Furman supplied the pulpit a year, and Rev. George W. Whitney four months from September 1, 1863.

Rev. James Orton of Thomaston, Maine, came in 1864, and remained five years. He was an interesting and instructive preacher. He accepted the Professorship of Natural History in Vassar College in March, 1869. April 18, 1867, the church edifice was burned. The people courageously set to work to repair the loss, and the present church was built on ground given by Justus Yale, Esq. The new church cost $15,000, and was dedicated June 23, 1872, four years after the people began to worship in it.

Rev. Henry Wickes began his ministry to this church November, 1869, and remained five years. He was highly esteemed for his personal excellencies and ministerial faithfulness.

The change to a Presbyterian church was made with unanimity September 21, 1870, and October 16, Elisha Y. Blossom, Harrison A. Lyon and Thomas B. Yale were elected ruling elders.

February 16, 1872, its corporate title was duly changed to "The First Presbyterian Church of Brighton."

Rev. Joseph R. Page, D. D., was installed February 25, 1875, and remained ten years. The most pleasant relations existed between him and his people. He was a faithful and conscientious preacher and an able Presbyter and counsellor.

Rev. James S. Root was installed May 12, 1885. The church prospered under his care. The congregation increased; members were added; the financial condition was improved. He resigned to accept a call to Emmanuel Church, Rochester, and was released by Presbytery June 13, 1887.

Rev. John McColl, called from the church of Brandywine Manor, Pa., began his ministry January 1, 1888, and was installed June 8, 1888.

The present number of members is 130. The Sunday School, organized by the first pastor, Mr. Allen, two years before any similar school existed in the city of Rochester, is in a flourishing condition under the superintendency of Mr. Theodore A. Drake. The missionary societies are prosperous, and temperance work is actively carried on. For an account of the godly men who served the church as deacons, and others to whom the church owes so much, readers are referred to Dr. Joseph R. Page's history of the church, from which this sketch is drawn.

BROCKPORT.

What is now the Presbyterian Church of Brockport was organized March 19, 1828, as a Congregational church, with six members; and it remained Congregational in its form of government for the first six years of its existence. But, in 1834, it was resolved to make a change, and adopt the Presbyterian form of government, and six ruling elders were chosen, namely, Moses Nash, Simeon Benedict, Jacob Sutphin, Silas Judson, Ralph W. Goold and Calvin McLueston. Some seven years later, the regularity of the proceedings in thus changing the church to Presbyterian was seriously questioned, and, as the best method to rectify the mistake and place the church on a safe basis, it was resolved, in 1841, to dissolve the old church and organize anew. Accordingly, this was done in due form, and new sets of officers elected. The ruling elders chosen at this time were Jacob Sutphin, Hollister Lathrop, Ralph W. Goold, John Efner, Ensign Bushnell, Simeon Benedict and Joseph Ganson. The deacons elected were Daniel Belden and Charles Wicks. From this date the church of Brockport has remained a thoroughly sound and firm Presbyterian organization.

But to return to the origin of this church: Not long after its organization in the Congregational form, steps were taken to secure a house of worship. A suitable lot for such an edifice was donated to the congregation by Mr. James Seymor, and thereupon, with commendable expedition, was built a substantial and convenient church at an expense of some $5,000. After rendering good service for about a quarter of a century, this was taken down in order to be replaced by a better. The new church was erected in 1852 at a cost of $6,526, and this, substantially, is the house now occupied by the congregation.

The ministers who have occupied the pulpit of this church and their time of service, as nearly as can be ascertained, were the following:

Rev. Eli S. Hunter, D. D., pastor from 1834 to June, 1837.

Rev. B. B. Stockton, pastor from August, 1838, to June, 1843.

Rev. Ebenezer Mead, S. S., from November, 1843, to August, 1844.

Rev. Hugh Mair, D. D., S. S., from December, 1844, to September, 1845.

Rev. Augustus W. Cowles, pastor from February, 1847, to July, 1856.

Rev. Joseph Kimball, S. S., from October, 1856, to February, 1863.

Rev. John Morron, S. S., from August, 1863, to February, 1865.

Rev. Horatio W. Brown, S. S., from December, 1865 to May, 1870.

Rev. George W. Rawson, S. S., from July, 1870, to July, 1871.

Rev. D. Henry Palmer, S. S., from May, 1872, to August, 1875.

Rev. David R. Eddy, S. S., from January, 1876, to present.

This church has been favored with a number of very precious revivals, the most noteworthy of which occurred in the following years, resulting in the hopeful conversion of the numbers set opposite thereto, respectively:

Revival of 1848, converted 17.
Revival of 1851, converted 39.
Revival of 1853, converted 31.
Revival of 1867, converted 53.
Revival of 1878, converted 37.
Revival of 1883, converted 65.

To indicate the present strength and past usefulness of this church, it may be stated that there have united with it altogether 958 persons. Of these, 468 joined on profession of faith, and 490 by letter. Of those who became members on profession, 311 were baptised in their infancy and 141 when received. The present number is 262, and among these remain Mr. George F. Barnett and Mr. William H. Seymour, who were members of the society at its first organization, and have resided in Brockport ever since.

A Sabbath school has been maintained in connection with this church from the day of its organization. The attendance at present is about 300, scholars and teachers included.

A ladies' " Missionary Society " was formed here as early as 1873; it has now a large and active membership, and through the years of its existence has accomplished much good.

A society named " Merry Workers " was formed in 1884, whose leading object is to raise funds for the improvement of the home church, and their efforts thus far have been rewarded by great success.

A young people's society of " Christian Endeavor " was organized in 1886, and has continued in a flourishing condition, having at the present time 49 active and 28 associate members.

A children's "Mission Band" also was formed in 1886, with 9 members, but now numbers 29. The meetings thus far have been very interesting and have proved of great benefit to the children.

This church has given to the world two ministers of the gospel—Rev. Corliss B. Gardner, now pastor of Westminster Church, Rochester, and Mr. George A. Eddy, son of the pastor of this church, who has lately completed his theological studies at Princeton.

The congregation owns a good parsonage, and owes no man anything save love.

The present ruling elders are Edgar Benedict, Joseph A. Tozier, Horace A. Metcalf, Addison Gardner, Henry W. Gardner and John N. Drake.

BUSHNELL'S BASIN.

Eleven miles southeast from Rochester, in the town of Perinton, is the great embankment over the Irondequoit creek. This embankment is one of the greatest works on the Erie canal. It is nearly a mile in length and from forty to seventy-six feet in height.

About 1820 a Mr. Pardee, objecting to the canal running through his farm, sold to Mr. Oliver Hartwell, and the place went by the name of Hartwell's Basin. Mr. Hartwell opened a grocery and warehouse, and built boats, doing quite a business. In a few years Bushnell, Lyman Wilmarth & Co. bought him out, and carried on the mercantile and forwarding business, employing many clerks and doing a large business for many seasons during the canal navigation. About one boat-load of flour was shipped daily from this place, being brought in from the various mills in the surrounding country. There are at present a grocery and shoe shop, a tavern, postoffice, and a short distance south a powder mill.

A school house was built in 1825. Previously, about 1800, one had been built a little farther east (District No. 1).

Mr. Charles Dickinson, who had commenced the mercantile trade by himself, in which he was very successful in after years, and Mr. Lyman Wilmarth, feeling the importance of observing the Sabbath, took it upon themselves, though non-professors, to gather the people, and conduct religious services by reading scripture, singing, and the reading of a sermon. Rev. Mr. Caulkins, of Victor, preached to them occasionally. Thus the first religious effort started in this place. In 1831, to a large extent aided by Charles Dickinson and Cyrus Leonard, a house of worship was built, which was dedicated as a Congregational church by Rev. Daniel Johnson, who left Victor in December, 1831, and ministered to this new church at Bushnell's Basin for nearly two years. This church was organized March 1, 1833, with twelve members, and was received by the Rochester Presbytery June 25, 1833. In 1834 it had increased to twenty-four members. Some of their members having removed West, and others having connected themselves with the Congregational church at Fairport, this church disbanded informally in the fall of 1834. Mr. Whittlesey was a deacon in the church. After the church had disbanded the house was occupied for many years as a mission by different denominations at different times. In 1863 the property was deeded to the Independent Methodists, and by them to the Episcopal Methodists, who, at last account, continued to occupy the property.*

---

* The above is compiled from "Half Century of the Presbytery of Rochester;" Rev. James H. Hotchkin's History of Western New York, and Prof. W. H. McIntosh's History of Monroe County, 1877.

CALEDONIA.

The First Presbyterian Church of Caledonia was organized March 4, 1805, by Rev. Jedediah Chapman, of Geneva, N. Y., with 52 members, 41 of whom were received by certificate, the remaining 11 by profession. Three elders were ordained to rule the church. The society was under the control of the Presbytery of Geneva, and supplies were furnished for over three years; said supplies consisting of Rev. Messrs. J. Chapman, Oliver Ayers, of Massachusetts, John Lindsley, of Geneseo, and Alexander De Noon.

June 14, 1808, a call was presented to Mr. De Noon to become the pastor of the church, which was accepted, and his ordination and installation took place August 16, of the same year. Mr. De Noon was born and educated in Scotland, came to this country about 1805, was licensed by the Presbytery of Albany, was one of the original members of the Presbytery of Ontario, was one of the most influential ministers of Western New York, and was greatly beloved and honored by the people of Caledonia. Mr. De Noon's labors were extended over a period of forty years, and considering the primitive condition of society at the commencement and the great hardships the early settlers had to endure, it may be regarded as a highly successful pastorate, an increase of 97 members being made during that time.

After the death of Mr. De Noon, the church was without a pastor for several years, when a successor was found in Rev. John W. Major, who remained from May, 1854, until some time in 1856. He was followed by Rev. William Evan Jones, who was installed May 20, 1857, dismissed in 1859. December 1st, of the same year, Rev. Malcolm Neil McLaren, D. D., began his pastorate, which continued until 1871; 82 members being added to the church. After leaving Caledonia, Dr. McLaren retired from the active ministry and took up his residence in Auburn, N. Y., where his death took place in 1887. He was one of the celebrated McLaren brothers, all three of whom were eminent Doctors of Divinity and able preachers of the gospel.

After an interval of three years, Rev. John Kennedy Fowler was chosen pastor, his ordination and installation taking place November 10, 1874. During the winter of 1875 a revival occurred, commencing with the week of prayer and continuing for several weeks, at which time 65 persons were received into the communion of the church. Mr. Fowler was assisted in these protracted meetings by a young class-mate, Rev. David Fay Stewart, who died a few years after in California. The pleasant pastoral relations existing between this church and Mr. Fowler were dissolved in 1877—he having accepted a call to Rockford, Ill. During this pastorate 106 persons were received into the church.

November 29, 1878, Rev. Thomas Stephenson was installed pastor of the church. At the same time, Rev. John P. Campbell, a son of Elder Peter P. Campbell, was ordained to the work of the gospel ministry, accepting a charge at Baltimore, Md. Mr. Stephenson remained pastor until March, 1882—40 members being received into the church during this period.

About this time the Presbyterian church at Fowlerville was organized, drawing several families from the Caledonia church, thereby decreasing the number of members.

Mr. Stephenson was succeeded by Rev. John M. Carmichael, who began his labors in April, 1882—was installed November 15, of the same year—continuing until November, 1886, when he was obliged to resign, owing to impaired health. There were thirty-nine accessions to the church during his pastorate.

After Mr. Carmichael's resignation the pulpit was supplied mainly by students from the Auburn Seminary; Rev. Johnson Henderson, of that institution, being engaged as stated supply during the summer of 1887. The following winter a call was extended to Mr. Henderson, and he was ordained and installed May 29, 1888, and is the present pastor. The present number of members is about 150.

At various times during vacancies the pulpit has been ably supplied. Among these supplies were: Rev. D. H. Palmer, D. D., now of Penn Yan; Rev. L. D. Chapin, formerly Chancellor of Ingham University; Rev. E. B. Walsworth, D. D., now of Livonia; Rev. Donald Grant, of Geneva, and Rev. T. M. Hodgman, of Rochester.

The following are the names of elders who have held office in the church since its organization:

Duncan McPherson, installed March 4, 1805.
Donald Anderson, " " "
Donald McKenzie, " " "
Archibald Gillis, installed August 16, 1808.
Peter Campbell, " " "
John McPherson, " " "
Donald Fraser, " " "
Donald Fraser, 2d, " " "
John D. McColl, installed May 19, 1842.
Alexander Fraser, " " "
Angus McKenzie, installed August 19, 1855.
Peter P. Campbell, " " "
Peter J. Campbell, " " "
James Hamilton, installed May, 1862.
Donald C. McPherson, " " "
William J. Williams, installed April 4, 1875.
Thomas Brodie, " " "
William E. Masterton, installed May 14, 1882.
James Fraser, " " "
Peter P. Campbell, " " "
Charles J. McKenzie, " " "
William S. McKenzie, " " "
Hugh McColl, installed January, 1888.
Arch. McColl, " " "

A flourishing Sunday school, with over 150 members, is one of the auxiliaries of this church. In January, 1881, a Young People's Christian Association was formed with a large number of members. This continued with great success until July, 1888, when it was reorganized as a Young People's Society of Christian Endeavor, with 32 active members, 14 associate members, and with the pastor as president. A woman's Missionary Society was organized April 9, 1873, which has a large number of members. A mission band known as the "Cheerful Workers" was organized January 4, 1874, with over thirty members. The present church edifice was erected in 1855, the parsonage in 1862.

CHARLOTTE.

In the year 1851, Rev. Thomas Bellamy of Penfield came to Charlotte and called a public meeting, with a view to establish a Protestant church there. At that meeting it was decided that the Presbyterians and Methodists should unitedly undertake the building of a house of worship; but with the understanding that the denomination which should raise the largest amount of money for the purpose should be the denomination of the church about to be established; which resulted in the success of the Presbyterians. The work was at once begun and vigorously pushed forward towards completion, which was accomplished in a brief period at an expense of about $2,000.

The church which was to occupy this new building was organized in June, 1852, by a commission from the Presbytery of Rochester, consisting of Rev James B. Shaw, D. D., Rev. M. J. Hickok, and Elders William Alling, H. C Fenn and David M. Chapin. The original members, or those who were at this time constituted into a Presbyterian church, were the following:

Joshua Eaton,
Adaline Eaton,
Phineas B. Cook,
Mary B. Cook,
William Rankin,
Mary Ann Rankin,
Joseph Wiggin,
Catherine Wiggin,
Nicholas Nelson,
Hannah Nelson,
Mrs. C. B. Colburne,
Mrs. Sarah Root,
Mrs. Sophia P. Stone,
Mrs. Marrette Allen,
Joseph D. Buck.

Total— 15.

The first ruling elders of this church were Joshua Eaton, Phineas B. Cook and Zenas Colburne.

The congregation was incorporated April 15, 1851, and its first board of trustees was composed of James S. Stone, Phineas B. Cook, Moses Wallace, George Lotta, William Rankin, Joshua Eaton and Henry H. Babcock.

The ministers who have occupied the pulpit and served this church are the following:

Rev. A. Ferguson, from June, 1852, to December, 1856.

Rev. A. T. Young, from April, 1857, to April, 1859.

Rev. Lemuel Leonard, from June, 1859, to September, 1860.

Rev. E. B. Van Auken, from January, 1861, to April, 1863.

Rev. Thomas Bellamy, from June, 1863 to November, 1866.

Rev. C. W. Ward, from May, 1867, for a few months.

Rev. O. P. Conklin, from April, 1869, to March, 1873.

Rev. A. B. King, from April, 1873, to April, 1875.

Rev. D. D. McColl, from May, 1875, to May, 1878.

Rev. R. J. Beattie, from June, 1878, to December, 1878.

Rev. D. M. Rankin, from February, 1879, to September, 1881.

Rev. T. B. Williams, from November, 1881, to June, 1885.

Rev. J. C. Henderson, from October, 1885, to the present time.

Of all the above ministers, two only were installed, namely, Rev. A. Ferguson and Rev. T. B. Williams.

During the ministry of Rev. D. D. McColl a religious interest was awakened in the congregation, which resulted in adding a goodly number of members, and this is the only revival that has occurred in the whole history of the church. .

A Sabbath school has been maintained in connection with this church from the date of its origin to the present day; but this, like the church, has had its times of prosperity and depression. At present the school is in a thriving condition, having within the past two years increased very considerably, both in numbers and efficiency. The present superintendent is the pastor, Rev. J. C. Henderson; secretary, Mr. Alexander Ferguson; treasurer, Miss Carrie Blacknell; librarian, Mr. George Swift.

The house of worship in which the church was organized is still occupied. It has since, however, been considerably repaired and improved. During the ministry of Mr. McColl the congregation bought a very comfortable parsonage, for which they paid about $2,500. Both the house of worship and the parsonage are entirely free from debt.

The trustees of the church at the present time are D. S. Messro, D. S. Denise, Alexander Ferguson, William Newcomb, Andrew Fallison, and J. J. Miller.

The eldership in this church is perpetuated on the rotary plan, each elder being elected to serve for the term of three years. The present elders are Richard Bemish, Alexander Ferguson and William Denise.

This church in the past has had to struggle against a combination of adverse influences, and its growth in consequence has been but slow. The population around it is and always has been largely Catholic; while the non-Catholic part are also, by local inheritance, largely non-church-going people.

Add to all this, Charlotte being a favorite resort for picnics, excursions and recreations for all classes from the neighboring city of Rochester, its Sabbaths, through the summer season, are sadly disturbed and desecrated. But the place is growing and improving, and the future of this church has never been so encouraging as at the present time.

CHILI.

This church originated in a religious "society," organized in the year 1816, at a meeting held in the house of Mr. Isaac Hemmingway, in the town of Chili, then a part of the town of Riga. This meeting was called "for the purpose of forming the professors of religion of the Congregational and Presbyterian order, in the vicinity, into a church of Christ." This purpose was there and then carried out under the direction of Rev. Hugh Wallis, a missionary sent out by the Geneva Missionary Society, Rev. Alanson Davidson, pastor of the First Congregational church of Riga, and Mr. Henry Smith.

The persons who were thus constituted into a church numbered eighteen, and were the following:

Abel Belknap,
Besha Belknap,
Patty Hemmingway,
Leah Marlin,
Lydia Potter,
Apollos Derry,
Timothy G. Baldwin,
Joel Baldwin,
Sarah Baldwin,
Mrs. A. Derry,
Lemuel Potter,
Daniel Clark,
Conrad Hartman,
Nancy Marlin,
Sarah Gridley,
Daniel Deming,
Fanny Deming,
Tamor Child.

The infant church held its first regular meeting July 24, 1816, at the house of Mr. John Wetmore, where Apollos

Deming and Joel Baldwin were chosen deacons, and Daniel Clark clerk. The first minister was the Rev. Mr. Chase.

The meetings for worship appear to have been held at private dwellings, and occasionally in barns, until some time in the year 1818, when Rev. Mr. Martindale was called to labor among them, and a small meeting-house was built upon the same site as that occupied by the present church.

At a meeting of the Presbytery of Rochester, held at Ogden, February 10, 1819, this "society" proposed to that body to unite with them on what was called "the accommodation plan;" this proposition was favorably regarded, and they were received under its care.

The first regular pastor of the church was the Rev. Chauncey Cook, who was installed December 27, 1821. During the following year there appear upon the records the names of from 96 to 103 members in full communion; but at the close of Mr. Cook's pastorate, 1827, there were but 87 members.

In the spring of 1828 Rev. Abner Benedict was invited to minister to the church for the term of one year, which he did, leaving the number of members a little less than he found it. Mr. Benedict was succeeded by Rev. Silas Pratt, who was called to be the pastor, and was installed November 25, 1829; under his ministry the number of members increased from 82 to 94.

In 1832 the congregation undertook the building of a new house of worship, measuring 40 by 60, which was completed at an expense of $2,600, and was dedicated January 2, 1833, Rev. Mr. Mead of Riga officiating.

About this time steps were taken to change the title of the congregation, and obtain a charter under that of the "First Presbyterian Society of Chili," which now appears on the county records, in Liber I, page 16 of Religious Incorporations. Shortly after this, May 25, 1833, the form of church government also was changed, by a nearly unanimous vote, from the Congregational to the Presbyterian system, the following persons being elected and ordained as ruling elders, namely, Alfred Schofield, Levi Campbell, Tunis Brokaw, Ira Andrews and J. A. Gillett. At the same time Alfred Schofield and Tunis Brokaw were chosen deacons. On the same occasion Levi Campbell, Judah Gridley and George Brown were elected trustees.

Of the church thus legally and ecclesiastically reorganized, Rev. L. Brooks became the first pastor, and remained such until 1837. Of the fruits of his ministry the records give no account. He was followed by Rev. C. B. Smith, whose pastorate, though short, only two years, was yet productive of great good. In the winter of 1837 and 1838, assisted by Rev. Mr. Avery, he held a series of meetings which resulted in the most fruitful revival in the history of the church, some seventy persons being received into communion on profession of faith.

After Mr. Smith's resignation, the pulpit was supplied for a brief period—the summer of 1840—by Rev. H. N. Short. Then came Rev. J. W. Fox, who was installed pastor and continued his services for four years.

From 1844 to 1848 Rev. R. Man was the pastor, of whose ministry no particulars are to be found in the church records.

The next pastor was the Rev. James Fenner, who was installed February 15, 1849. His ministerial labors extended through a period of eleven years.

From 1860 to 1866 the pulpit was successively occupied by Rev. C. E. Furman, Rev. J. H. Phelps, Rev. Mr. Southworth and Rev. R. Man, of whose labors nothing of marked importance is recorded.

In 1866 and 1867 extensive alterations and repairs were made in the house of worship, at an expense of about $1,600. Further repairs were made in 1874 and 1876, costing $450.

From 1868 down to the present time, this church has had a succession of temporary supplies and short pastorates.

Rev. J. D. Lane served during the year 1868; Rev. H. N. Short from 1869 to 1871; Rev. Mr. Hicks during 1872; Rev. James Robertson during 1873; Rev. George Craig from 1874 to 1877; Rev. Wm. L. Milliken from 1878 to 1882; Rev. John Mitchell from 1883 to 1884; Rev. T. M. Hodgman and others in 1885; Rev. T. D. Hunt from 1886 to 1888, and, latterly, students from Rochester Theological Seminary.

There has been a Sabbath school in connection with this church since the year 1821. A Young People's Society of Christian Endeavor also was organized a few years since. But this church has not retained its former strength and standing, and its future is not promising. Deaths and removals have greatly reduced the number of its members. The springing up of other churches—Methodist and Baptist—in the immediate neighborhood has also contributed to its decline.

Present elders are J. Allen Andrews and Benjamin F. Bowen.

Present trustees—George Sheldon, Herbert Short and B. F. Bowen.

CHURCHVILLE.

A commission, duly appointed by the Presbytery of Rochester, consisting of Rev. Joseph Penny, D. D., Rev. Ralph Clapp, and Elders Ayel Ensworth and Moses Hume, met at Churchville on the 10th day of July, 1832, for the purpose of organizing a Presbyterian church at that place.

The commission having been duly constituted for the performance of this duty, there appeared before them 36 persons, who presented letters of dismission and recommendation from several different churches—some from the Presbyterian church of Riga, some from the Congregational church of Ogden, and some from the Dutch Reformed church of Schuylerville. These persons presented their letters for the purpose and with the request that they be organized into a new and separate church ; and this was done after the usual manner, Hubbard Hall, Daniel Hall and George Redfield being elected as ruling elders.

The first minister of this church was Rev. W. Wright, whose labors extended through about two years, during which there were added to its communion about 35 persons. He was followed, for longer or shorter periods, by Messrs. Rev. G. W. Ellicott, Richard DeForest, David Slee, Josiah Pierson, L. Brooks, S. Carver, R. W. West, Charles Kenmore, E. W. Kellog, — Thompson and H. L. Stanley, the united ministries of whom covered a period of eighteen years, and bring down the history of the church to the year 1850. Thus it will be seen that the average stay of her ministers did not exceed a year and a half ; yet during the ministry of nearly all of these more or less additions were made. The highest number ever attained was 80 members.

The records left by this church are scanty and defective : but two facts, which are scattered through them, may serve to indicate its condition and strength as it advanced through the years of its brief history, namely, the *number* of its members and the *amount* of its benevolent contributions to the Bible, tract and missionary causes. These were as follows :

Number of members—In 1833, 57 ; in 1837, 67 ; in 1841, 80 ; in 1843, 73 ; in 1845, 76 ; in 1847, 55.

Contributions— In 1833, $50.68 ; in 1842, $55.05 ; in 1843, $47.00 ; in 1844, $42 00 ; in 1845, $51.60 ; in 1846, $65.43.

The volume containing the records of this church is

largely occupied with complaints and charges against members, and with the conduct of vexatious trials and processes of discipline on the part of the session—a condition of things which could not but prove detrimental to the spiritual welfare of the church.

The last minister employed by this church as their preacher was Rev. H. L. Stanley, and the last item of his ministry entered in the records is dated October 6, 1850. After this we have no account of the doings or condition of this congregation. But some twenty years after this date, we find appended to the records of the session the following memorandum, penned, apparently, to account to the generations to come for the end and extinction of the Presbyterian church at Churchville:

"N. B.—Master Stanley was the last minister employed by the church. The church became feeble and unable to support preaching, and withdrew in due form by letter, and united with a new organization in Churchville, just formed by general consent, made up in part by all the old members. This new organization is called the 'Union Congregational Church of Churchville.' They built a new meeting-house, and have prospered unto this day, and made a wise and good arrangement for themselves and children, and for the cause of Christ in this village. So ends this Book of Records of the Presbyterian church of Churchville.

"Attest,   LEMUEL BROOKS,
       "Minister and Clerk,
"Churchville, January 3, 1871."

CLARKSON.

The church of Clarkson was organized on the first day of April, 1816, by a council, under the Congregational form of government, and under the name and title of "The First Congregational Society of the Town of Murray." The original members numbered sixteen, of whom four only were males. The first board of Trustees was composed of the following persons, namely, Nathaniel Rowell, Joshua Field, Witter Steward, Abel Baldwin, Moody Freeman and John H. Bushnel.

The church was received under the care of the Presbytery of Ontario, February 10, 1819; and on the next day, Rev. John F. Bliss was installed as its first pastor.

At a meeting duly called, and held on the 6th of May, 1823, the name of the church was changed, and it was now called "The First Congregational Church of Clarkson," part of the Town of Murray having been formed into a separate township under this name.

In the year 1825, the church engaged the Rev. William James as their minister. The next year we find Rev. Stephen V. R. Barnes in charge of the congregation. During the ministry of the latter, namely, in 1826, the society built them a comfortable house of worship.

This church, at a certain date, which the writer of this narrative cannot give, withdrew from all connection with the Presbytery, and for several years acted as a strictly Congregational body. In 1868, however, it changed its polity to that of pure Presbyterianism, by a vote of 15 to 5; and the following members were elected to be its ruling elders, namely, Chauncy Allan, Hugh Johnston, Jonathan Wadhams, Henry E. Lawrence, Luther H. Johnston and Joseph Tozier.

In addition to the ministers already named, this church has been served, either as pastors or stated supplies, by the following: Rev. Charles E. Furman, who was installed in February, 1831, and continued his services until 1836. Mr. Furman was succeeded by Rev. Norris Bull, D. D., who was installed in June, 1837. Then followed, for longer or shorter periods, Rev. Charles McCarg, Rev. R. S. Goodman, Rev. Ebenezer M. Toof, Rev. J. McNulty, Rev. Corlis B. Gardner, Rev. Francis Rae, Rev. N. Marcellus Clute, Rev. Charles E. Furman (a second term), Rev. Alfred A. Graoley, Rev. Elijah H. Bonney, Rev. Nathan B. Knapp, Rev. J. Q. Collen and Rev. John Reid, the present occupant of the pulpit. Of all these three only were installed pastors.

This church has been favored with several very precious outpourings of the Holy Spirit. Revivals of pure and undefiled religion were had during the ministries of Messrs. Lane, Furman, Bull, McNulty, Toof, Goodman and Graoley. Other but less notable seasons of refreshing from the presence of the Lord have been enjoyed. The church continued to grow till its roll of communicants numbered 176, which was the highest number it ever attained.

The church of Clarkson organized a Sabbath school at an early day, and has kept it up through its whole history. This has generally been flourishing, and in the course of its existence has accomplished much good. The present attendance is 85, teachers and scholars included.

This church, sad to state, is not now what it once was; its present number of members is reduced to 55, of whom only 12 are males. Several causes have contributed to bring about this decline, among which may be named, the construction of the railroads and the canal, which have diverted trade to order points; and the coming into the town of a new class of inhabitants, largely foreigners, who are of a very different religious faith and practice, or of no religion at all. But for all this, to its credit be it said, the church still supports its minister without any aid from the Home Missionary Board.

The congregation now owns a comfortable parsonage, and also a house of worship valued at about $6,000. Moreover, the society is free from debt.

The eldership has been and still is perpetuated on the rotary or term system; those acting at present are Chauncy Allan, Edward P. Corlett, Thomas Breckenridge and William B. Steele.

DANSVILLE FIRST.

The origin of the church named above is well defined in the following extract from the sessional record bearing date March 25th, 1825. "At a meeting holden this day pursuant to notice given, at the new school house in the village of Dansville, N. Y., for the purpose of organizing a Presbyterian church, there were present the following persons, viz: James H. Hotchkin, Robert Hubbard and Stalham Clary, ministers, members of the Presbytery of Bath, and Rev. Silas Pratt, member of the Ontario Presbytery; the meeting was opened with prayer. An application from Willis F. Clark, Calvin E. Clark and Samuel Shannon, members of the church in Sparta, and residing in this village, to the Presbytery of Ontario, in behalf of themselves and others, for leave to be organized into a Presbyterian church to be known by the name of the Presbyterian Church of Dansville Village, was read, together with the act of said Presbytery granting this petition; whereupon the following persons, members of the church of Sparta, N. Y., viz: Willis F. Clark and Charity his wife; Samuel Shannon and Sarah his wife; Calvin E. Clark and Harriet his wife, Mrs. Mary Rowley, Mrs. Elizabeth Pickell, Nancy

Pickell, together with Stephen Franklin and Sarah his wife, members of the——Presbyterian Church of Buffalo, N. Y., presented themselves to unite in church fellowship, and having agreed to adopt the Presbyterian form of government and discipline, and having made solemn profession of their faith, and entered into covenant with God, and each other, were after prayer, declared to be a church of Christ by the ministers present."

The society thus organized immediately entered upon the duties and privileges of church membership under the ministry of Rev. Robert Hubbard, who continued to hold office, as stated supply, to this church, from March, 1825, to April, 1834, a period of nine years.

The first board of ruling elders, elected to serve this church, comprised the following persons: Stephen Franklin, Willis F. Clark, who were ordained to this office by Rev. Mr. Hubbard on Sunday March 27th, 1825. Samuel Shannon was elected clerk of session. During the administration of Rev. Mr. Hubbard the church seems to have enjoyed constant growth and prosperity. From the charter members of eleven in 1825, the number enrolled as communicants increased to over two hundred in 1834, with a net gain of something over a hundred. Accessions to the church were made from year to year, the most noteworthy of these occurring during the years 1831-2, when there were received into communion 109 persons, of whom 104 were upon profession of faith. Regarding the period covered by Mr. Hubbard's ministry the following extract is taken from the History of the Presbyterian Church of Dansville, prepared by the pastor, Rev. George K. Ward, in the year 1876.

Additions were made to this feeble church (charter members eleven), during its connection with the Bath Presbytery, until the summer of 1827, when the church dissolved its relation to that body, and united with the Presbytery of Ontario, Synod of Genesee. At this time they numbered forty-six members; they had no place of worship except an old school house, which stood on the west side of Main street, on the vacant lot south of the Clinton house. Upon the completion of the new school house (on the site now occupied by the Episcopal Church) they had for a time, quite a convenient place of worship, but this soon became inadequate to the accommodation of their increased numbers. At this time Mr. Joshua Shepard, a leading merchant of the village, very kindly donated a lot on Main street and $1,000.00 to erect a church, which offer was accepted by the society, and a building was erected at a cost of $3,500.00, opened and dedicated to divine service in the year 1831. In 1832, the first protracted meeting was held in the new church, under the direction of Rev. Wm. Curry. As a result of this effort between 60 and 70 persons united with the church. In the summer of 1834, the Rev. Robert Hubbard resigned his charge, and was settled over a church in Fowlerville, where he died in 1840. The Rev. Elam H. Walker who had been employed as a missionary among the Choctaw Indians in the South, left that field of labor, on account of poor health, accepted a call and was installed pastor of the Dansville Church by the Presbytery of Ontario in September, 1834. Seventy additions were made at different communion seasons during his pastorate up to 1840, when, through disaffection growing out of circumstances attending a protracted meeting conducted by Rev. Augustus Littlejohn, an unfortunate division of the congregation occurred. Fifty-six communicants adhered to Mr. Walker and the old church. Sixty-six left the fold and organized a new society.

The old church continued to carry out its functions under the ministry of Mr. Walker until his death, which occurred in the year 1849, after intense and protracted sufferings from disease and surgical operations, which he bore with

Christian patience and resignation. Succeeding Rev. Mr. Walker were the following ministers who labored as stated supplies over the church for brief periods until 1855, viz:

Rev. Wm. Powell, 1849–50.
Rev. Jno. Parker. 1850–52.
Rev. John W. Ray, 1852–53.
Rev. Chas. L. Hequemburg, 1853–55.

On the 31st day of March, 1854, the church edifice was destroyed by fire, which deprived them of their beautiful house of worship. Services were continued, however, at Canaseraga Hall and at the English Lutheran Church until 1855, when Rev. Mr. Hequemburg's ministry over the church came to a close. From that time until 1861, there was no regular pastor or stated worship. In June of that year, by mutual consent of the two branches of the old society, known respectively as the First and Second Presbyterian Churches of Dansville, they were consolidated by the Presbytery of Ontario under the pastorate of Rev. Samuel Jessup.

DANSVILLE SECOND.

The Second Presbyterian Church of Dansville owed its formation to a division of sentiment among the members of the First Church which led to a separation in the year 1840. In that year sixty-six members of the old church seceded therefrom, and formed the nucleus of what was afterward known as the Second Presbyterian Church. This organization, having no church edifice, occupied for a time an upper room in the Stevens block upon Main street. In 1842 a house of worship was erected at a cost of about $4,000.

This church was ministered to by the following pastors and stated supplies:
Rev. Jno. N. Hubbard, S. S., 1840.
Rev. Leveret Hull, S. S., 1840—1842.
Rev. D. N. Merritt, Pastor, 1842—1844.
Rev. Joel Wakeman, S. S., 1844.
Rev. W. F. Curry, Pastor, 1844—1849.
Rev. Chas. L. Hequembnrg, Pastor, 1849—1853.
Rev. John N. Hubbard, S. S., 1853—1857.
Rev. S. M. Campbell, D. D., S. S., 1858.
Rev. Dr. Seager, S. S., 1859.
Rev. Mr. Ford, S. S., 1860.
Rev. Samuel Jessup, Pastor, 1861:

This Second Church enjoyed a fair degree of prosperity during the twenty years of its existence, the number of its members having nearly doubled during that period. Periods of special religious awakening occurred under the ministry of Rev. Leveret Hull in the year 1840, when 102 persons were received into the church at the four seasons of communion. During the succeeding pastorate of Rev. D. N. Merritt, in the year 1843, about forty more names were added to the roll. In addition to the sixty-six members constituting the original number, there were added by certificate and upon profession of faith, 300 persons from 1840 to 1860.

This church was taken under the care of the Presbytery of Angelica, July 15, 1840, soon after its organization, and was transferred to the Presbytery of Ontario, Feb. 13, 1855.

DANSVILLE. (Consolidated.)

Extract from the Minutes of the Presbytery of Ontario at its session in Dansville, June 4th, 1861:

"The committee appointed to inquire into the condition of the First Presbyterian Church in Dansville, and whether any action of Presbytery is called for in regard to it, reported as follows : That they have had an interview with the First Presbyterian Church in Dansville, and finding them destitute of the means of grace, and of a house in which to worship, and with no prospect of being able to support an independent organization, recommend that the First and Second Churches of Dansville be consolidated under the name of the Presbyterian Church of Dansville; that the pastor and officers of the Second Church be the pastor and officers of the consolidated church. This report was accepted and adopted, and the Rev. Samuel Jessup was appointed to communicate this act to the two churches.

"(Signed)   J. BARNARD,
"*Stated Clerk.*"

This action was ratified by both churches, and the forty-four remaining members of the First Church became thereby a part of the Consolidated Church. At this time Rev. Samuel Jessup was pastor, having entered upon his duties in the fall of the year, 1860. The board of elders consisted of the following persons : Willis F. Clark, Dr. Wm. H. Reynale, Samuel Lemen, Calvin E. Clark, Wm. Perine, Edward S. Palmes.

Mr. Jessup's pastorate continued for eleven years and was in every way successful. The church edifice was enlarged, a neat, commodious chapel was built, the services were well sustained and there were additions to the church to the number of 222, forty-four of these coming in a body under the act of consolidation. During the winter and spring of 1866, there was a special religious awakening following upon daily union meetings of the four Protestant churches. From the beginning to the close of that year there were over sixty additions to the church, chiefly upon profession of faith in Christ. Mr. Jessup's administration closed in the year 1872. Following his resignation, the church was supplied for a year by the following ministers of the gospel: Rev. Messrs. Geo. K Ward, John Jones, D. D., and Jno. H. Brodt.

In the spring of 1873 Rev. Mr. Ward was called to the pastorate of this church, over which he was ordained and installed June 4th, 1873.

Under Mr. Ward's administration the society has increased to nearly four hundred members. The chapel has been enlarged and connected with the church, and the following auxiliary societies have been organized: Woman's Foreign Missionary Society, Ward Home Missionary Society, Willing Workers, Young People's Society of Christian Endeavor. The Sabbath school is large and prosperous. A parsonage has been purchased in which the pastor has resided for the last ten years.

A special season of revival occurred in the year 1884, when fifty-one were received into the church.

At the communion season of March, the present year (1889) twenty-four were received.

The church is in good working order, and pastor and people are united. A monthly paper, *The Presbyterian Church Herald*, commenced its issue in April, 1889. The present elders are: David D. McNair, Geo. W. DeLong, Geo. W. Shepherd, Wm. T. Spinning, James M. McCurdy, Alexander Edwards.

FOWLERVILLE.

On the 16th of November, 1832, at their own request, the following persons were set off from the Presbyterian Church of York to form a church at Fowlerville: Amos Skinner, Olive Skinner, Ezekiel Morely, Sally Fowler, Joseph Tosier, Alfred Collins, Nancy Weller, Elizabeth McKnight, Clarissa Janes, Mary Eastman, Lavinia Roberts, Mary S. Eastman.

Rev. John Eastman acted as moderator, and Rev. John B. Whittlesey preached the sermon from Cant. VI: 10.

The Rev. John Eastman was the first minister, who, as stated supply, remained until 1832 or 1833, and was followed by Rev. Mr. Walker for a short time. Rev. Robert Hubbard was reported as stated supply in 1834, who, was followed by Rev. Messrs. Powell, Hezekiah B. Pierpont, Jacob Burbank, Orange Lyman, Mr. Slic, and E. H. Stratton.

Rev. John P. Foster was ordained and installed pastor by the Presbytery of Ontario, Sept. 21, 1842, which relation was dissolved Jan. 30, 1844. He was followed by Rev. Messrs. Robert Laird, Bridgeman, Chapin, Henry Snyder, Timothy Darling, Thomas A. Wadsworth, Moses Powell, Yeomans and W. M. Modesit. During the ministries of Pierpont, Laird and Wadsworth there were quite extensive revivals.

During the ministry of Rev. Thomas A. Wadsworth in the year 1856, the church withdrew from the care of the Ontario Presbytery and became distinctively Congregational, it having before this been connected with Presbytery since Aug. 25, 1829, on the "Accommodation Plan," as the Second Presbyterian Church of York.

In the year 1878, this Congregational Church having become very weak, the Presbytery of Rochester in response to an overture to that effect, reorganized the same by setting off from the First Presbyterian Church of Caledonia sixteen members, who, uniting with twenty-three of said Congregational Church, three from the United Presbyterian Church of Caledonia, four from the United Presbyterian Church of York, two from the Presbyterian Church of Ireland, and four on profession of faith, fifty-two, in all, were constituted, April 22nd, 1878, the First Presbyterian Church of Fowlerville, by Rev. Samuel M. Campbell, D. D., of Rochester.

Of the church thus organized the Rev. Eugene G. Cheeseman acted as stated supply for one year; Rev. Frederick

D. Seward as stated supply from April 1, 1879, to Oct., 1881, and Rev. Sybrant Nelson as stated supply from April 9, 1882, to April 9, 1886. Then followed brief supplies for a year when, May 25, 1887, Rev. Bevard D. Sinclair was ordained and installed pastor, which relation was dissolved April 21, 1889.

The pastorate of Mr. Sinclair was blessed with a revival. In seven months thirty-five were received on profession of faith, twenty-two of whom were received at one communion. The following persons were deacons while the church was Congregational, viz: Amos Skinner, Ezekiel Morely,   Merrill,   Eastman, Israel Casoey, and   Sackett.

The Sunday-school superintendents during the same period were: Joseph Tosier,   Merrill, Miss Polly Hubbell, James Fowler, John P. Casey, B. F. Dow, F. F. Dow.

There have been the following elders since the reorganization in 1878: William Fraser, Gerrit S. Casey, F. F. Dow, Theodore Freeman, Matthew Ralph, and Hugh B Agar.

A Total Abstinence Society in connection with the church existed as early as 1837.

A Woman's Missionary Society, both Home and Foreign, has existed since 1879.

A Young People's Society of Christian Endeavor was organized by Rev. B. D. Sinclair in 1887, which still continues in vigorous operation.

A Young Ladies' Mission Band was organized in 1885, which is in full vigor at present.

The present board of trustees is composed of Robert Vallance, John W. Horn, George McPherson, Leroy Budlong and John Hunter. The first church building was erected about the year 1833, on the public park, and was destroyed by fire April 13, 1836, supposed to be the work of an incendiary, and resulting from abolition meetings which had recently been held in the church. Another building was erected in the immediate rear of the former in 1838. In 1882 quite extensive repairs were made at an expense of about $3,100. The church as thus renovated, having a pleasant lecture-room in the rear, was re-dedicated, with a sermon by Rev. Josiah E. Kittridge, D. D., Oct. 27, 1882. The society also owns a good parsonage.

YORK.

Hotchkin's History, which is dated 1848, says: "This church is first noticed on the records of the Presbytery of Ontario, Oct. 14th, 1828. Rev. Johnson Baldwin was then stated supply. In 1830 it numbered fifty-five members; in 1836, one hundred and sixty-six, and in 1840 one hundred and sixty. This is the last enumeration known to the writer. Rev. Johnson Baldwin was its stated supply as early as the year 1826, and continued to the close of 1828. He was succeeded by Rev. John B. Whittlesey, who was installed as pastor Nov. 18, 1830, and continued till Jan. 15, 1833, when he was dismissed. In 1836 Rev. John H. Carle was reported as the stated supply, and the next year Rev. Caleb Burge. Rev. Silas C. Brown was installed pastor Jan. 23, 1838, and officiated till May 5, 1841, when he was dismissed from his charge. In 1832 forty-five members were reported as having been added, by profession, to the church during the preceding year, indicating that the church had been visited with a gracious effusion of the Holy Spirit. In the support of Messrs. Johnson and Whittlesey, the church was assisted a number of years by the American Home Missionary Society. They have an appropriate house of worship which was erected in 1830."

To the foregoing statement of Mr. Hotchkin may be added that the last reference to this church by the records of Ontario Presbytery is under date of Oct. 28, 1844, when its records were approved, and it is thought that soon after this the church withdrew from Presbytery and existed for about twenty or twenty-five years as a Congregational church, when, having become very weak, the organization was abandoned and the building used for other than church purposes.

A strong United Presbyterian Church in the village of York traces its origin as far back as 1811, and a Reformed Presbyterian Church was organized in 1832, both vigorous churches at the present time.

GATES.

The brevity of the space allowed for this narrative and the number of particulars to be embraced in it demand a concise plan, and the writer adopts the following:

Origin. "The first Presbyterian Society of the town of Gates," as a corporate body, dates from October 15, 1828, when according to the provisions of law, three trustees were duly elected, namely, Matthias Garrett, Amasa Kellog and William Jameson. But that "society," for some unrecorded reason was not organized as a church until March 8, 1831. The original members were but five—Nathaniel B. Lord, Sarah Ford, Oliver Noble, Dr. Ezra Butterfield and Nabby Butterfield; N. B. Lord being chosen as "deacon" and Dr. Butterfield as "clerk."

Edifice. Their first place of worship was the ball-room of a tavern, kept by Eliezar Howard. After statedly assembling in this place for some three years, a small frame church was built, costing about $400, the site together with the ground for the adjoining cemetery being donated to the society by Mr. Howard. Ten years later, a new and more commodious house of worship was built on the same spot, at an expense of some $1,000. This was dedicated, January 23, 1845. After occupation for a quarter of a century, repairs became necessary; and in 1871, these were undertaken, and great changes and improvements made in the interior, all accomplished mainly through the influence and agency of Mr. Thomas S. Joslin. Other improvements have been made since. This church is situated just four miles directly west of the centre of Rochester.

Pastorate. Of those who ministered to the infant church during the first seven years of its existence we have no account, save of one, Rev. George G. Sill, who was the prime mover in the erection of the first house of worship. But from the year 1838 to 1845, its pulpit was supplied, for varying periods by Rev. Messrs. Hilam W. Lee, Dr. K. Gally and Hugh Wallace, whose services extended over three years. In 1845, Rev. James Ballentine was called to be their minister, who served the church with great fidelity for sixteen years, and was the only installed pastor it has ever had. From 1861 to 1866, the desk was occupied successively by Rev. Messrs. Francis Surbridge, Ezra F. Munday, — Bishop and Gavin L. Hamilton, also several students from the Baptist Seminary. In 1867, Rev. Charles E. Furman became the supply, and served for something over two years. He was followed by several transient supplies, or those whose terms of service were quite brief, among the latter were Rev. Messrs. John E. Baker, Edward B. Van Auken, Henry M. Morey and Willis C. Gaylord. In the spring of 1874, Rev. Henry Wickes became the preacher, and labored with them till the fall of 1876. Then followed a period of eight years, during which students and transient ministers occupied the pulpit, the last of whom was Rev. John Mitchell, who remained with them for a year and a half.

In November, 1884, Rev. Herbert W. Morris, D. D., was asked to preach to them for a few Sabbaths, while they

HISTORY OF ROCHESTER PRESBYTERY.   169

looked for a suitable supply; this not appearing or not sought for, at their urgent request, he has continued ever since to render them all pastoral services, though not installed.

Eldership. For three years from its organization, the only officers known in the church were a deacon and a clerk. Its first ruling elders were elected and ordained in 1834, who were Matthias Garret, Ezra Butterfield, Calvin Sperry and Rufus J. Bushnell. In 1842, through deaths and removals, the church was so reduced that Presbytery authorized the male members to act as a session. This state of things continued till 1845, when a new board of elders was organized. Subsequently we find James C. Van Nest, Henry L. Monroe, John Gardner and George B. Sperry acting as members of the session. The elders at the present time are Thomas Roe, Thomas S. Joslin, Franklin S. Hinchey and S. W. Hulbert. These have been elected for limited terms.

Membership. The growth of the church in numbers has not been great or rapid at any period. As stated, it was organized with five members. At the end of the first ten years it had 26 members, of the second 82, of the third 76, of the fourth 63, of the fifth 58, and at the present time it has 99. Had it enjoyed the services of settled pastors, its growth and usefulness doubtless would have been much greater.

Sabbath School. This church has had its Sabbath school, embracing Bible classes through the whole period of its existence. The entire Sabbath school membership at the end of the first decade was 25, of the second 115, of the third 75, of the fourth 90, of the fifth 57, and at the present is 83. Its earlier superintendents were Calvin Colt, Rev. Hugh Wallis, Asahel Pratt and Calvin Sperry. The last named held the office for 23 years, resigning in 1867. This servant of God had for his successors Franklin S. Hinchey,

John Gardner, Isaac Simmons, Thomas Roe, Jeremiah Smith and Edward M. Behan, who is the present incumbent. This school, though small, has been a power for good, and its records present much that is interesting and instructive, such as the following items: "Cyrenia Baker recited 1289 verses, Ansell Mills, 1341 vs. and William Colt 1507 vs." Again "*A* class of girls recited 5204 vs.; *B* class of boys recited 5884 vs." Members of this school fought and fell on many a bloody field in the war of the great rebellion. For September 14, 1862, we find this sad record, "Our young men's Bible class is broken up, most of them having joined the army." Again, later, "Theodore Sperry, after suffering all the horrors of a rebel prison was with us to-day"—"Alexander Patterson was carried to the hospital where he expired"—"George Rowe died from his wounds,"—etc.

Missions. This church has also its Missionary Society, which, as an auxiliary of the Women's Missionary Society of Rochester Presbytery, is active and earnest in its efforts to promote the good cause. Its president is Miss Carrie M. Smalley, secretary Miss Myrtie Beman, and treasurer Miss Jennie Curry.

Trustees. The present board of trustees are Alfred J. Rudman, Henry Patten and Frank Booth.

GENESEO FIRST.

Lakeville is a small village situated at the foot of Lake Conesus (from which it derives its name) six miles northeast from Geneseo, the shire town of Livingston county, N. Y. Among the first to settle in this locality were James Haynes and Daniel Kelly, from Pennsylvania. These were followed a few years afterwards by Benjamin Wynn,

Abraham Duffenbacher, Abraham McClintock and Duncan Sinclair. Time passed on and there came from Connecticut and from the eastern part of the State, several emigrant families, among whom were R. Wattles, E. Bigelow and A. C. Knight, with the households of M. Armstrong, W. Price, W. McClintock and R. Densmore, who settled in Livonia. The descendants of many of these original emigrants still hold and occupy the homesteads.

The First Church was organized with twelve members in 1795 by Rev. Daniel Thatcher, a missionary of the " Presbyterian General Assembly." Its title was " The First Presbyterian Church of Geneseo," which name it still bears. It was the earliest of all the churches in this part of the county. The first members were nearly all Presbyterians, the place of worship being a small building on " Temple Hill," above the village of Geneseo. In course of time several joined by letters from Congregational bodies in the Eastern States. In order to avoid friction and secure unity of feeling, the elders resigned. The " Plan of union adopted by the General Assembly and the General Association of the State of Connecticut being adopted, with a standing committee in place of a church session." But this measure was not attended with success. There was no real harmony. Acting wisely under the circumstances, the Congregationalists asked and obtained letters of dismission, and organized another church, which, after several changes, is now known as " The Presbyterian Church of Geneseo Village." The original Presbyterian element removed to the eastern part of the town, where they met for worship during several years in a school house during the winter months, and in a barn in summer. In the year 1824 a house of worship was erected—a plain, unpretending structure, but was the spiritual birthplace of many persons, some now living and many more above.

In the year 1855, the commodious and attractive building,

where services have since been held, was completed and dedicated to the worship of the Triune Jehovah; a sermon of characteristic scholarship being preached by the late Samuel H. Cox, D. D., at that time chancellor of Ingham University, Le Roy. The old structure still stands, though for uses secular but not unsacred. It is a barn alike in kind with the place where the church convened in its early days. The older members of the parish cannot look upon it without a moved heart and a tearful eye.

Pastors and Stated Supplies.—Revs. Samuel Thatcher, 1795; John Lindsley, 1806–1817; Silas Pratt, 1824–1827; Horace Galpin, 1827–1831; Elijah Woolage, 1831–1832; Merrit Harmon, 1832–1842; Sidney S. Brown, 1843–1845; —— Chamberlain, 3 months, 1845; Charles Richards, 1845–1849; E. M. Toof, 1849–1853; Chas. Livingston, 6 months of 1853; Lafayette Dudley, 1853–1854; William Reed, 3 months, 1854; Edwin Moore, 1855–1860; Geo. W. Mackie, 1860–1861; Dwight Scovel, 1861–1867; Alvin Baker, 1867–1871; John Jones, D. D., 1871–1872; John Mitchell, 1873–1879; Newton J. Conklin, 1879–1883; F. De W. Ward, D. D., 1883–1889.

Elders.—Daniel Kelly, John Haynes, John Ewart, 1795; Duncan Sinclair, Abram Duffenbacher, John Haynes, Abraham McClintock, Robert Clark, John R. Haynes, Epaphroditus Bigelow, Richard A. Riley, Joseph Haynes, Enoch Babcock, Abraham H. Williams, James Haynes, James S. Wells, M. D., Revilo Bigelow, J. Hunter Haynes.

Trustees.—James Haynes, E. Bigelow, Wm. McClintock, Robert Clark, R. T. Sinclair, Hugh Gray, Joseph Haynes, Roger Wattles, William Haynes, Samuel Carman, Jonathan Hill, Amos Schofield, John Price, R. A. Riley, Peter Dopp, R. Beckwith, L. H. Williams, G. E. Hill, L. F. Olmstead, A. C. Knight, E. Hillman, H. Hillman, Daniel Bosley, R. Densmore, J. H. Haynes, W. C. McClintock, Charles Price.

REV. F. DE W. WARD, D. D.

Officers in 1888.

Minister.—Rev. F. De W. Ward, D. D., for twenty years pastor in Geneseo.

Elders.—David Densmore, C. P. Weeks, S. N. Knight, Daniel Bigelow.

Trustees.—William Harris, R. Bosley, Edgar Gray.

Sunday School.

Superintendent, Charles D. Neff; *Assistant,* Edward R. Bosley; *Treasurer,* C. Knight.

Within the parish boundaries are fifty families, some of them dating back before the present century. Attendance upon Sabbath and neighborhood services, the Sabbath School and regular contributions to all the church boards, indicate a fair amount of prosperity; additions are made at almost every communion.

GENESEO.

I. Second Presbyterian Church of Geneseo.*

This church was organized May 5, 1810, with 21 members as follows: Elizabeth Reed, Mary Rew, David Skinner, Jerusha Skinner, David Kneeland, Mercy Kneeland, Cephas Beach, Dolly R. Beach, Delight Finley, Samuel Finley, Lucy Finley, Louise Chappell, Abigail Case, Alice Skinner, Betsey Finley, Candice Beach, Sylvia Kneeland, Annie Alvord, Russell Lord, Nabby G. Kneeland, Sibbil Lawrence.

David Skinner was chosen moderator, Samuel Finley clerk, and David Skinner and Cephas Beach deacons.

*The history of *The Presbyterian Church of Geneseo Village* (1880-1889) naturally embraces sketches of the related ecclesiastical organizations, the *Second Presbyterian Church of Geneseo* (1810-1880) and the *Central Presbyterian Church of Geneseo* (1858-1880). These sketches follow in their natural order.

The original settlers in this region were Presbyterians from Pennsylvania. The first religious society was thus Presbyterian and was organized in 1795 by Rev. Daniel Thatcher, a missionary of the General Assembly. The new organization was Congregational. Its members were Congregationalists from New England. Withdrawing from the First Presbyterian church, they were organized as a new church by Rev. Daniel Oliver, a missionary of the Massachusetts Home Missionary Society. In 1814, the church adopted the confession of faith of the Presbyterian church and came under the care of Geneva Presbytery on what was called the "accommodation plan." In December, 1817, the Presbyterian form of government was adopted in full, the church took its name as the Second Presbyterian Church of Geneseo, and elected Jonathan Ellis, Reuben Weeks and Oliver Skinner, elders. Frederick Hill was elected elder in 1819, and Norman Bushnell deacon the same year. In 1820, Elijah Dresser was chosen deacon; in 1824, Reuben Weeks, and in 1829, John Colt, Eben N. Buel and Oliver Skinner. The church again formally adopted the Presbyterian form of government September 3, 1834, and elected on the rotary plan the following board of nine elders: Charles Colt, Cyrus Wells, Jr., Jacob B. Hall, Samuel A. Hubbard, Chauncey Parsons, Levi Goddard, Freeman Hastings, William H. Stanley and Owen P. Olmsted. A year later, there were added to fill vacancies Frederick W. Butler, Samuel F. Butler and Russell Austin. Samuel Gardner was elected deacon.

The town house was the first place of worship. This had been moved from the public square on Main street to Temple Hill a few years before and now came under the control of the church and was called their meeting house.

The ecclesiastical society was incorporated under the name of the "Geneseo Gospel Society," September 11, 1815, with Joseph W. Lawrence, Samuel Finley, Isaac

Smith, William H. Spencer, Samuel Loomis and Timothy P. Kneeland, trustees. The year following Aaron Skinner, Elijah Dresser and Jonathan Ellis were elected to fill vacancies, in 1817, James Wadsworth and Charles Colt, in 1818, Orlando Hastings and in 1819, Norman Bushnell.

In 1811, a novel expedient was adopted for supporting the gospel. It was known as the sheep fund. The flock began with 48 sheep contributed by several persons. In 1817, it had increased to 324. In 1820, the proceeds were invested in landed security, and six years later amounted to about $300. These funds were used in building the first session house which stood on Centre street where now stands the house of Dr. W. E. Lauderdale, Jr.

The Genesco Gospel Society received from Mr. James Wadsworth, April 13, 1816, a deed of 100 acres of land. This gift testified his practical interest in religious and educational matters and redeemed a promise that he, with other land proprietors, had made to make such grant to the first regularly incorporated religious society that should be organized within the township. From the first he and his brother Gen. William Wadsworth greatly aided this church in Genesco. He was accustomed to give $100 a year for the support of the minister.

In 1816, the subject of erecting a meeting house was agitated. In December, an association was formed composed of the Messrs. Wadsworth and fifty others. These subscribed 353 shares at $10 each, Mr. James Wadsworth taking 120 shares and his brother, besides superintending personally the work, presenting a good bell. The house was a plain structure 45 by 55 feet, built of the best timber and furnished with 50 pews. Its entire cost was $6,000. It was raised in June, 1817, and completed in December of the same year. The first day of January, 1818, the house was dedicated. This was an event of great interest. The sermon was preached by Rev. Daniel C. Axtell of Geneva.

The Sunday following, the first elders elected received ordination. This building, long known as the "White Church," stood opposite the public square near the south end of Main street. It was enlarged one third in 1854, and again greatly improved within and without in 1870. For two generations it was used as a church, the last service being held within its walls, December 4, 1881. In 1884, it was taken down by Mr. J. D. Lewis and its site occupied by the residence of Mr. William A. Stevens.

On the 12th of July, 1817, Rev. Abraham Foreman (Union College, 1815) was installed as the first pastor of the church. The exercises took place in the unfinished house, which was enclosed and fitted for the occasion. Here also at the same time Loring D. Dewey, A. M., was ordained an evangelist. Rev. Ebenezer Fitch, D.D., then pastor at West Bloomfield, and formerly for 22 years the first president of Williams College, preached the sermon. Until this time the church had had no settled pastor. It had enjoyed, however, these six years, the ministrations of several transient ministers, among whom were Daniel Oliver, John Lindley, Aaron C. Collins, Robert Hubbard, Stephen Wheelock, Silas Pratt, Bartholomew Mills and Daniel S. Butrick.

Rev. Mr Foreman came in October, 1816, as tutor in the family of Mr. Wadsworth, and was employed by the church to preach from that date. The following spring he was called to be pastor on a salary of $500, and remained as such until November 17, 1819, when at his own request he was dismissed. He continued to reside in Geneseo, till his death, August 20, 1854. With marked personal eccentricities, Mr. Foreman was a good sermonizer and a man of rare scholarship and kindness of heart.

About 1820, the Sunday school was organized. The first teachers were Jacob B. Hall, Orlando Hastings, Mr. Fairchild, Miss Harriet Wadsworth and Miss Mary Lawrence. Orlando Hastings was the first Superintendent.

After a few years he was followed by Chauncey Parsons, who continued to hold the office for over thirty years. Four or five years earlier, however, in 1816, Rev. Daniel S. Butrick held the first Sunday school in town, the sessions being on Saturday afternoon in the school house on Temple Hill, and the exercises mostly recitations of the catechism.

Rev. Norris Bull (D. D., 1846, Union; grad. Yale, 1813), of the Presbytery of Troy, came to Western New York as a missionary in 1818, and was called to the pastorate April 22, 1822. He was ordained and installed June 19 of the same year. For over ten years he was pastor until July 3, 1832, when he was dismissed to the Presbytery of Genesee and took charge of the church in Wyoming. From 1837 to 1847, he was pastor of the church in Clarkson. In both these places he was also principal of the town Academy a part of the time. Early in 1847, he became pastor at Lewiston, where he died, quite suddenly but triumphantly, December 8, 1847.

It was early in his pastorate, in 1824, that the Wednesday evening meeting of prayer was first established. It was at the suggestion of a missionary, who with Dr. Bull met a few of the male members at the house of Dr. Cyrus Wells. These were John Colt, Jacob B. Hall, Erastus Parsons and Wilbur Turner. They entered into a covenant to sustain the meeting and to spend some time every day in prayer for a revival. It was held from house to house. Soon the female members of the church sought admission. Then the impenitent became interested, the doors were thrown open and the great awakening of 1824-5 followed. April 3, 1825, was a memorable communion Sabbath. Ninety-one persons, embracing many of the leading men and women of the village, entered into covenant with the church. In 1824, the number of members was 92; in 1825, 191; and in 1831, after the great revival of 1830, 206.

"The Livingston Co. High School," afterward known as

Geneseo Academy, was established and its substantial brick buildings erected on Temple Hill in 1826. It was incorporated March 10, 1827. In this enterprise Mr. James Wadsworth took the liveliest interest. This school came to be under the care of the Synod of Buffalo in 1849, and continued a recognized power of good, educational and religious, for nearly half a century. Its first principal was C. C. Felton, LL. D., afterward president of Harvard University, and its last, Henry D. Gregory, Ph. D., now of Girard College, Philadelphia. It ceased to exist in 1875, four years after the opening of the State Normal School.

The attempt of Unitarianism, though abortive, to gain a footing in Western New York in connection with the establishment of the Academy, was a sore trial to the church. The unusual mode of building by an association instead of trustees, brought on serious financial complications. During the same time church discipline was also extensively undertaken. Yet by the signal blessing of God and under the guidance of Dr. Bull, a man of consummate ability, courage and devotion to truth, the period of his ministry was one of unwonted spiritual growth.

In September, 1833, Rev. John Chase Lord (D. D., 1841, Hamilton; grad. Hamilton, 1825) began his labors, and was ordained and installed July 31, 1834, the sermon by Rev. James Richards, D. D., and the charges to pastor and people by Rev. Norris Bull, D. D , and Rev. John Barnard, D. D., respectively. In October, 1835, he was called to the Central Presbyterian church, Buffalo, and was dismissed the 28th of the same month. He died at Buffalo, January 21, 1877. His Geneseo pastorate though brief was greatly blessed. A powerful revival resulting in over 100 additions signalized his ministry in 1833-4. The church now numbered 258.

Rev. John Nitchie Lewis, A. M. (grad. Yale, 1828) followed Dr. Lord in the pastorate, October, 3, 1838. The church was supplied statedly in the interim by Rev.

Theodore Spencer, Rev. Elam H. Walker and Rev. Henry Snyder successively. Rev. Mr. Lewis' ministry continued to April 5, 1841. Loss of voice compelled release from pulpit labor for 2½ years. His subsequent charges were at Newburgh, Bethlehem, Monticello and New York city. While assistant pastor of the Brick church his death occurred very suddenly, October 5, 1861.

In 1843, November 8th, Rev. Benjamin B. Stockton succeeded to the pastorate which continued five years. He was dismissed September 26, 1848, was pastor at Phelps several years, entered later the United States Navy as chaplain and died at Brooklyn, June 10, 1861. October 9, 1842, Hugh McBride and Cornelius Shepard, Jr., were ordained elders and Elihu N. Faxon, deacon; and in 1845, October 21, Felix Tracy and Ephraim Cone were ordained elders and Chauncey Watson, deacon.

The trustees of the Geneseo Gospel Society, elected from 1819 to 1848 were as follows: 1820, Philo C. Fuller; 1822, Samuel F. Butler and Oliver Skinner; 1823, Ogden M. Willey; 1825, Owen P. Olmsted; 1827, William Finley; 1828, Alfred Birge; 1830, John Colt and Freeman Hastings; 1831, Frederick W. Butler; 1832, Cyrus Wells and Russell Austin; 1833, Jacob B. Hall; 1834, Allen Ayrault; 1835, Edward P. Metcalf and Ebenezer Walker; 1836, Cornelius Shepard; 1838, William H. Stanley; 1841, William M. Bond; 1842, Walter E. Lauderdale, M. D.; 1844, Ephraim Cone and 1848, Samuel Finley.

Rev. Ferdinand DeWilton Ward (D. D., 1861, Washington; grad. Union, 1831) was invited to Geneseo in 1848, having just returned from a ten years' residence as missionary in Southern India. He was installed September 26, 1850, Rev. John Barnard, D. D., preaching the sermon, Rev. Henry Kendall, D. D., giving the charge to the pastor and Rev. C. H. A. Buckley that to the people. His ministry was continuous from November 5, 1848, to the division of the church, October 31, 1858. During this period 243 were added to the church roll, which now numbered 234 members. Ephraim Cone and Mortimer Buell were ordained deacons, Sunday, September 14, 1851. The church edifice was greatly enlarged in 1854, a clock was placed in the tower, a Hook organ was introduced supplanting the bass viol, and a new session house, now known as the Ward Annex, was built on Second street. Scott Lord was elected to the board of trustees in 1853, James S. Orton and Charles Colt, Jr., in 1858 and Sidney Ward in 1859. Chauncey Parsons was chorister for many years until 1854, then William Cushing until his removal from Geneseo two years later and Charles O. Beach from 1856 to 1875. The organists were Benjamin Cushing (1854-5), Catharine M. Austin (1856-1867), James A. West, M. D. (1867-1876), Kate McArthur (1876-1878) and Myron A. Rector from 1878.

The church called Rev. George Palmer Folsom (D. D., 1881, Williams; grad. Williams, 1847) from Attica, December 7, 1858. The installation occurred Wednesday, February 2, 1859, the sermon being preached by Rev. Grosvenor W. Heacock, D. D., of Buffalo. He remained pastor of the church until September 20, 1868, when at his own request he was dismissed. During this pastorate the system of rotary eldership gave place, by vote of the church October 12, 1865, to that of permanent eldership. For twenty years there had been no election of elders. The board at this date consisted of Jacob B. Hall, Charles Colt, Russell Austin, Frederick W. Butler and Ephraim Cone. Three additional members were chosen, Elijah N. Bacon, James S. Orton and William Walker, who were ordained October 22. There were received to church membership 138. After the division there were 130 members. The present number of members was 166. A comfortable manse on Main street, and a new church bell which is still in use, were purchased in 1866.

July 7, 1867, William A. Brodie and Elisha W. Hudnutt were ordained elders and John Davidson, deacon. The writer is greatly indebted to Dr. Folsom, as also to Dr. Ward, for material for this historical sketch. After leaving Geneseo, Dr. Folsom was for several years pastor at Baraboo, Wisconsin, and at Iowa City, Iowa. His present pastorate since 1887 is at Carroll, Iowa.

Rev. Isaac Newton Sprague, D. D. (1865, Middlebury; grad. Middlebury, 1822) was called November 16, 1868, entered on his work January 17, 1869, and was installed February 2, following. Rev. James B. Shaw, D. D., of Rochester, preached the sermon. During his ministry of a little more than eight years, 210 were added to the roll. This numbered at the close of his ministry 232. Revival blessing was enjoyed in 1870-71; union church services were promoted; systematic beneficence developed and contributions largely increased. The church name was changed to the First Presbyterian Church of Geneseo Village, by vote, December 22, 1869, and the building was renovated in the summer of 1870 at an expense of $2,000. June 18, 1871, James J. Cone, Adoniram J. Abbott and John R. Strang were ordained elders. March 20th of the same year James S. Orton was chosen church treasurer. Services commemorative of the completion of fifty years of continuous labor in the ministry by the pastor were held Sunday, September 14, 1873. Dr. Sprague was dismissed to the Presbytery of Detroit, April 10, 1877. For six years he was pastor at Wyandotte, Mich. In 1886, he went to Poultney, Vermont, where honorably retired he makes his home, now at the ripe age of almost 89 years.

Charles O. Beach was elected trustee in 1862. Elijah N. Bacon and Charles F. Doty, in 1865; William Walker, in 1866; James J. Cone, in 1870; Nelson Janes, in 1871; Theodore F. Olmsted, in 1876 and Orrin F. Sherwood, in 1878.

April 10, 1877, Rev. Josiah Edwards Kittredge (D. D., 1884, Univ. of N. Y.; grad. Yale, 1860) was received to Rochester Presbytery, and on the 18th inst., was installed pastor of this church, Rev. J. Lovejoy Robertson preaching the sermon. In the three following years 63 were added to the roll, which then numbered 261, the number of Sunday school members rose to 319 and the spirit of Christian love prevailed. On the 30th of March, 1880, the union of the two Presbyterian churches was happily consummated and this church was merged in the *Presbyterian Church of Geneseo Village*.

II. CENTRAL PRESBYTERIAN CHURCH.

The Presbytery of Genesee River, in response to a petition signed by 113 petitioners, organized this church by commissioners previously appointed, in the Methodist church, Thursday, October 21, 1858. The commissioners were Rev. Thomas Aitken, of Sparta, chairman, Rev. William E. Jones, of Caledonia, Rev. James M. Harlow, of Moscow, and elders Wm. W. McNair, of Sparta, Zephaniah Lewis, of Scottsville, and Edward B. Miller, of Warsaw, who was appointed clerk. A sermon was preached by Rev. W. E. Jones, and devotional services conducted by Rev. Thomas Aitken, W. E. Jones and D. D. McColl, of Scottsville, after which, the church was duly constituted with 82 members. Oliver Skinner, Cornelius Shepard, Jr., Gulielmus Wing, Andrew W. Butterway, clerk. Scott Lord and George Fridd were elected elders, and Edward Thomas and Francis C. Sage, deacons.

The ordination of Andrew W. Butterway and Scott Lord as elders, and of Edward Thomas and Francis C. Sage, as deacons, followed with their installation, together with that of Oliver Skinner, Cornelius Shepard, Jr., and Gulielmus Wing, already ordained. The prayer of installation was offered by Rev. W. D. McKinley, of Tuscarora.

The first public service was held Sunday, November 7th, in Concert Hall, Rev. Thomas Aitken preaching the sermon. A Sabbath school was organized, and Rev. Ferdinand De W. Ward, (D. D., 1861, Washington; graduate, Union, 1831,) was unanimously elected pastor of the church. The first communion service was observed at the same place, where, for fourteen months, the congregation worshipped. Sunday, January 2nd, 1859, the pastor elect presiding. The church now numbered 109 members.

The installation of Dr. Ward took place February 16, 1859; Rev. Joseph Kimball, of Brockport, preached, Rev. Joseph E. Nassau, D. D., of Warsaw, gave the charge to the pastor, and Rev. J. Carroll, of Groveland, that to the people. George Fridd was installed elder on the same occasion. In the afternoon Rev. Charles Ray was inaugurated principal of Geneseo Academy, with addresses by Rev. Albert G. Hall, D. D., of Rochester, Rev. Mr. Ray and Hon. Allen Ayrault, of Geneseo.

March 29, 1859, the ecclesiastical society was incorporated under the name of The Central Presbyterian Church of Geneseo, with Walter E. Lauderdale, M. D., Samuel Finley, Wallace R. Walker, Peter Miller, Chauncey M. Dake, M. D., M. Luther Heath, John Crossett and James D. Crank, trustees. Richard Champ was added to the board in 1864.

July 18, 1859, the church was called to mourn the death of Oliver Skinner, its senior elder. Measures were taken promptly to secure a church edifice. Funds were subscribed at a parish meeting June 12, 1859, and the corner stone was laid July 6, with appropriate exercises, the pastor delivering the address. The building was after the plans of Messrs. Upjohn & Son, of New York, and was a fine structure of brick (40x85 feet), situated at the corner of Second and Centre streets, and provided with tower and bell. It was dedicated Jan. 3, 1860, the dedicatory sermon by

Rev. Nicholas Murray, D. D., of Elizabeth, N. J. The church now numbered 170 members.

The pastorate of Rev. Dr. Ward continued until November, 1861. In 1862 he took the chaplaincy of the 104th New York Volunteers in the field. During the five following years the church was statedly supplied by Rev. Henry Neill, D. D., of Detroit. He was regarded as a man of marked pulpit ability and decided social qualities. He prosecuted his labors with the church until April, 1866, when he entered upon the work of the Board of Aid for Presbyterian Churches at the South. From 1869 to 1871 he was pastor of the Second Church at New Brunswick, N. J. His death occurred at Philadelphia, Pa., April 21, 1879, at the age of 63.

Rev. Dr. Ward was at once recalled and was re-installed December 4, 1866, Rev. Malcolm N. McLaren, D. D., preaching the sermon, and Rev. Thomas Aitken and Rev. Joseph E. Nassau, D. D , delivering the charges to pastor and people. On August 5, 1866, Walter E. Lauderdale, M. D , and Samuel Finley were ordained elders, and Richard Clamp, deacon.

A union service was held in the church, January 20, 1867, when, on invitation of the session, Rev. Mr. Folsom, of the Second Church, preached. The church received the special blessing of God in revival in the winter of 1870-71. April 2, 1871, was a Sabbath made memorable by the admission to the communion for the first time of 51 persons; 71 were received during the year. The church roll increased to 304.

December 15, 1872, occurred the installation of Henry D. Gregory, Ph. D., and Edward E. Sill, as elders, and of Nelson J. Griswold and John LaMarsh, as deacons.

The pastor again resigned his charge, to take effect from November 9, 1873, in order to act as district superintendent of the American Bible Society for Western New York.

Dr. Ward supplied statedly a number of neighboring churches for several years, when failing health in the spring of 1889 compelled release for a while. Mrs. Ward, his devoted companion for more than half a century, died, greatly mourned by all, in October, 1886. Though now retired from responsible service, Dr. Ward is still active with voice and pen, and honored and beloved, resides in Geneseo, which for over forty years has been his chosen home.

During this period the Woman's Missionary and Aid Society, auxiliary to the Woman's Foreign Missionary Society of Philadelphia, was organized, mainly through the efforts of Mrs. H. D. Gregory, and also the Butler Band, named for Rev. John Butler, once a member of the church, and from 1860 to 1885 a missionary in China. He died at Ningpo, Oct. 11, 1885, at the age of 48.

A call was extended July 3, 1874, to Rev. Charles Stoddard Durfee, A. M. (graduate Williams, 1864,) of the Presbytery of Troy. His installation took place September 10, 1874. The sermon was preached by Rev. Teunis S. Hamlin, D. D., of Troy; Rev. William H. Millham, of Livonia, gave the charge to the pastor; Rev. F. DeW. Ward, D. D., the charge to the people, and Rev. I. N. Sprague, D. D., offered the installing prayer.

October 4, 1874, William J. Milne, Ph. D., principal of the State Normal School, was ordained elder, and September 19, 1875, Nelson J. Griswold and Thomas Elliott to the same office. A much needed organ was procured in 1874. The church was called to suffer the loss by death of elder Samuel Finley, February 9, 1875, and again, January 12, 1879, of elder Cornelius Shepard at the age of 84.

The trustees of the church were John Crossett, Norman W. Rose, Andrew J. Willard, James W. Clement, Nelson J. Griswold, Charles Fridd, Walter E. Lauderdale, M. D., and Samuel Finley. During the ministry of Mr. Durfee the church continued to grow in its devotion to Christian missions, to the cause of temperance and all matters of true social reform.

Rev. Mr. Durfee remained the faithful and beloved pastor for nearly six years until the union of the two churches. He devoted himself to this union with a most rare unselfishness, so shining a characteristic of the man. Without this personal effort of his, no union was then possible, but the large interests of Christ's cause moved him to great singleness of heart to promote it. He was conscientious always and fearless, a man of studious habits, a preacher clear and convincing, and a warm hearted, genial friend. He was three years at Liverpool when, in 1884, he became pastor at East Bloomfield. Here in 1887, the 24th of December, he died in triumph. His funeral service was attended by a large delegation from the church that he had helped so signally to make one.

The congregations of the two churches met simultaneously, each in its own place of worship, Monday afternoon, January 19, 1880, at one o'clock, and voted with great unanimity for the union of the churches. Special church meetings were also held Wednesday, January 28, at which identical resolutions requesting Presbytery to consummate this union were adopted, and elder Nelson J. Griswold of the Central Church, and elder John R. Strang of the First Church, were appointed to present the petition to that body. The union was happily effected March 30, 1880, and this church was merged in the *Presbyterian Church of Geneseo Village.*

III. PRESBYTERIAN CHURCH OF GENESEO VILLAGE.

From the record book of the church the following preliminary, historical note is taken:

On the 30th day of March, A. D. 1880, the Presbytery

PRESBYTERIAN CHURCH OF GENESEO VILLAGE.

of Rochester, at a special meeting held at the Central Presbyterian Church in Geneseo, called for the purpose of considering the union of the two Presbyterian Churches there located, took action affirmatively on the following minute which had been duly adopted by both these churches:

"*Resolved*, that the Presbytery of Rochester be requested to unite and consolidate the two Presbyterian Churches now existing in the village of Geneseo, and known as the First Presbyterian Church of the Village of Geneseo, and the Central Presbyterian Church of Geneseo, so that the same shall hereafter constitute one church, to be known as The Presbyterian Church of Geneseo Village upon the following terms and conditions, viz:

"First. Rev Mr. Durfee desiring to withdraw in case a union can be effected, the Rev. Josiah E. Kittredge to be pastor of said united church.

"Second. The elders of each of such churches at the time of such union to retain their offices as such in the united church.

"Third. The deacons in office in each of such churches to retain their offices in the united church."

The church thus constituted numbered 472 members. Its officers were as follows: Pastor, Rev. Josiah E. Kittredge (D. D. 1884, Univ. of New York; graduate, Yale, 1860); elders, Adoniram J. Abbott, Frederick W. Butler, Andrew W. Butterway, William A. Brodie, clerk, Thomas Elliot, George Fridd, Nelson J. Griswold, Elisha W. Hudnutt, Walter E. Lauderdale, M. D., William J. Milne, LL. D., James S. Orton, treasurer, John R. Strang; deacons, John Davidson, Nelson J. Griswold, John La Marsh. The trustees were those of the incorporated Geneseo Gospel Society up to September 6, when a new board was elected, consisting of James S. Orton, chairman and treasurer, Nelson J. Griswold, Nelson Janes, clerk, William J. Milne, LL. D., Theodore F. Olmsted and John R. Strang. The Sunday school superintendents were John R. Strang, William A. Brodie and William J. Milne.

The first service of the united church was held with the celebration of the Lord's Supper the Sunday after the union, April 4th, 1880, in the "White Church." Here for a year and nine months the church worshipped. Arrangements were at once set in motion for the erection of a new and suitable edifice in connection with the Brick Church at the corner of Second and Centre streets. Subscriptions were secured and plans matured so that on the 14th of September ground was broken, and the corner stone was laid the 8th of November, with appropriate services. Rev. Dr. Ward read the Scriptures, Rev. Mr. Durfee offered prayer, the pastor delivering the address.

December 8th, 1881, occurred the dedication of the house. Rev. Henry Darling, D. D., LL. D., president of Hamilton College, preached the dedicatory sermon at the service in the afternoon. A social service of praise and prayer followed in the evening, Rev. Dr. James B. Shaw, of Rochester, presiding, and addresses were made by Rev. Dr. Ward and Rev. Dr. Folsom, former pastors, Rev. Dr. J. R. Page, Rev. Dr. Levi Parsons and others.

The new edifice was of brick with trimmings of Ohio sand stone, slate roof and stained glass windows, built in Roman gothic style with tower after architectural plans of Lawrence B. Valk, of New York. It was 55 x 95 feet, and was so united with the former church building as to make one harmonious structure 95 x 98 feet, and to secure complete provision for the Sunday School and all the social needs of the church. The main audience room was furnished with 127 pews, arranged in circular form, with seating capacity for 650 persons, floor sloping towards the pulpit, and an excellent Steere & Turner organ valued at $4,000. The cost of the new building including organ was $26,000, the value of the entire structure with site, about $40,000.

December 4th, 1881, the church worshipped for the last

time in the old White Church, and the following Sunday, December 11th, gathered in the new church home a congregation that overfilled the audience room.

In the winter of 1883-4, the church rejoiced in a Pentecostal blessing. Rev. Edgar E. Davidson was with the pastor and labored assiduously. As a result of this outpouring of God's spirit more than 200 united with the church; 167 persons were received into membership on confession of faith, Sunday, April 6, 1884, and 80 adults were baptized; 76 were received to the church in 1888, 47 on confession of faith. The members at this date, October, 1889, number 630, and of the Sunday school 486. The average beneficence per year for the nine years since union, has been $2,670, and the average expenses for the same time, including the cost of its new edifice, nearly $7,000.

In September, 1887, a new and delightful manse on Centre street was purchased at an expense of $6,000.

The present officers of the church are the same as in 1880, except that the senior elder at the reunion, Frederick W. Butler, died May 10, 1884, at the age of 89. John R. Strang is church treasurer. The trustees are John R. Strang, chairman, Elisha Bacon, Myron N. Foster, clerk, Nelson J. Griswold, William J. Milne, LL. D., and Theodore F. Olmsted. Charles W. Fielder is treasurer of the society. The Sunday school superintendents are Charles W. Fielder, Elisha Bacon and James R. Coddington. For the entire period Jay C. Merrill has been chorister and Myron H. Rector, organist.

Connected with the church is a Young People's Society of Christian Endeavor, organized, January, 1887, the successor of the Young People's Association, a Ladies' Missionary Society (1880), a Young Ladies' Missionary Society (1880), Mission Band (1880), Society of Systematic Givers (1885), and the Young Men's Missionary Association (1889).

GROVELAND.

This church was organized in 1809 by Rev. John Lindsley, and consisted of sixteen members and three elders, which are believed to have been as follows, although the original records prior to August 13, 1820, were lost: John Jones and Margaret, his wife, Hugh Harrison and Phebe, his wife, Abraham Harrison and Mary, his wife, John Harrison and Mary, his wife, Thomas Begole and Mary, his wife, Samuel Stillwell and Margaret, his wife, David Robinson and Agnes, his wife, Adam Wisner and Margaret, his wife; with John Jones, Hugh Harrison and Abraham Harrison, as elders. The following is the list of ministers with their terms of service as nearly as can be ascertained:

Rev. John Lindslay, 1809–1818.
Rev. Silas Pratt. Sept, 1818–June. 1828.
Rev. Isaac Crabb, March 10, 1831–Aug. 28, 1833.
Rev. George E. Sill, Nov., 1833–Oct., 1834.
Rev. George Freeman, Jan., 1835–Nov., 1837.
Rev. Orin Brown, Jan., 1838–May, 1841.
Rev. Silas Pratt, May, 1841–May, 1843.
Rev. Lewis Cheeseman, Aug., 1843–June, 1845.
Rev. Richard Kay, Nov., 1845–Nov., 1848.
Rev. J. C. Van Lew, Feb., 1849–April, 1860.
Rev. E. Sturges, Oct., 1850– 1853.
Rev John J. Carroll, June, 1854–Oct., 1862.
Rev. Stuart Mitchell, April, 1863–July, 1864.
Rev. Henry L. Doolittle, Oct., 1864–Oct., 1867.
Rev. Thomas Dobbin, May, 1868–Aug., 1875.
Rev. David Conway, Sept., 1876–July, 1877.
Rev. Christian P. Murray, July, 1878–April, 1879.
Rev. A. N. Hardy, July, 1879–July, 1880.
Rev. F. Swartz Crawford, Oct., 1881–April, 1888.
Rev. Lucius F. Badger, Sept., 1888.

Of these twenty the Rev. Messrs. Crabb, Carroll, Dobbin, Crawford and Badger, were installed as pastors; the last still retaining that relation. In addition to the three ruling elders already named, the list is as follows:

Hugh McNair.
Samuel Culbertson, Jan., 1819–Aug., 1827.
Thomas Ward, Aug , 1820– 1834.
John Jones, September, 1820–April, 1833.
Abraham Harrison, Sept. 1820–July, 1846.
Michael Johnson, Jan., 1824–June, 1835.
William Leaming, Jan., 1824–July, 1847.
John Vance, Feb., 1836–May 8, 1843.
Samuel C. Culbertson, Feb., 1836–Jan., 1858.
J. J. Groesbeck, Feb., 1836–May, 1883.
Daniel Kelly, Feb., 1836–Aug., 1861.
Peter Teitsworth, June, 1842–Sept., 1858.
John Kuder, June, 1842–Oct., 1883.
J. R. Roseburgh, Oct., 1852–Feb., 1864.
John Gray, Oct., 1852–June, 1864.
John Magee, Oct., 1852–Oct., 1882.
Samuel Vance, July, 1861–Jan., 1879.
Orimel Bigelow, July, 1861.
Fort Benway, Aug., 1877.
David Gray, Nov., 1885.
John P. Teitsworth, Nov., 1885.

The only deacons ever elected by this church were Aaron T. Henderschott and Peter Ebenriter, in 1852.

This church was taken under the care of the Presbytery of Ontario, January 20, 1819, where it remained until, in April, 1838, the time of the division of the New and the Old School, the session decided not to be represented in Presbytery.

On the 10th of March, 1842, the church united with the Presbytery of Caledonia, O. S., though not without a vigorous protest from the minority, who organized a separate church to remain with the Presbytery of Ontario, which was duly recognized by the same, but soon ceased to exist. The other church maintained its connection with the Old School assembly up to the time of reunion, first with the Presbytery of Steuben, which was formed Oct. 19, 1842, and subsequently with that of Genesee River, which was formed Sept. 27, 1853.

The use of tokens was dispensed with on the 20th of April, 1821.

In 1834 occurs the record of a "Sacramental occasion which lasted five days, consisting of preaching services and prayer meetings, and on the third day (Sunday) the Communion." A similar record appears again under date of January, 1857.

In 1842 the session took action on temperance, and themselves with twenty of the church members signed a total abstinence pledge. In the same year the session adopted vigorous measures for promoting the missionary spirit by a systematic plan of giving.

In 1825 the church reported forty-five members; in 1827, sixty-four; in 1837, one hundred and thirty-one; in 1846, one hundred and twenty-one; in 1876, one hundred and forty-three, and in 1888, one hundred and seventy-eight.

Its larger accessions have been: in 1821, thirteen; 1831, fifty-six; 1835, twenty-three; 1864, twenty-five; 1871, twenty-four; 1883, twenty-four; 1888, eighteen.

The first mention of the Sunday school in the records is under date of June 16, 1838, though it is certain that the school had been organized quite early.

The Ladies' Missionary Society was organized May 15, 1872; the Young Ladies' Aid Society, Aug. 26, 1882; the Band of Willing Workers, 1881, and the Boys' Mission Brigade, 1888.

The present house of worship was erected in 1829. The builder was Henry Vroman, and the trustees were G. N. Morrill, Daniel Kelly, John Harrison, A. Harrison, Michael Johnson and George Bennet.

The present trustees are George S. Ewart, William G. Wilson and Charles F. Arner.

In 1872, the building was thoroughly repaired and many improvements made, at an expense of $4,000. This was done during the ministry of Rev. Thomas Dobbin, and was largely attributable to his persevering efforts.

The society owns a commodious parsonage not far from the church. This church though rural in its location, being about four miles from the nearest railroad station, and composed almost entirely of farmers, has increased in members and apparently so in pecuniary ability, furnishing a very happy exception to other churches similarly situated. Without asking for missionary aid it has furnished a liberal support for its pastors, and taken rank among the foremost of the churches, in proportion to its numbers, in the amounts contributed for missionary purposes.

HENRIETTA.

In 1810, Rev. Solomon Allen, pastor of the Pittsford Presbyterian church, preached a missionary sermon, on a Sabbath, to his congregation. A collection was taken, which amounted to $10. It was to be devoted to sending the gospel to the heathen. There being no convenient way to send it to a foreign field, the pastor was requested to preach two Sabbaths to the destitute people of West-town (Henrietta), and appropriate the $10 to remunerate himself. These efforts were followed by others in 1812, at which gatherings deacon Moses Sperry read sermons furnished by his former pastor in Connecticut. These meetings were supplemented by occasional preaching by himself and deacon Ellis, in the school house near the latter's residence.

Soon a strong religious interest was evoked and May 20, 1816, in the same school house, the Congregational Church of Henrietta was organized with 20 members. So far as known the following are the persons identified with the church at that early date:

Deacons Moses Sperry and Ellis; Betsey Stannard, Fanny Sheldon, Polly Burr, Hannah Kelsey, Asa Munn, Olive Remington, Polly Gooding, William Ellis, Lorinda Burr, David Deming, Sally Deming, Margaret H. Jones, Elizabeth Brown, Mary Ellis, Amos Edgerton, Levi Jackson, Isaac Seeley, William Sternberg, Nancy Titus, Lydia Gillette, Sally L. Tinker, Matthias L. Angle and Mary Angle. Rev. John F. Bliss, who subsequently became pastor of the Baptist church, was actively interested in furthering the organization. He and Rev. George R. King preached occasionally in the school house, but there was no regular preaching until 1823, when Rev. John Taylor preached half of his time in the log meeting house erected south of the former residence of Thomas O. Jones. Afterwards the meetings were held in Academy Hall, in the east village.

There were no considerable accessions to the church until the revival of 1831, which commenced in Rochester under the preaching of Rev. Charles G. Finney, at which time 25 persons united with the church, and among them James Sperry, Ebenezer Gooding and Joseph Brown, who became active and substantial members. Under the impetus of such accessions the society, in the same year, purchased a lot of the trustees of Monroe Academy, and erected a new church building, with sheds attached. In 1865, these buildings upon which there was no insurance were burned, and the year following the present building was erected. The church united with the Rochester Presbytery, under the accommodation plan, June 27, 1833, and was dismissed to the Genesee Consociation, July 1, 1835. In 1834, the church numbered 114 members. Rev. George R. King, under the patronage of the American Home Missionary Society, officiated as stated supply two years from August, 1826. Following him, were Revs. William P. Kendrick, John Thalheimer, Roswell G. Murray (July 11, 1833—July 1, 1835), Edward Wheeler, Harvey A. Sackett, Silas H. Ashmun, Orlow Bartholomew, William Bryant Brown, S. W. Streeter (1848–'57), Albert Worthington, Byron Bosworth and George R. Merrill. Since Mr. Merrill left, the church has had no regular pastor for any considerable time.*

HONEOYE FALLS.

The Presbyterian church of Honeoye Falls (originally West Mendon) was organized March 1, 1831, under the ministry of Rev. George G. Sill, who began his work here under the auspices of the General Assembly's Board of Missions in 1828, about thirty years after the first settlement of the village Six persons received by letter from other churches, united in forming the church: Charles Foot, Simeon S. Johnson, Moses Rowell, Louisa W. Sill, Marcia M. Blaisdell and Asenath Dixon. Within one month thereafter five were added by letter and twelve by confession of faith. Since that time, ten persons have served as ruling elders: Moses Rowell, Horace Wheeler, James Smith, who served for twenty-nine years, Harry Allen, fifty-two years, Albe C. Allen, Asa Pride, forty-six years, Samuel Chipman, Zenas W. Smith, Charles Bickford, and James Edwin Allen. Of these Charles Bickford, residing elsewhere, and Albe C. Allen, the only ruling elder of the church at present (1888) are now living. The last named has served the church over

*Compiled from Prof. McIntosh's History of Monroe County, 1877; Half Century of the Presbytery of Rochester, and Hotchkin's History of Western New York.

forty-eight years, having also during that period, filled the offices of clerk and treasurer of the congregation. Other elders named have served for periods less than ten years. The term of office is for life.

Of the fifteen ministers who have served the church, those indicated have been installed: George G. Sill, 1828-32; Richard Dunning, 1832; Jacob Hart, 1834-39; S. J. McCullough, (installed) 1839; Ephraim Strong, (installed) 1840-43; Thomas Riggs, 1843-46; O. C. Beardsley, 1846-57; Ira O. De Long, 1857, six months; J. W. Wood, 1858; L. B. Rogers, 1860; Henry M. Hurd, 1861; Edwin B. Van Anken, (ordained) 1863-5; Ira O. De Long, (second term) 1865-8; John E. Baker, 1868; Samuel Alden Freeman, 1869 to the present, 1889 (installed 1872).

The Sabbath school, opened in 1831, has continued without intermission to the present time. The entire number of members of the school by the last annual report, was 153. The Ladies' Aid Society has for many years rendered effective assistance in keeping the interior of the church edifice suitably furnished, and in other like work. A Ladies' Missionary Society has existed for the last ten years. Mission Bands have been maintained for the last six years. Since 1885 a Temperance Society has existed in connection with the Sabbath school, which holds meetings and circulates the Total Abstinence Pledge in the school once a month. "The church began in a revival," marked by fifteen or twenty hopeful conversions. Other years of especial ingathering have been 1843, 39; 1849, 19; 1859, 30; 1864, 27; 1876, 28; 1887, 38. The first church edifice, 40 ft. x 24, was erected 1831, upon a lot in the rear of that now in use. The present church, 70 ft. x 42, was completed in 1842, at a cost of $4,500. The lot was given by Doctor Harry Allen, and his wife Lydia N. They were also among the largest contributors to the cost of its erection. The original building was first sold and then in 1864 repurchased and is now annexed to the rear of the main edifice at a cost of $600. The bell was placed in the steeple in 1864, and was purchased as a memorial, with funds left by Theodore H. Jameson, a member of the church who was killed at the second battle of Manassas, August 30, 1862. Considerable repairs were made on the church in 1873. In 1877, a new desk and other furniture were provided for the pulpit. In 1880 stained glass windows were put in, and a pipe organ purchased. In 1874 sheds were built, and in 1887 others were added. A manse was erected in 1832, but was sold a few years later, and in 1876 another was bought for $1,500. In 1887 this building was remodeled with handsome additions at a cost of about $1,800.

The first board of trustees were Harry Allen, James Dixon, and James Smith. The present board are John Ferguson, Clarence A. Gilmore, Christopher Eberly, Andrew Y. Earl, and Christian Nau. Fifty-eight persons have served in this capacity. Five persons, originally members of the church, have entered the ministry. Chauncey Leavenworth, (deceased, Presbyterian); Dr. Leonard Swayne, (deceased, 1869, Congregational, Providence, R. I.); Edwin Allen, Presbyterian; Horace H. Allen, Presbyterian, and Edward Gibbs Bickford, (deceased, 1877, Presbyterian missionary at Marash, Asiatic Turkey).

About ten years after the organization of this church, several persons left to unite with St. John's Protestant Episcopal Church, then organized. A Christian church formed about the same time with the Presbyterian, having disbanded a few years since, several of its members united with this church. In a like manner were received, former members of a German Reformed Church which had existed here for a time. Friendly intercourse and co-operation with other churches in the community have marked the life of the church, especially during its more recent history. Severe financial reverses have more than once seriously affected the growth and prosperity of the town. The Roman Catholic population has increased. In every desirable respect, there has been a continuous, if not rapid, advance of the town, which this congregation has, in its measure, both promoted and shared.

In 1887, the church reported 137 communicants, a larger number than at any time before in its history. The whole number of communicants from the beginning is 578. Up to 1869, 182 by confession, and 213 by letter. Since 1869, and during the present pastorate of twenty years, 110 by confession, and 73 by letter.

LIMA.

The name of this town was Charleston, until 1808, when it was changed to Lima. The church was organized Oct. 1, 1795, by Rev. Daniel Thatcher. The first elders were Elisha Wade, Solomon Hovey and William Williams; and the first deacon was Thomas Lee.

Among the early members were Miles Bristol and wife, Joseph M. Gilbert and wife, Huldah, wife of Judge Warner, Mary, wife of Abel Bristol, Elijah Gifford and wife, Charles Rice, Mrs. Daniel Warner, Mrs. Clark Brockway, Guernsey W. Cook and wife.

Being without a pastor, and having largely fallen into decay, the church was reorganized as Congregational by the Rev. Jacob Catlin, Dec. 27, 1799, and prior to 1804 belonged to the Ontario Association, and after the dissolution of that body in 1813, was received under the care of the Presbytery of Ontario, June 20, 1820, with which it was subsequently merged into the present Presbytery of Rochester.

Prior to 1804 the church had little more than occasional preaching, and ministers who were employed for short terms,

LIMA PRESBYTERIAN CHURCH.

the Rev. James H. Hotchkin, stating in his history that he preached to this congregation one half of the time for more than six months of the year 1802.

In November, 1804, the Rev. Ezekiel J. Chapman was employed as stated supply for about two years, who was succeeded by Rev. Mr. Leavenworth for a short term. Mr. Chapman afterwards returned and was installed pastor, Jan. 12, 1809, and remained until 1814 He was succeeded by Rev. John Brown, who served for a short time and was followed by Rev. Mr. Cook.

Rev. John Barnard was installed February 3, 1819, which relation was dissolved September 18, 1856, of whose life and character an extended sketch is found in connection with the history of Presbytery.

Rev. Robert R. Kellogg was installed pastor June 22, 1857, which relation was dissolved July 22, 1859.

Rev. Alphonso L. Benton was ordained and installed March 6, 1861, which relation was dissolved September 18, 1870.

Rev. Albert H. Corliss was installed December 27, 1870, which relation was dissolved December 30, 1875.

Rev. Henry N. Payne was installed, May 1st, 1877, which was dissolved, February 10, 1879. The Rev. James Robertson immediately succeeded Mr. Payne as stated supply for about two years, when ill health compelled him to resign.

Rev. Alfred K. Bates was installed, October 25, 1882, which was dissolved, October 2, 1883. The present pastor Rev. Benjamin F. Willoughby commenced his labors, January 1, 1884, and was installed, May 12, 1884.

The elders which were elected, May 21, 1820, when the church became fully Presbyterian, were Abel Bristol, Gurdon W. Cook, Elijah Gifford and John Dixon; also Henry Look and Nathan Rogers, deacons.

The rotary eldership was adopted, February 5, 1887. And the present elders are William R. McNair, Justin S.

Goodrich, Andrew J. Warner, Edward Salmon, Henry E. Lawrence and William H. Day. The deacons are Edwin Warner, Joseph Foreman and Charles D. Miner. The rotary system does not apply to the deacons.

During the ministry of Rev. Dr. Barnard the records show that revivals occurred in 1828, when 23 were received on confession; in 1838, when 28 were received, and in 1842, when 57 were received. The loss of the records from 1831 to 1842, prevents greater particularity in regard to the spiritual condition of the church at that time. The long ministry of Dr. Barnard will, however, be well remembered for its great ability and success.

In 1858, during the ministry of the Rev. Robert R. Kellogg, the church shared in the general revival with which the country was blessed, and 27 were added. In 1862, during Mr. Benton's ministry 36 were added. In 1876, in connection with the ministry of Mr. Payne, 22 were added; also in 1878, when he was assisted by Rev. E. E. Davidson, the Evangelist, 27 were added.

During the summer of 1884, a Young People's Association was formed. This was at first an independent organization, but was afterwards resolved into a Young People's Society of Christian Endeavor in connection with the general organization of that name.

November 10, 1874, a Ladies' Missionary Society was organized. This society especially undertakes to contribute fifty dollars per annum towards the support of Mrs. Fannie M. Smith, formerly Miss Fannie Strong. who went from this church as a missionary to Peking, China, and is still in China in the missionary work.

The religious society connected with the church was first organized as the Charleston Congregational Society, January 5, 1802, when the following trustees were chosen: David Morgan, Willard Humphrey, Abel Bristol, Manasseh Leech, Asahel Warner and William Williams. The name of the society was changed in 1851 to "The Lima Presbyterian Society."

In the early part of the century, the church was feeble and able to pay but a small salary and a part of that in produce; and at a later period was in great financial straits, which were attributable to failures in business, removals of families and hard times, but about the year 1850, affairs took a more favorable turn. The church originally met for worship in a school house.

The first church building was completed in 1816, at a cost of seven thousand dollars, and occupied a central and very commanding location. The same was re-roofed and remodeled during the pastorate of Mr. Benton, and a large organ was purchased. This was succeeded by the present beautiful and spacious brick edifice, the corner stone of which was laid, August 12, 1873, during the pastorate of Mr. Corliss. There is a convenient lecture room in the rear, and a dining room and kitchen in the basement.

The society owns a very pleasant and commodious parsonage. The present trustees are Justin S. Goodrich, Charles Warner, Henry E. Lawrence, Horace E. Gilbert, Hiram B. Warner and Edward Salmon.

LIVONIA.

In the year 1790 a settlement was made at the outlet of Honeoye Lake. The first man who moved there was Peter Pitts, whose family were the only white persons for four years. Then many came from Massachusetts, Connecticut and Vermont, before the close of the century. The first sermon was by Rev. Samuel Mills in 1792. In 1801 the Rev. Zadoc Hunn, who for several years had given one-eighth of his time to the people of Pittstown, died. There was a revival of great power during his ministry, and so many were converted that ever after religious worship has been maintained. The western part of the above named settlement, called Livonia, was chosen as the center, or site, for a village. Log cabins were built about the square, which was set apart as the place for the church. The first pioneer in Livonia was Solomon Woodruff, grandfather of Mr. S. G. Woodruff. In the year 1803, the first religious services of record were held by Rev. John Rolf. These services were continued by himself and Mr. Lane, a Methodist preacher, till the year 1806. In December of that year seventeen persons were organized into "The Second Congregational Church, of Pittstown," by Rev. Aaron C. Collins. The original members were Jeremiah Riggs, Aaron Childs, Selah Stedman, Damann Blake, Oliver Woodruff, Benjamin Cook, Thankful Parsons, Lucy Childs, Mary Stedman, Irene Clark, Rachel Gibbs, Nancy Benton, Lydia Gibbs, Anna Woodruff, Sally Fenand, Sally Blake and Rebecca Blake.

The church thus formed was received by the Ontario Association in 1807. The Lord's Supper was administered for the first time February 22, 1807. Till a house of worship could be built, the Sabbath was honored by prayer, praise and conference in log cabins, barns, and in a school house on Buel's Hill. When no preacher could be had a "reading meeting" was held. In the year 1808, Pittstown was divided into Livonia on the west, and Honeoye on the east. As the Ontario Association was dissolved May 25, 1813, the church at Livonia took the name of First Presbyterian, which it has since retained. On the 7th of July, 1813, it was received into Geneva Presbytery, but in 1817 it was transferred to Ontario Presbytery. Its first elders, elected that year (1813), were Asa Woodford, Zara Blake, Selah Stedman and Oliver Woodruff. Its first deacon was John Warner, elected 1810, and its second, Oliver

Woodruff, elected 1812. Its first house of worship was raised May 30, 1814. The cost was $3,000. The church then had but thirty members. The Rev. Mr. Collins supplied them about eight years. He was followed by the Rev. Ebenezer Everett for two years. A revival of great power occurred during his ministry. He was succeeded by Rev. Ezekiel Chapman, a scholar, who published a book of value, of "Critical Notes on Select Passages of the New Testament." His ministry of about eight years was fruitful in blessings.

In 1823, Joel Stone, Wm. Ticknor, David Doolittle and Alfred Beecher, were ordained elders. In 1826, Elisha Clark was elected elder. April 30, 1828, Rev. Jeremiah Stow was installed pastor. His pastorate was only four years. He died at the age of thirty-four, greatly honored and lamented. Seventy were added to the church during his ministry. In 1829, Jonathan Kingsbury was elected elder, and Alfred Beecher, deacon. In 1830 the church petitioned Presbytery for leave to adopt the Congregational form of government, remaining with Presbytery on the "Accommodation Plan." This request was granted on Dec. 19, 1832. One month after its pastor's death the church edifice was burned. In a year and a half after, the present building was raised, being the first in the town raised without liquor. It was dedicated free from debt. The next pastor was Rev. Justus S. Hough for seven years, during which, one hundred were added to the church, mostly by letter. Rufus E. Hill, in 1833, was elected deacon, and in 1846, Adna S. Gibbs. In March, 1843, Rev. Benjamin G. Riley was installed pastor, and remained about twelve years. Seventy were added to the church. In 1859 Horatio Reed was elected deacon.

On the 9th of January, 1856, Rev. Anson H. Parmelee was installed pastor. There were revivals in 1858 and 1867. Mr. Parmelee was pastor for thirteen years, during which time 138 were added to the church, 107 on profession. In

1865 Benjamin Coy was elected deacon. For two years the pulpit was profitably supplied by Prof. U. P. Coddington of Genesee College. At this time the church building was repaired, costing about $5,000. Oct. 5, 1871, Rev. Wm. H. Millham was installed pastor, and remained till the close of the year, 1885, when he was called to Hillsdale, Michigan, where he was most successful till his death, April 28, 1888. The ministry of Mr. Millham of thirteen years was most useful. During it, the manse was built, which, with the land, cost about $6,000. There were revivals in 1872 and 1875, in which, over 100 united with the church. Since the church was organized about seven hundred and fifty persons have been added to its communion by letter and profession. Twelve of its members have entered the gospel ministry. This church has always been self-supporting. It had a Sabbath school as far back as the year 1818, which was known as the "Catechetical Society of Livonia." It was instituted by Joel Parker, then a member of this church and teacher of the district school, afterwards the Rev. Joel Parker, D. D., of New York, New Orleans and Philadelphia.

The Rev. Edward B. Walsworth, the present pastor, was called July 11, 1886.

MENDON.

Among the early settlers of Mendon were Jonas Allen, from Stockbridge, Mass., in 1797; Timothy Barnard, Ezra Sheldon and Thomas Ewer. Doctor Nathan Wadsworth, a Presbyterian from Vermont, arrived in August 1807. As early as January 1, 1809, he and Mr. Cornelius Treat, a Baptist, and others, including four families, met at the house of Mr. Treat, and held religious worship, by singing, praying, and a sermon read by Dr. Wadsworth. From this time meetings were held each Sabbath for some months. Soon after these meetings had been started, the eloquent speaker and gifted Dr. Wadsworth died, and on December 21, 1809, the Baptists formed the first religious society. January 5, 1815, at the residence of Ezra Sheldon, Jr., a Congregational Society was organized, with the following named trustees: Marvin Smith, M. Barrett, Jonas Allen, Timothy Barnard, Ezra Sheldon, and Thomas Ewer.

Rev. John Taylor appears to have ministered to this church as early as 1816. January 3, 1820, a schism occurred on a difference of opinion as to the location of the new church building to be erected. Mr. Taylor and a part of his flock organized the "Central Congregational Society," and worshipped in a church near the school house on Taylor street, the others of the old society continued in the school house. July 4, 1822, those worshipping in the school house were organized into a Presbyterian church by Rev. Aaron C. Collins, of East Bloomfield, and Rev. Reuben Parmele, of Victor. "The following named members of the original Congregational church, were constituted a Presbyterian church: Elder Ezra Sheldon, and Eunice, his wife, Elder Thomas Ewer, Harmanus Courter and Jane, his wife, Mrs. M. Wilson, Mrs. C. De Garno, Mrs. Phoebe and Miss Harriet Barnard, Mrs. Libbie Spear, Mrs. Charlotte Beers, Elder Asa Robbins, and Mrs. James Doyen.

Messrs. Sheldon, Ewer and Robbins were ordained elders. The two first were the original organizers of the former Congregational church, and this new organization was a perpetuation of the same as a Presbyterian church. This church was received into the Rochester Presbytery July 2, 1823.

Rev. Mr. Pierson ministered to this branch of the original Congregational church, from March 5, 1821. Rev. Elijah Wollager succeeded him on the 21st of the following November. September 13, 1824, a movement was made to build a church. The corner stone was laid July 13, 1825, by the Masonic fraternity, in presence of a large concourse of people. The church numbered but a score of members, and opened a Sabbath school in April, with 20 scholars, and by June had increased the number to 110. At the time there was a Ladies' Missionary Society of over 50 members. The first meeting in the new church was on June 26, 1826, and the dedicatory sermon was by Rev. A. D. Eddy, of Canandaigua. In 1839, the church was moved from the hill to where it now stands in the valley. In 1828, under the ministry of Mr. Jones, was the first large addition under a revival. He had been sent by the Presbytery upon the humble and urgent petition of the church, and during the one year of his ministry over 40 united with the church, and they proved to be a great support to the church for years, and among whom was Timothy Barnard, one of the earlier and most prominent settlers of the town. He was elected an elder and held the office for 52 years. During the six years' pastorate of Rev J. M. Sherwood, there were additions to the church, benevolent gifts were increased, the parsonage built, and the Sabbath-school prosperous. The church, declined in numbers from 123 in 1848, to 47 in 1859, notwithstanding 45 new names had been added to the roll. In 1857 Frederick Probst was elected and ordained an elder, which office he has held faithfully and still continues to hold. During the ministry of Rev. Dwight Scovel, 1867, there was much improvement in spiritual things, and in church property. A chapel was built, meetings were held in out-lying stations, extra Sunday schools were maintained ; and again it became apparent that when the church was doing most for Christ's cause beyond its borders, it was doing most for itself. This church has had the experience of the ups and downs of a country village church. It is largely dependent upon one man for its financial support. During Mr. Hubbard's ministry, improvements were made in the church and new sheds built.

The following is the roll of ministers who have served this church: Rev. George G. Sill, June, 1825, to February, 1828; Rev. William Jones, March, 1828; Rev. Elisha D. Andrews, January, 1830; Rev. Ezra Scovil, December, 1831; Rev. John Thalheimer, June, 1833, to August, 1835; Rev. Elijah D. Wells, October, 1836, to October, 1837; Rev.   Snyder, June, 1838; Rev. J. M. Sherwood, August, 1840; Rev. Rankin, July, 1845; Rev. Robert W. Hill, October, 1848; Rev. L. W. Billington, May, 1853; Rev.   Overhizer, August, 1857; Rev. Nathaniel Hurd, August, 1860; Rev. E. B. Van Auken, May, 1865; Rev. Dwight Scovel, June, 1867; Rev. Alexander Douglass, 1868; Rev. H. H. Morgan, 1872; following him Rev. W. G. Hubbard, 4 years; Rev. John N. Kilbourn, began in the fall of 1881, and continued until the spring of 1887. He left the church with a larger roll of members and a larger Sunday-school, and had made certain church improvements, outwardly as well as spiritually. Rev. Theodore B. Williams, the present incumbent, began his ministry in July, 1887. By the will of the late Mrs.   Zyler, the church receives $1,000. A timely gift, wisely and generously given. No history of this church would be complete, without mention of the service and kindly interest of Mr. Marvin Gates, who for many years held the office of trustee.

Present Session, Elders: Frederic K. Probst, Henry Scribner, Curtis M. Gates.

Present Board of Trustees: John Eckler, Sheldon Strong, Theodore D. Rupert.

Compiled from Mr. Theo. B. Williams' sketch, Hotchkin's History of Western New York: McIntosh's History of Monroe County.

MOSCOW.

The first ministerial labors in this village, were those of Stephen M. Wheelock, a licentiate, about the year 1814; who at that time was supplying the church at Mount Morris. He was followed in the year 1816, by Rev. Elihu Mason, of Barkhampstead, Mass., who also preached at Perry and the district then known as the Holland Purchase. By his efforts, the Presbyterian church was organized in June, 1817, by Rev. Abraham Foreman, and was connected with the Presbytery of Ontario.

The original members were as follows: Asahel Munger, Asahel Munger, Jr., Hinman A. Boland, Asa R. Palmer, Ahijah C. Warren, Eunice Munger, Lydia Munger, Amanda Munger and Bathsheba Warren. The first elders were Asahel Munger, Ahijah C Warren and Asa R. Palmer.

The Moscow Presbyterian Church Society was organized in July, 1818, and the following six trustees were elected: Asahel Munger, Ahijah C. Warren, Asa R. Palmer, Samuel Miles Hopkins, Nicholas Ayrault and Hezekiah Ripley; the latter was the publisher of the Moscow *Advertiser*, the first newspaper published in the county of Livingston.

During the ministry of Mr. Mason, which continued to April, 1819, nine besides the original members were added to the church. The first of these was Mrs. Polly Dutton, daughter of Capt. Joseph Smith, who was captured by the Senecas, while serving in the Revolutionary War; she was the first white female child born west of Utica. Another of these early members, was Samuel M. Hopkins, who founded the village, was an elder of the church, and was also a member of the 13th Congress. Another, who was also an elder of the church, was Col. Jerediah Horsford, who taught a mission school among the Seneca Indians at Squakie Hill, and was employed by the Presbytery of Geneva, to erect a school house for them.

Following Mr. Mason in the supply of the pulpit were Rev. Samuel T. Mills, 1820 to 1826; Rev. Amos P. Brown, 1826 to 1829 and Rev. John Walker, 1829 to 1833. During Mr. Walker's ministry the church edifice was built, and seventy were added to the members.

Among the pioneers who at this time were interested in the church, were Eleazar D. Parker, Noah Cooley, Dr. Daniel P. Bissel, Henry A. Wilmerding, Felix Tracy, George W. Patterson, William Lyman, Harvey Wheelock, W. T. Cuyler, Job Holbrook, Nathaniel Wilder, Jesse Waddams, Martyn Starr and C. Ames.

After Mr. Walker, the pulpit was supplied for a short time by Rev. Mr. Schaffer, who was followed by Rev. Samuel Porter from November, 1833, to 1835. Immediately following him, was Rev. John H. Redington, during whose ministry, in August, 1837, the church was divided into two separate churches, new and old school. The new school being in the majority, and numbering 59, retained the church edifice, and the original church organization, and secured Rev. M. Gillet as their minister from 1838 to 1841, and Rev. Ebenezer H. Stratton from 1841 to 1845; while the old school, numbering 39, organized a separate church, retaining Mr. Redington as their minister, and built a small edifice at the east end of the public square, and united with the Susquehanna Presbytery. Mr. Redington was their pastor until his death in September, 1841, who was followed by Rev. John W. McDonald, who was installed in 1843. During his ministry in the O. S. Church, and that of Rev. E. H. Stratton of the N. S. Church, by the efforts of the latter, and his willingness to retire from the field, a reunion of the two churches was effected, February 5th, 1845, under the Presbytery of Wyoming, O. S., and the united church worshipped again in the old sanctuary, retaining Rev. J. W. McDonald as their pastor until 1848.

After Mr. McDonald, the pulpit was supplied by Rev. L. Leonard from 1849 to 1856; Rev. Walter V. Couch for three months; Rev. James M. Harlow, 1857 to 1864; Rev. F. DeW. Ward, D. D., for two months; Rev. George R. Howell, 1864 to 1865; Rev. Washington D. McKinley as pastor, 1866 to 1873; Rev. Jerome Allen, 1873 to 1874 and Rev. Fisher Gutelius as pastor, 1874 to the present time.

The present elders, who are chosen for terms of four years each, are Daniel T. Barnum, Newton H. Crosby, F. Stuart Gray and William Holbrook.

Those who in their youth were members either of the congregation or church, and have entered the ministry, are Rev. John B. Dales, D. D., Rev. Elam H. Walker, Rev. Herman N. Barnum, D. D., son of elder D. T. Barnum, and for thirty years a missionary at Harpoot, Turkey, Rev. William Wilder and Rev. Charles Ferry.

Two ladies who were born here, went as missionaries to foreign nations: Mrs. Emily (Redington) Montgomery, who went to Central Turkey, and is now at Adana, and Miss Sarah Dales, who was sent out by the U. P. Church, and was subsequently married to Dr. Lansing, and is now laboring in Cairo, Egypt.

The whole number of members has been 401. The present number is 91. The largest number was before the separation, which was the time also of greatest prosperity to the village. During the division, fewer were added to the churches than at any period of like length in its history; and at the reunion of the churches, the number of members was considerably less than at the separation.

Religious services were first held in the Brick School house for about three years, and subsequently for about thirteen years, in the Female Academy; which was then a flourishing institution. The present church edifice, 65 by 45, was built in 1832, at a cost of $3,300, and in 1868 was modernized and refurnished at an expense of $3,000.

In 1876, a new pipe organ costing $2,500 was placed in the church.

The Sabbath school, organized about 1833, and continued ever since, was never more prosperous than under the present superintendency of Austin W. Wheelock.

The church in the summers has sustained mission schools and preaching in outlying districts.

MOUNT MORRIS FIRST.

Mount Morris was settled in 1794 by Gen. Wm. A. Mills.

The First Presbyterian Church was organized April 29, 1814, by the following individuals: Jesse Stanley, Jonathan Beach, Luther Parker, Enos Baldwin, Abraham Camp, Luman Stanley, Russel Sheldon, Almira Hopkins, Lucy Beach, Martha Parker, Sarah Baldwin, Mary Camp, Patty M. Stanley and Clarissa Sheldon.

Ministers: Mr. Stephen M. Wheelock, a licentiate, was the first minister, and continued about three years after the organization. His successors have been as follows:

Rev. Silas Pratt, from 1817 to 1818.
Rev. Elihu Mason, 1818 to 1820.
Rev. Bartholomew F. Pratt, 1821 to 1825.
Rev. Wm. Lyman, D. D., 1825 to 1827.
Rev. Abel B. Clary, 1827 to 1828.
Rev. James McMaster, 1828 to 1830.
Rev. Calvin Bushnell, 1830 to 1831.
Rev. James Wilcox, 1831 to 1832.
Rev. George W. Elliott, 1832 to 1834.
Rev. Clark H. Goodrich, 1834 to 1838.
Rev. John Van Buren, 1838 to 1839.
Rev. Cyrus Hudson, 1839 to 1846.

Rev. C. H. A. Bulkley, D. D., 1847 to 1851.
Rev. Darwin Chichester, 1851 to 1855.
Rev. Levi Parsons, D. D., 1856 to the present time.

Ruling Elders: The first ruling elders were Jesse Stanley, Abraham Camp and Jonathan Beach. Those subsequently elected were in 1818, James Coe and Luther Parker; 1820, Asa Woodford and Oliver Stanley; 1829, John Pratt and James Conkey; 1831, George Kemp, Jr., and George Hastings; 1834, Harry H. Evarts and James H. Rodgers; 1836, Reuben Weeks, Reuben Sleeper and Charles W. King; 1842, Marsena Allen; 1844, Henry Sheldon, Charles Holmes and Levi Goddard; 1853, Samuel J. Mills, Loren J. Ames, Milo H. Maltbie and Stilwell Burroughs; 1857, Loren Coy and Pomeroy Sheldon; 1862, Jonathan E. Robinson, Samuel L. Rockfellow and Justine Smith; 1871, Elijah N. Bacon, Frederick E. Hastings, Ziba A. Colburn and Jay E. Lee; 1875, Reuben S. Weeks and Wilder Silver; 1883, Miles B. McNair; 1886, Henry M. Swan and Joshua C. Weeks; 1887, Robert Crawford.

The term-eldership was adopted in 1875.

Deacons: The first deacons were Jesse Stanley and Jonathan Beach. Those subsequently elected have been as follows: 1831, Asa Woodford, William Marvin and Abraham C. Camp; 1834, James Conkey and Marsena Allen; 1861, Robert E. Weeks; 1862, Esek M. Winegar; 1871, James Beggs and Milo H. Maltbie; 1879, Wilder Silver; 1886, Willard A. Weeks; 1887, Jacob Tallman and Amos Austin.

Members: The whole number of members by catalogue is 1,359, being an average annual addition of 18$\frac{1}{3}$. The present number reported is 262. Baptisms, 189 adults, and 450 infants; total, 639.

Choir: The first choir consisted of Dea. Jesse Stanley, leader, Luman Stanley and wife, Mrs. Mark Hopkins, Mrs. Parmerlee, Abraham C. Camp, Moses Camp and Harlow Beach.

The succession of leaders is as follows: Harlow Beach, Moses Camp, Wm. H. Stanley, Cicero Camp, John Pratt, Harry Evarts, George Hastings, Henry Sheldon, Loren Coy and Thomas Hudson. Mr. Coy was a very faithful leader for more than thirty years. The organ was purchased in 1864. Mrs. Merab A. Scott was organist from 1864 to 1867. Mrs. Ruth M. Hastings, from 1867 to 1883, and Miss Helen Coy, from 1883 to the present time.

Sabbath School: As early as 1814 or 1815, Mrs. Oliver Stanley, and Emily, daughter of Luman Stanley, gathered numbers of poor children and instructed them upon the Sabbath. As the result of these efforts a permanent organization was effected in 1817. Allen Ayrault was superintendent in 1818. Among the early teachers were Abraham C. and Moses Camp, Harlow Beach, Mr. and Mrs. Alvah Beach, Sylvia Coe. Lucina Baldwin, Deacon Conkey and Asa Mahan. Some Indian girls were among the pupils. Newton Robinson was superintendent about 1826, and was succeeded by Abner Dean and John Pratt. The office, with slight exceptions, was filled from 1831 to 1866 by Harry Evarts and Hon. George Hastings, the former from 1831 to 1841, and the latter from 1841 to 1866, the time of his death. He has been succeeded by Dea. Milo H. Maltbie, Wm. P. Heston, A. M. Bingham, Esq., Dr. L. J. Ames, James Vanderbilt, Wm. H. Pease, F. E. Hastings, Joshua C. Weeks and Miles B. McNair.

Missionary Societies: The Youth's Missionary Association was organized in 1856, and continued for about seven years.

"The Ladies' Church Missionary Society," was organized January 10, 1872. Mrs. Harriet M. Parsons, president; the "Young Ladies' Missionary Society," April 16, 1882, Anna M. Maltbie, president; and the "Cyprus Mission Band," June 9, 1882, Carrie Lowery, president, all of which are well sustained up to the present time, having made annual contributions for missionary purposes.

Society of Christian Endeavor: A Young People's Society of Christian Endeavor was organized in January, 1888, which has increased to about 90 members and is doing very effective work for the Master.

Missionaries: In 1855, the Presbytery of Ontario ordained at this place two members of this church, the Rev. Orson P. Allen, as a foreign missionary, who immediately sailed to Kharpoot, Turkey, and the Rev. Herman N. Barnum, D. D., as a home missionary. Mr. Barnum followed Mr. Allen to Kharpoot in about two years, where the two have been associated as missionaries up to the present time.

Another member, Frank Gaylord Weeks, son of Dea. Robert E. Weeks, was ordained as a home missionary, Nov. 3, 1885, and since that time has labored in Minnesota.

Revivals: The larger additions have been in the following years: 1816, forty-two; 1822, eighty-four; 1831–5, one hundred and fifty-seven; 1839, forty-five; 1843, fifty-three; 1848, forty-seven; 1853, twenty-nine; 1856, sixty-seven; 1858, thirty-one; 1864, forty-one; 1870, forty-one; 1878, fifty-two; and 1882, thirty-two.

Religious Society: The First Presbyterian Society was incorporated about the year 1816. The first trustees were Wm. A. Mills, Elisha Parmerlee, Phineas Lake, Jerediah Horsford and Luman Stanley.

Church Buildings: The church was organized in a school house located upon the west side of what was then an open square, and about thirty rods to the south-east of where the present church stands.

The first church edifice was 64 by 44, located on the north side of the square and dedicated in January, 1832, Rev. S. H. Gridley, then of Perry, preaching the sermon. In 1841, this building was moved about twenty rods south and enlarged, a separate lecture room, 40 by 24, being erected at the same time a short distance to the east. Both these buildings were destroyed by fire, September 29, 1852.

The present building, 80 by 52, was erected about forty rods west of the former one, and dedicated, February 1st, 1855. Rev. Darwin Chichester preaching the sermon. The present lecture room, 24 by 40, was built in 1860.

Presbyterial Relation: This church was received by the Presbytery of Geneva, February 12, 1817, and after the organization of the Presbytery of Ontario in March, 1818, was transferred to that body, which it followed when the same became a part of the present Presbytery of Rochester in 1870.

A history of this church written by Rev. Darwin Chichester was published in 1855, and another written by the present pastor was published in 1876.

MOUNT MORRIS SECOND.

The Second Presbyterian Church of Mount Morris, was organized by a committee of the Presbytery of Ontario, in 1830, and received under its care in January, 1831. Among its original members were Moses Marvin and Ann, his wife, Harriet Speas, Fanny Roland and Anna Sharp.

Sylvester Richmond and Lucy, his wife, and Milo H. Maltbie and Jerusha, his wife, united soon after the organization.

Rev. Elam Walker was the first minister, whose labors were greatly blessed. He was followed by Rev. Messrs. Hall, Ward and Lindley.

The ruling elders were Moses Marvin, Sylvester Roland and Clark Mather.

The deacons were Moses Marvin and Sylvester Roland.

The church maintained a prayer meeting, also a Sabbath school, of which Sylvester Roland and J. McCreery were superintendents.

The largest number of members at any one time was about fifty.

This society never erected a church edifice, but united with a school district in the erection of a house, which was used both for church and school purposes, and which was situated five miles south of Mount Morris village, on the west side of the State road.

Owing to the organization of a Dutch Reformed church in that neighborhood, this church was disbanded about the year 1839.

NUNDA.

The First Presbyterian Church of Nunda, is situated in the village of Nunda, town of Nunda, county of Livingston, state of New York.

It was organized October 6th, 1831, in a school house near Deacon Wisner's, two miles north-east of the present site. Services were held here and in the Page school house about half a mile east of the village for two years. The following ministers and elders were present at the organization:

Ministers: Robert Hubbard, Abel Caldwell, Ludovicus Robbins.

Elders: Joseph Waldo, Silas Olmstead.

The number uniting in this organization was fourteen; ten by letter and four by profession.

By letter: John Chapin, Clarrissa Chapin, Jas. Patterson, Sarah Patterson, Zaddock Herrick, Betsey Herrick, Eliza Gay, Mille Pierce, Celestia J. Hills and Abraham Van Sickle.

By profession: Sillah Lee, Lucinda Booth, William R Duryee and Larry Duryee.

Until May 21, 1835, *i. e.* for four years, they conformed mostly to Congregational usages, transacting their business by church meetings. It does not appear that they elected any officers until August 25, 1833, when David Shager and John Chapin were elected deacons, the latter declining.

At a meeting on May 25, 1835, the organization was perfected by the election of six elders and four deacons.

Elders for one year: Samuel Swain and Russell Barnes.
For two years: Elihu Dickinson, Ephraim Smith.
For three years: John Chapin, Abraham Burgess.
Deacons: G. Wing, David Thayer, Erastus Buck, Josiah Phelps.

The church was under the care of the Presbytery of Angelica until October 8, 1844, when by an act of Synod it was transferred to the Presbytery of Ontario.

It had been the custom of the church to meet its expenses by taxing the property of the church and society. Those not agreeing to this plan gave by subscription. It was a difficulty growing out of this plan of taxation and refusal to pay resulting in a case of discipline, which went to Presbytery and Synod, that finally led to the transfer of the church to the Ontario Presbytery, though an underlying cause was O. S. and N. S. differences.

Church buildings: In 1833, the first church building was erected on the corner of East and Church streets at a cost of about $2,200. Those most prominent in the enterprise were S. Swain, N. Chandler, G. Wing. Up to this time, the church had had only one-half of the minister's time; now he gave them his full time. In 1846, they sold their old church building to the M. E. society, and began the erection of the present building. To Mr. Alfred Bell, now of Rochester, is accredited an especial influence in orginating and aiding the work of constructing this second and commodious house of worship.

The cost of construction was about $6,000, and is of wood, 50 by 80, with a seating capacity of 650. It was dedicated June, 1847, by Rev. Edwards Marsh, a former pastor.

Session house: The first session house was built in 1838, on the present site of the parsonage, at a cost of $800. The upper story of this was for years used for school purposes. It was sold in 1872 for $600, and the site used for a parsonage.

The present chapel was built in 1886, in the rear of the church, and combines kitchen, etc., being used for social gatherings as well as for prayer and church meetings. Mr. Alfred Bell again stepped forward with a generous gift. Cost of erection, $1,000.

Parsonage: This was built by contract by F. D. Lake, at a cost of $3,000.

Before proceeding to give the succession of pastors and elders it is proper to state that the churches of Nunda and Oakland, the latter being O. S., were united by action of the Presbytery of Rochester, at Dansville, the 13th of September, 1871, by request of both churches, so that "The members of the church of Oakland were added to the church of Nunda."

PASTORS.

Ludovicus Robbins, October, 1831-32.

Wm. P. Kendrick, October 25, 1832-33.

Asa Johnson, S. S., three months. Installed February 26, 1834-37.

Wales Tileston, P., November, 1837, May 13, 1840.

Edwards Marsh, S. S., 1840-46. Installed March, 1846-47.

Wm. Lusk, P., June 7, 1847, to February 26, 1852.

Pliny F. Sanborne, S. S., December 11, 1852, to May 1857.

Levi G. Marsh, S. S., June, 1857, to September, 1860.

Ira O. De Long, S. S., 1860-63.

Levi G. Marsh, P., February 9, 1864, to December, 1871.

T. Dwight Hunt, P., February, 1872, to September, 1875.

Bentley S. Foster, P., March 1, 1876, to June 1, 1879.
Newton H. Bell, March 1, 1880, to September 14, 1884.
John V. C. Nellis, Ph. D., P., October 30, 1884, to July 1. 1888.
John M. Carmichael, P. E., November 17, 1889.

Elders: Samuel Swain, Russell Barnes, one year; Elihu Dickinson, Ephraim Smith, two years; John Chapin, Abraham Burgess, three years; May 21, 1835. Erastus Buck, 1838; Wm. R. Duryee, May 21, 1839; Charles W. King, June 23, 1840; Jos. Waldo, December 31, 1841; Chas. V. Craven, Stephen Baldwin, Earl J. Payne, January 10, 1846; Alfred Bell, John Gilmore, George H. Bailey, March 5, 1864; J. Brinkerhoff, Chas. T. Metcalf, December 31, 1870; Adam Potts, Geo. Arnold, James M. McNair, July 6, 1872; John T. Van Ness, May 6, 1876; Arnold G. Galley, Augustus C. Dodge, Clement J. McNair, June 18, 1881.

Deacons: David Shager, August 25, 1833; Wm. R. Duryee, July 2, 1836; Zaddock Herrick, September 4, 1837; Chauncy Ladd, May 21, 1839; John Briggs, December 31, 1841; Chas. V. Craven, Erastus Buck, January 10, 1846; Geo. H. Bailey, A. B. Lockwood, March 6, 1864; C. T. Metcalf, April 8, 1871.

Revivals: Of revivals there have been three of very marked power. The first under Rev. Asa Johnson, conducted by the evangelist, Littlejohn. This was in 1837. The second under Rev. Wales Tileston in 1840, when 97 were received into the church on profession of faith. The third under Rev. Edward Marsh in 1843, when 56 were received. The fourth under Rev. L. G. Marsh in 1858, when 30 were received. The fifth under Elder Knapp in 1872, when 25 were received. There have been other seasons of quickening, but none of especial note. The whole number uniting with the church since its organization has been about 934. Sixteen for each year of the church's existence.

OAKLAND.

The Presbyterian Church of Oakland was organized Sunday, Dec. 5, 1819, by Rev. Elihu Mason, of Mount Morris, with the following members: Arad French and Lucinda French, Richard W. Robinson and Charlotte Robinson, Mrs. Laura Strong, Wm. Totten, Enoch Miller, Mrs. Rosanna Marks, Mrs. Hannah Moses, Samuel Swain, and Mrs. Elisabeth Tuthill.

Elders: Arad French, R. W. Robinson, Samuel Swain.
Deacon: Arad French.

Mr. French was chosen clerk also, and served in this office for over twenty years, and it is added, kept a model record. Jan. 18, 1820, the church became a member of the Presbytery of Ontario, as the church of Nunda. To this church Mr. Mason ministered for about two and a half years and then Rev. John Lindsley became pastor in the spring of 1822, and although he gave up his charge in 1828 he continued to live at Oakhill until his death, which occurred Dec. 4, 1838. He had the reputation of being "a deep thinker and a very exemplary man." He was a native of Connecticut, and though an old man he was a missionary in western New York, where his name is found in the history of most of the old churches. In 1828 Phineas Smith, a licentiate, supplied the pulpit, and though the church numbered more than 100 members they had no building, but continued to worship in school houses and barns at Oakhill and Hunt's Hollow.

Though these two churches had separate organizations until 1848, when the church at Hunt's Hollow was merged in that of the O. S. at Oakland, under the Presbytery of Wyoming, they were ministered to by the same pastors or preachers. They are mentioned together, they seem to have been organized at the same time and by the same man, Rev. Elihu Mason, and joined the Ontario Presbytery at the same meeting. The records of the church Hunt's Hollow, if they ever had any separate minutes, have been lost. In 1830 they built a church at Hunt's Hollow. The church then became a member of the Presbytery of Angelica.

In 1827 a church was organized in Portageville, and in 1831 in Nunda, and though these both drew from the church at Hunt's Hollow, yet it prospered and grew until 1835, when it reached its highest membership, 130.

In 1848 they sold their church and parsonage to the Baptists for $800 and uniting with the O. S. of Nunda, formed the church of Oakland and joined the Presbytery of Wyoming. In 1850 they built a church and session room in Oakland, which was dedicated Oct. 3, 1850.

Succession of pastors and stated supplies of these organizations up to the time of the organization of the O. S. church in 1848: Elihu Mason, 1819–22; John Lindsley, 1822–28; Abel Caldwell, 1829–37; Leonard Rogers, 1837–40; Abram C. DuBois, 1840–41; Abel Caldwell, 1841–42; Lewis Hamilton, 1843–44; John M. Bear, 1845–47.

Succession of pastors and stated supplies in the O. S. church in Oakland, up to the time of union with the First church in Nunda, 1871: Richard Kay, 1848–52; Isaac Oakes, 1852–57; Wm. Hall, 1857–58; H. B. Thayer, 1858–60; Pliny Twitchell, 1861–64; E. W. Kellogg, 1864–68; R. W. McCormick, 1868–69; L. G. Marsh, 1870–71.

The elders in the church of Oakland at the time of organization, 1848: G. Wing, David W. Thayer, Silas Olmstead, E. S. Olmstead, J. Preston, J. B. Hewitt.

Deacons, W. T. Totten, Tracy Ensworth.

During the fifty years of their existence there were about 450 names on their records.

OGDEN.

The early records of this church are scanty and defective, and all that can be gathered and offered from them is a bare outline of its history.

The First Presbyterian Church of Ogden was organized, by whom or in what manner is not recorded, in the year 1811, with ten members, namely, Samuel Davis, Daniel Arnold, James Ferrington, Josiah Mather, Jabes Busley, Phebe Finch, Lydia Mitchell, Betsey Nichols, and two names not given.

The first deacons were Samuel Davis and Josiah Mather; and the first ruling elders were Sylvanus Willey, Diodati Lord, Charles Church, Austin Spencer, H. D. Vroom and A. Norton.

Of those who served this church as its ministers during the first seven years of its existence we have no record; but from that date forward the following were the successive occupants of its pulpit, either as pastors or stated supplies:

Rev. Ebenezer Everett, pastor, from 1819–22.
Rev. Avelyn Sedgwick, pastor, from 1824–33.
Rev. John Carle, stated supply, during 1833 and 1834.
Rev. Conway P. Wing, pastor, from 1835–38.
Rev. Avelyn Sedgwick, pastor, from 1838–49.
Rev. Charles Jerome, stated supply, part of 1849.
Rev. Darwin Chichester, stated supply, in 1850.
Rev. Edward Perkin, stated supply, in 1850.
Rev. Mr. Ely, stated supply, in 1851.
Rev. William A. Fox, pastor, from 1851–65.
Rev. Alexander McA. Thorburn, pastor, from 1865–82.
Rev. A. S. Hoyt, pastor, from 1883–88.
Rev. Glenroie McQueen, is the present incumbent of the pulpit.

This church has been favored with many precious revivals, the most notable of which occurred in the following years, resulting in the number of converts set opposite thereto respectively:

Revival of 1827, converted 63; revival of 1831, converted 131; revival of 1834, converted 14; revival of 1836, converted 44; revival of 1838, converted 17; revival of 1840, converted 59; revival of 1843, converted 33; revival of 1853, converted 69; revival of 1858, converted 25; revival of 1866, converted 28; revival of 1869, converted 30; revival of 1874, converted 47; revival of 1878, converted 21.

Of the members of this church, four have become ministers of the gospel, namely, Nelson E. Spencer, Ephraim Strong, Francis W. Lord and John Q. Adams.

The Sabbath school of the Church of Ogden was organized in the year 1819; and those who have been received as members to communion with the church, during the last thirty-five years, have been largely from those who have been taught the Word of God therein.

A "Woman's Missionary Society," was organized in this church in September, 1872, which at first was connected with the Philadelphia Board, but in March, 1885, was transferred to that of New York.

A "Christian Endeavor Society" also was organized in December, 1886. This now numbers 50 active and some 25 associate members; these hold general meetings weekly, and consecration meetings monthly. This society has already been the means of great good among the young in the congregation; twelve of its associate members have united with the church during the past year.

The first house of worship owned by this congregation was built in 1823; its dimensions being 40 feet by 50 feet. This served them until the year 1849, when it was enlarged and improved at an expense of $2,723. This house was again thoroughly repaired in 1868, and a Sabbath school and lecture room added to it, costing altogether $3,343. In 1887, the church and lecture room were once more thoroughly repaired and refurnished at an expenditure of $1,206.

The present ruling elders are: James N. Arnold, W. W. Nichols, George Comstock, Horace Rann, William Lowery.

The present Board of Trustees are: Lewis Corser, Henry Vannest, John Kincaid, Henry S. Dyer, Horace Rann, and Charles Smith.

OSSIAN.

The Presbyterian Church of Ossian was organized by Rev. Robert Hubbard in 1818, with the following members: James Haynes, Mary Haynes, Thomas Lemon, Jane Lemon, Minerva Faulkner, Mrs. Rhoda Clendenin, Timothy Osborne and wife, and Addison Sill, and probably a few others whose names cannot be positively given.

The first elders were James Haynes and Addison Sill.

The Rev. Robert Hubbard supplied the pulpit from the time the church was organized until 1830. Other ministers succeeded him as follows:

Rev. Ludovicus Robins for one year.
Rev. William P. Kendrick for two years.
Rev. David Cushing for two years.
Rev. Jacob H. Endress for two years.
Rev. Dwight Twitchell for three years.
Rev. John A. Littlejohn for one year.
Rev. —— Darling for two years.
Rev. Nathan Hammond for six years.
Rev. —— Richardson for one year.
Rev. —— Hard for one year.
Rev. Willis Clark Gaylord for one year.
Rev. —— Calkins for three months.
Rev. —— Boyd for three months.

Rev. James H. Board for six years.
Rev. James L. Box for three years.
Rev. George W. Craig for two years.
Rev. William C. Brass for two years.

The Sabbath school was organized soon after the organization of the church, and has been sustained the most of the time since.

The present superintendent is Isaac Hampton, who has been superintendent most of the time for the last twenty-five years.

There have been special revivals as follows: In 1840, about forty were received; 1855, ten; 1875, eight; and in 1878, twenty-two.

The church edifice was erected in 1835, its dimensions being 30 by 42, and costing $300. In 1878 it was enlarged by an addition of twelve feet to its length, and the building was renovated at an expense of $1,500, at which time it was re-dedicated, the Rev. Levi Parsons, of Mount Morris, N. Y., preaching the sermon.

The present elders are Jacob Clendenin, David McCurdy, and Matthias Rolison.

The first trustees were Jacob Clendenin, Timothy Osborne and Thomas Lemon.

The present trustees are Freeman Court, Mansfield More, Edward Burrill, John Scott and Lemuel Price.

Present number of members, 42.

This church was received under the care of the Presbytery of Ontario, June 10, 1868.

Mr. Hotchkin, referring to this church, says: "For many years the church was small and feeble, and enjoyed very little ministerial aid, except an occasional service from Rev. Robert Hubbard, who had the charge of two extended congregations. The church is uniformly with one exception reported vacant until 1837. On the 13th of September, of that year, Rev. Ashbel Otis was ordained and installed pastor of the church. On account of the failure of his health he was dismissed February 26, 1839. The church has since been reported as having a stated supply, but the name is not given. In 1832, twenty-five members were reported as having the preceding year united with the church by profession. These were the fruits of a revival enjoyed by the church. The years 1837 and 1840 were also years of revival.

"In looking at the reports of the American Home Missionary Society, the author finds the names of Rev. Messrs. Ludovicus Robbins, William P. Kendrick, Robert Hubbard, Ashbel Otis and A. C. Dubois, as missionaries appointed to labor on this field at different periods."

PARMA CENTER.

This church was organized March 4, 1829, by a commission of the Presbytery of Rochester, consisting of three ministers, Rev. Joseph Penny, D. D., Rev. Chauncey Cook and Rev. Abelyn Sedgwick, and two lay delegates, Mr. John Arnold, and Mr. John Granger.

The original members, all of whom presented letters from different churches, were the following: Daniel Clark, Daniel Clark, Jr., Emilia Clark, Orpha Clark, Clarissa Patterson, Harriet VanSise, Nicholas Kipp, Nancy Kipp, Jane Post, Isabel VanTuyl, Hannah Pulis, Phebe Gager, Lucius Peck, Abby Peck.

Of these, Daniel Clark, Nicholas Kipp and Lucius Peck were elected and ordained as ruling elders; while the first two were also named to discharge the special duties of deacons. The organization services were had in the Atcheson school-house.

The first house of worship owned by this church was erected in 1831, which for some time served both as a church and a town house. The ground on which this edifice stood was donated to the congregation by Mr. Roswell Atcheson.

At first the pulpit was occupied by such chance supplies as could be obtained. In 1832, Rev. Silas Pratt is named in the records as being their stated preacher, and the number of members is said to have been 73. During the year 1833, Rev. Samuel Griswold and the Rev. Richard De Forest each preached for a few months. Toward the close of this year, Rev. Chandler Bates was engaged to preach, whose ministery extended through a period of some three years. In 1837, the church secured the services of Rev. Beaufort Ladd, who remained with them about two years. In 1840, Rev. William P. Kendrick was called to occupy the pulpit, whose ministry was also limited to a term of two years.

The Rev. Chandler Bates, a former pastor, continued a resident in the town and gratuitously served the church at various intervals, to the end of his life. And Mrs. Bates, like her faithful consort, whom she survived, loved the church to the last, leaving it a handsome legacy when she followed him and went to her rest and reward.

In the spring of 1842, Rev. Shubael Carver became the minister of Parma Church. He was an Oberlin man, and held the doctrine of Christian perfection, and by his way of presenting this, created a division in the church, when he had been its preacher but a few weeks. At this time the members numbered 61, of whom 24 became his avowed adherents, and managed to get and keep possession of the building. Shortly after this rupture, these formed themselves into a Congregational church, which, however, survived only three years.

During the continuance of these troubles, those who

remained firm Presbyterians worshipped in different school houses until 1844, when a substantial house of worship was built, which still remains and is in fact the one now occupied by the congregation. This was erected by great sacrifice and self-denial. The site was donated by the Rev. Mr. Bates, and the building was put up almost entirely by the joint labors of the members. While the male members hewed the timbers, quarried the stone and drew the materials to the spot, the female members came together to knit and sew, to win what funds they could, and those outside the pale of the church, catching the general spirit of activity and co-operation which prevailed, came forward and helped on the work. Thus, by the fall, the house was completed without a dollar of debt. The erection of the church was accomplished during the ministry of Rev. Daniel Johnson, which extended over a period of four years. This worthy man was succeeded by the Rev. George Freeman, who served the church about six years.

In 1850, the church had on its roll 59 members; but ten years later we find that it had declined to 55.

In 1856, the pulpit was occupied by Rev. H. G. Miles; and from 1858 to 1861, by Rev. J. H. Phelps. Early in 1862, Rev. Edwin Allen became the minister, who continued his labors nearly five years, and under his preaching 36 members were added to the church. From 1867 to 1870, Rev. A. G. Wilcox was the preacher; in 1870 and 1871, Rev. Joshua D. Lane; in 1872, Mr. Lewis H. Morey and Mr. George Smith, both students; in 1873, Rev. E. W. Kellogg.

In 1874, a call was given to the Rev. George C. Jewel, who was ordained and installed, and continued the pastor for four years. He was succeeded by Rev. D. W. Marvin, who remained two years. Then followed a number of transient supplies. In 1880, Rev. G. L. Hamilton became the preacher, whose labors extended through a period of one year. Then the Rev. William G. Hubbard was called, who, Nov. 3, 1881, was installed, and held the office of pastor for a term of two years and a half. From the time of his departure, Rev. Theodore B. Williams, who was settled at Charlotte, engaged to preach to them on Sabbath afternoons, which he continued to do down to June, 1885. For the next succeeding eight months the pulpit was supplied by a student from the Rochester Theological Seminary.

In November of 1886, Rev. G. L. Hamilton, for the second time, became the preacher, and though residing in Rochester, continues to be the stated supply down to the present time.

The membership is now reduced to 27, but the congregation owns a parsonage and owes no debts.

PENFIELD.

The First Presbyterian Church of Penfield (originally Northfield, embracing the present towns of Perrinton, Pittsford, Henrietta, Brighton, Irondequoit, Penfield, Webster, and that part of the City of Rochester lying east of the Genesee River,) was organized by Rev. Reuben Parmele, pastor of the Victor church, on February 7, 1806, and was received into connection with the Ontario Association, June 10, 1806, and continued such connection until the dissolution of that body. It was organized a Congregational church, with fifteen members: Elisha Sheldon, Sarah Sheldon, Huldah White, Abraham Bronson, Mary Bronson, Thomas Brooks, Esther Brooks, William Spears, Love Spears, Daniel Wilson, Esther Wilson, Josiah Kellogg, Rachel Perrin and John Stroger. It is claimed that prior to the above date a Congregational church had been gathered which continued until merged in this new organization.

Josiah Kellogg and Thomas Brooks were elected the first deacons of this new organization.

In the beginning of the year 1814, the church adopted the Presbyterian form of government, and was received into the Presbytery of Geneva, April 19, 1814. From this Presbytery it was transferred to the Presbytery of Ontario, and subsequently to the Presbytery of Rochester, on the erection of those Presbyteries. February 13, 1850, the church joined the Buffalo Presbytery. It was set off to the Rochester Presbytery, Oct. 7, 1851, and received by that body June 2, 1857.

During the two years succeeding the organization, twenty-nine members were added to the church. Under Mr. Carpenter's ministry in 1818, a precious season of revival added twenty-one to its membership. In 1825 it reported fifty eight as the whole number of members. In 1831, thirty-nine were added, and the whole number, 107; in 1837, 100 members. During its existence of more than seventy years the church was blest with many revivals. At one communion season forty-one were received; at another, fifty-two. From its organization until 1816, there were no regular stated administrations of gospel ordinances; the preaching of the gospel and administration of sacraments, was only occasional, but the church maintained regular stated worship upon the Sabbath. Its Sunday school was at one time large and flourishing; in 1836 it numbered 150; and in 1838, 156.

In 1814, the first elders elected and ordained were Thomas Brooks, Josiah J. Kellogg, Levi Warren, Isaac Barnum and Gersham Dunham.

· The following named ministers have been in charge of the pulpit; Rev. Asa Carpenter, 1816–25; Rev. Garret Hallenback, 1825–27; Rev. Eber Child, 1828; Rev. Lemuel Brooks, Dec., 1828, and was ordained and installed March 18, 1829, and dismissed Oct. 19, 1830. After the dismission of Mr. Brooks, Rev. Elijah Buck, Rev. Simeon Peck, Rev. Conrad Ten Eyck, and Rev. Moses Ordway were severally employed as stated supplies for one year, or about that period." They were succeeded by Rev. Albert G. Hall, then a licentiate, in May, 1835, who was ordained and installed pastor of the church, Feb. 24, 1836. Dr. Hall was dismissed Feb. 5, 1840. During the pastorate of Dr. Hall the church enjoyed its season of greatest prosperity. Its membership ranged from 107 to 160, its congregation filling the church. "The church was aided by the American Home Missionary Society in the support of Mr. Hall."

Connected with its congregation and membership were such prominent men of their day as Daniel Penfield, Hon. Henry Fellows, Richard Ely, Isaac Raymond, Alexander Canada, Ralph Camp, John Weaver, Jacob B. Bryan, John Cole, Julius Warren, Leonard Adams, Edmond Parmenter, Thomas Myers, Ami Carpenter, Moses Wisner, Levi Duncan, Daniel Lewis, Jacob Hallenback, Henry Ward, Isaac Chichester, Horace Bush, Samuel Scovil and others. Dr. Hall was succeeded by Rev. Edward Ray, who, in 1842, was followed by Rev. George Delevan, and he, in 1843, by Rev. Ralph S. Crampton, and he, in 1845, by Rev. John H. Young, and also Rev. Thomas Bellamy, 1849-53; Rev. Allen McFarland, 1853-57; Rev. Alvan Ingersol, 1857-58; Rev. Royal Mann, 1858-60; Rev. Jeremiah Woodruff, 1860-66; Rev. Wm. W. Collins, 1866-67; Rev. C. H. Wheeler, 1867-75; Rev. Elisha B. Sherwood, temporarily; Rev. Levi G. Marsh, 1876.

In 1828, dismissions by letter to form churches in Brighton, Perrinton, Webster, Pittsford and Henrietta, reduced the membership to forty-six. It is remarkable that in so short a time this church should have given birth to so many new enterprises, which, in the main live, while the mother church has become extinct, a memory to be cherished.

The officers of the society in 1876 were:

Elders: William Fellows, Doctor Thomas A. Brown, Charles Leonard.

Trustees: William Fellows, James Harris, Horace P. Lewis, George R. Leonard, George W. Raymond.

The ground upon which the church stands was donated by Daniel Penfield, one of the first settlers in the town. The deed of the conveyance of this piece of ground is dated April 7, 1820. The building was erected in 1823, and dedicated in 1825. It was a brick edifice capable of seating from six to eight hundred persons. In 1864 it was repaired at considerable expense. July 26, 1831, the property was sold by virtue of a *Fi-Fa*, for $390 and costs. September 19, 1832, it was redeemed by Laura M. Ely, a judgment creditor, and Dec. 1, 1832, was sold by her to Leonard Adams, Elias D. Brooks, Levi Warren, and Ralph Camp, for $2,000, with the special provision in the deed of conveyance, that they covenant and agree that it shall not be disposed of for any other purpose, or converted to any other use than a Presbyterian meeting-house so long as there should be a Presbyterian society in Penfield holding stated meetings and supporting stated preaching. It is stated that the decline of the church is largely due to isolation from canal and railroad facilities. While the church lived it had been a means of good, and it died full of years and honor. In its declining years it received financial help from the Board of Home Missions. Finally, being unable to support public services, the house was closed and the chapel of the church was sold, Feb. 11, 1884, for sixty-five dollars and removed from the ground. The bell was donated to the North Church in Rochester, April 14, 1884, and the church with its lot was deeded to Charles N. Leonard, on 12 December, 1884, for five hundred dollars, to be used by a German Lutheran Church. The proceeds of the sales, with interest on them, was, by vote of Presbytery, paid on 15th April, 1886, one-third to each Board, the Home Missions, Foreign Missions, and Church Erection, $194.98.

The above sketch is compiled from an historical address by Hon. C. M. Hawley, delivered by request, July 2, 1876, and from the history by Rev. James Hotchkin, and from the records of the church, on file with the clerk of Presbytery.

PIFFARD.

Mr. and Mrs. David L. Haight, of New York, whose daughter, Mrs. David Piffard, had settled in the Genesee Valley, Livingston County, in 1824, became, in consequence of frequent visits to Western New York, greatly interested in the welfare of the people in the near neighborhood of her daughter's home. Feeling a deep religious sympathy with those about them, and bending with noble energy every power to the work, they succeeded in establishing a church of their own denomination—Protestant Dutch Reformed. On the 13th of July, 1843, it was duly constituted the Dutch Reformed Church of Piffard. On the second Saturday of September, 1843, the corner-stone was laid, with appropriate ceremonies by the Rev. Dr. Gustavus Abeel, of Geneva, N. Y. The basement was soon afterward completed and the Rev. J. Hammond, of Mt. Morris, was engaged to supply the pulpit, which he did every Sabbath until the spring of 1846. In May of 1846 the church edifice was completed. It was solemnly dedicated to the service of the Triune God, on Saturday, August 1, 1846. The Rev. Dr. Wycoff preached a most interesting and appropriate sermon from Isaiah, 60th chapter, 13th verse, "*And I will make the place of my feet glorious.*" The act of dedication was then performed by the Rev. J. C. Van Liew, the minister in charge. Services were then held in the church. Dr. Abeel preached the sermon, the text taken from 1st Timothy, 3rd chapter, last clause of the 15th verse: "*Which is the Church of the living God, the pillar and ground of the truth.*" Following the sermon the elders and deacons were ordained in their respective offices. At a meeting after the services the following wardens were elected: David Piffard, Edwin Breckridge and B. C. Nichols.

Elders: The first elders were Thomas Boyd and Chauncey Van Vliet.

Deacons: Jacob N. Clute and George Sinclair.

Present Elders: T. N. Shattuck and W. A. Sackett.

Trustees: Nina H. Piffard, T. N. Shattuck and W. A. Sackett.

The Rev. J. Hammond, of Mt. Morris, supplied the pulpit from October 1, 1843, until the spring of 1846. The Rev. J. C. Van Liew, from the middle of May, 1846, until October, 1847.

The Rev. James M. Compton, through application to the Classis of Cayuga, entered soon afterwards on his charge as missionary pastor, but later on, aid which had been promised being withdrawn, he resigned the 16th of November, 1850.

In June, 1853, the Rev. Charles Ray, Presbyterian pastor, took the charge, and under his influence and that of others, it became a "Society" connected with the Presbytery of Wyoming, and took the name "The First Presbyterian Congregation of Piffard." He continued in charge for several years.

Subsequent to the removal of the Rev. Charles Ray, who resigned to take the principalship of the Geneseo Academy, the Rev. F. De W. Ward, D. D., succeeded, and labored faithfully for twenty-five years. He resigned to go as chaplain in the 104th New York Volunteers during the late war (ad interim), resuming the pastorate on his return.

Following a period of quiescence which succeeded Dr. Ward's leaving, mission services were held nearly every Sabbath during the summer months for several years, the clergymen in the vicinity contributing most kindly their services, Mr. Slack taking the pulpit for the winter months during the interval years. Again a period of inaction succeeded. During the early spring and summer of 1884, a number of the members of Dr. Kittredge's congregation [Presbyterian Church] in Geneseo, held weekly meetings in

Piffard with such success that out of the new life instilled through their labors, the church started afresh with every sign of enduring success.

During that summer the following trustees were elected: Nina Haight Piffard, T. N. Shattuck and Robert M. Ferris. Subsequently, in the place of Mr. Ferris, resigned, Mrs. Charles F. Wadsworth was elected. Later Mrs. Wadsworth resigned and W. A. Sackett was elected to fill the vacancy. In the autumn of 1884, the Rev. Fisher Gutelius, of Moscow, N. Y., began to hold regular services, increasing and strengthening the newly grown interest, until a resident minister could be secured, which was done during the fall of 1885.

On the 1st of September, 1885, the Rev. John M. Wolcott, of New Haven, Conn., was called and accepted, and he remained until the 1st of July, 1887. During his pastorate was regularly organized, November 16, 1885, the "First Presbyterian Church of Piffard," with twenty members. On the 17th of July, 1887, the Rev. Fisher Gutelius was again called and accepted, taking the parish as before, in connection with his own church in Moscow.

A Sabbath school was formed long prior to the church congregation, Mrs. Piffard starting one in 1826 or 1827, and which has been regularly kept up ever since, her grandchildren teaching the grand-children of those whom she instructed.

The services, at present, are a Sunday school at noon, an evening service, and a weekly prayer meeting—two in fact, a children's, just before the regular meeting—of 45 minutes. A large and very active society, "The Ladies' Aid Society," of about twenty-five members, is doing some very good work; it has been in existence some two years. A small society, "The Little Christians," meet for prayer, singing and religious readings and recitations. These "little ones" purpose to follow closely in the wake of their elders, and I am confident they will do so.

Donations: In 1853 Mrs. David L. Haight [Ann Matilda] placed in the hands of Levi A. Ward, of Rochester, as a gift to the church, the sum of $1,500.00, the interest of which was to be used for various church expenses.

The church edifice and grounds belonged to the estate of David Piffard, now deceased, and was obliged to be sold. Certain of the heirs resigned all claim, each adding as much more to assist in the purchase. Some members of the Presbyterian Church in Geneseo, most nobly and generously bought and donated said church for the use of the village of Piffard, to be held by the trustees for such purpose, subject to certain conditions. This was in the autumn of 1884. In the summer of 1885, the Ladies' Missionary Society of the Presbyterian Church in Geneseo gave to the Piffard church a beautiful Meneely bell in loving memory of Miss Sarah E. Piffard, whose loss was the sorrow of a community, and whose life the crown of a Christian mother's shining example.

The "Ladies' Aid Society" is now building a town hall for the benefit of the village. It was deeded to the church, and held by the trustees. Miss A. M. Piffard donated the site.
N. H. P.

PITTSFORD.

Pittsford formerly constituted the centre of business for the original town of Northfield, which town was organized in 1794. In 1798, the name was changed to Boyle. In 1813, it was divided into three towns, named Perrinton, Penfield and Smallwood, the latter embracing the territory now constituting the towns of Pittsford, Henrietta, Brighton, Irondequoit, and that part of Rochester which lies East of the Genesee river. Afterwards Smallwood was divided into Pittsford and Brighton. In 1818, Henrietta was set off from Pittsford. The settlement of Pittsford began in 1790. The first school, taught by Mr. Barrows, was instituted in 1794, and held in a log house one mile south of the village, which served both as school house and place for worship. The first sermon preached in Pittsford, was by a traveling missionary, said to be from Virginia, who visited them on a week-day during harvest. The service was held in a barn. Occasional preaching was enjoyed thereafter. Rev. James H. Hotchkin preached six Sabbaths, between November 8, 1801, and February 1, 1802. The organization known as The First Presbyterian Church of Pittsford, N. Y., began with the "Congregational Society of Northfield," instituted 1807, at the house of Glover Perrin. Trustees were chosen, consisting of Orange Stone and Thomas Kempshall for one year; Abram Bronson and William Spear for two years; Glover Perrin and Samuel Stone for three years: Thomas Ramsdell was chairman of the meeting and Josiah J. Kellogg, clerk. In February, 1808, this society voted to settle Rev. John Stewart, "if enough money could be raised." In 1809, Rev. Solomon Allen was engaged at a salary of $250 annually.

May 11, 1809, "The Second Congregational Church of Northfield" was "constituted" by Rev. Solomon Allen, of the following members—"they having given satisfactory evidence of true piety and soundness in the faith," viz:— Andrew Miller, Joseph Farr, Michael Beach, Thomas Ramsdell, Samuel Stone, Glover Perrin, Joseph Shepard, Henry E. Dennis, Hannah Miller and Leah Packard. Thomas Ramsdell and Samuel Stone were chosen deacons of the church. The following June the church was received into connection with the "Ontario Association," and after the dissolution of that body, it was received under the care of the Presbytery of Geneva on the accommodating plan, April 20, 1814. From this Presbytery it was subsequently transferred to the Presbytery of Ontario, and from that to the Presbytery of Rochester upon its organization in 1819. In 1818, there were 37 members; in 1826, forty-two; in 1831, 159; and in 1846, 195. Rev. Solomon Allen was stated supply for two years. In 1811, Rev. Silas Hubbard labored with this church a short time. In its early years, the church was without regular preaching much of the time, and neighboring ministers and transient preachers supplied the pulpit; baptised and received members. The town was named Pittsford by Col. Hopkins, one of its prominent citizens, after the place of that name in Vermont, whence he came. This changed the name of this church to that by which it was known for over fifty years. Rev. A. C. Collins, of Bloomfield, supplied the pulpit a part of the years 1817–18; after him Rev. Ezekiel J. Chapman for a few months. Rev. Chauncey Cook was stated supply for two years. Rev. John Taylor served the church from 1820–24, and also preached at Mendon. Rev. Ralph Cushman followed for one year. His ministry was blessed with a revival, and 38 were added to the church. Rev. William F. Curry, a licentiate from the South, followed Mr. Cushman, and was ordained and installed July 14, 1825. In the same year, the society of this church was incorporated. Mr. Curry was dismissed, July 4, 1826. In 1827, Rev. Homer Adams came and preached for two years. He was succeeded by Rev. Asa Mahan, who was installed November 11, 1829, and was dismissed March 4, 1831. Rev. Alfred E. Campbell followed as stated supply, for one year. His successor Rev. Elijah Buck remained nine months. Rev. John B. Richardson began his labors June 2, 1833; was installed February 16, 1834, and left in 1850. During his ministry the church was especially blessed and built up. The years 1830, '31 and '32, seem to have been years of revival, during which time about 100 were added on confession. Rev. Job Pierson accepted a call to this church in 1850; was ordained and installed February 12, 1851. Resigned on account of health in 1856. Then came Rev. A. North for a season. Rev. Mr. Crittenden followed. In 1799, the inhabitants of Northfield built a large log-house, a little north of the present village of Pittsford, in which town business was transacted; and public worship held upon the Sabbath. In 1816, a frame building was erected one mile South of the village, and dedicated as a place of worship. In 1826, the Presbyterian congregation built a commodious house of worship on the site occupied by the present edifice. It was a well built stone structure, 60 ft. by 40, with a spire of great symmetry and beauty. The ground was donated by John Acer, Esq. This building was burned in 1861. The present building was erected in 1862, which with subsequent improvements cost $12,000, and was dedicated May 13, 1863. The bell was donated by Mrs. Chloe Wilcox. Rev. C. R. Wilkins was, at this time, acting pastor. Rev. Dr. James B. Shaw, of Rochester, preached the sermon. Rev. Messrs. North, Pierson and Richardson, former pastors, took part in the services. The parsonage of this church was donated chiefly by Mrs. Lydia Bushnell. July 15, 1869, the ecclesiastical order of this church was unanimously changed from Congregational to Presbyterian. For 60 years it had been a Congregational church connected with Presbytery. Rev. G. L. Hamilton was serving the church faithfully and well, in April, 1866. He was followed by Rev. Henry M. Morey for two years, under whom the church prospered. For short periods Rev. George G. Smith and others followed him. In September, 1874, Rev. Lewis H. Morey, a brother of Henry, was called to this field, was ordained and installed May 25, 1875, and left in 1880. His labors were blest. May 3, 1880, Rev. J. Edward Close was called. He served the church with great acceptance for eight years, without installation. During his ministry over 100 united with the church. The Sabbath school early became an institution in this church, and has proved a great blessing. It last reported to the General Assembly 176 members. This church sustains a Ladies' Missionary Society, The Mission Band for Children, The Temperance Loyal Legion, and The Band of Mercy. It was active in the Anti-Slavery Cause, and as early as 1836 took strong temperance ground. Its present membership numbers 194.

ROCHESTER FIRST.

This church was organized on the 22nd August, 1815, as "The First Presbyterian Church of Gates in Rochesterville," by a commission appointed by the Presbytery of Geneva, consisting of Rev. Daniel Fuller and Rev. Reuben Parmerlee and elders Isaac B. Barnum and Samuel Stone. It consisted of the following 16 members: Sibel Bickford, Warren Brown, Henry Donnelly, Hannah Donnelly, Elisha Ely, Hannah Ely, Oliver Gibbs, Jane Gibbs, Aaron Lay, Sarah Lay, Charles Magne, Polly Magne, Huldah Stoddard, Arbela Starks, Daniel West and Elizabeth West.

At the same time Warren Brown and Henry Donnelly were elected elders and Oliver Gibbs and Daniel West were elected deacons, and all were then ordained.

This congregation at that time was the only church in a tract of about 400 square miles.

This church being the oldest ecclesiastical body of any denomination in the place, it has naturally been a mother of Churches. Most or all of the other Presbyterian congregations that were formed during the first forty years of the existence of Rochester, were colonies from the old First.

It was natural, too, from its having been earlier and longest in the field, that the First Church should have contained from the beginning and should still contain a con-

FIRST PRESBYTERIAN CHURCH, ROCHESTER.

siderable element of the stable intelligent and prominent Presbyterians of the city.

The pastors of this church have been as follows: Rev. Comfort Williams, installed January 7, 1816, was dismissed June 6, 1821; Rev. Joseph Penny, D. D., was installed April 3, 1822, and dismissed April 26, 1833; Rev. Tryon Edwards, D. D., was ordained and installed July 22, 1834, and dismissed July 26, 1844; Rev. Malcolm N. McLaren, D. D., was installed Aug. 27, 1845, and dismissed Feb. 2, 1847; Rev. Joshua H. McIlvain, D. D., was installed July 13, 1848, and dismissed Oct. 1, 1860; Rev. Calvin Pease, D. D., was installed May 13, 1862, and died Sept. 17, 1863; Elias R. Beadle, D. D., of Philadelphia, Pa., was elected pastor that fall, which he accepted, and after supplying the church one year returned to his old charge; Rev. Casper M. Wines was installed May 22, 1866, and dismissed July 14, 1868; Rev. J. Lovejoy Robertson was installed Dec. 7, 1870, and dismissed June 11, 1877; Charles E. Robinson, D. D., was installed May 14, 1878, and dismissed Dec. 6, 1886; Nelson Millard, D. D., began his pastoral labors here Sept. 15, 1887, and was installed April 24, 1888.

The First church edifice was of wood and stood on Carroll, now called State street, where the American Express building now stands.

That portion of Rochester which now is the heart of the city, was then like much of the central section of the town, wet and marshy. Indeed, where now stand massive and splendid business blocks was then almost a swamp. The church was raised a few feet from the mucky ground and stood on posts or blocks. It was not uncommon for dogs, hens, and other creatures of the street to find shelter underneath the building and sometimes even on Sunday, to make themselves heard in a manner non-conducive to reverence. From such beginnings have grown both the city and the church, now so strong and so substantially built.

The second and better edifice of the First Church, which

was of stone, was erected in the year 1825, on Fitzhugh street, just north of the Erie canal, on the site now occupied by the City Hall. It was capable of holding about 850 persons. Its first chapel, built of brick, stood east of the church edifice, and was erected in 1831. It was removed in 1859 to furnish room for widening Irving place.

A second chapel was then built of stone in 1860, west of the church near the east line of Fitzhugh street. This was demolished with the old church to make room for the City Hall. In 1871 the present beautiful and commodious edifice which is also of stone, and stands at the corner of Plymouth avenue and Spring street was erected. It was dedicated June 23, 1872. Its cost, with that of the parsonage adjoining, was about $110,000. The lot on which the buildings stand is 112 by 132 feet or 15,783 square feet.

The first Sunday school that was established in Rochester was organized by the First Presbyterian church in the year 1816, that is the next year after the organization of the church itself. The school was held in a district school house, that stood on the site of the present Free Academy. The church also used the school house for conference or social meetings until their first chapel was built.

This church also organized the first infant school in Rochester in the winter of 1830-31. Mrs. Margaret Penny and Miss Harriet Hatch were particularly active in inaugurating it. They made special efforts to gather in the neglected little children from the highways and resorts of dissipation. The lady members of the church furnished a band of devoted helpers while the church sustained the enterprise with liberal contributions, so that the work was prosecuted with much vigor and success.

This missionary feature has prevailed in the Sunday school from the first and still continues in both the infant and the older departments. The superintendent is Thomas Chester, assisted by Charles P. Ford. Mrs. Marion L. Olds is at the head of the infant department.

In June, 1873, the First Church organized, at the corner of Plymouth and Frost avenues, a mission Sunday school. A suitable building was completed in 1874. The organization was very vigorously and successfully maintained and continued to grow with that part of the city, until, in 1887, an addition was made to the original structure, very much enlarging and improving it. On May 2, 1887, a church was organized called the Emmanuel Presbyterian Church and elders were chosen and ordained. The cost of the lot and building amounting to about $9,000, was provided for by the First Church.

The session of the First Church is constituted on the rotary plan. Its present elders are George C. Buell, Albert G. Bassett, Thomas Chester, Henry Goold, David M. Hough, Arthur Hamilton, Charles F. Pond, and George D. Olds. The present trustees are Gilbert Brady, John Durand, Charles P. Ford, James C. Hart, George C. Hollister and Menzo Van Voorhes.

A goodly spirit of benevolence has prevailed in the church from the first, as evinced by their yearly contributions. This moreover has manifested encouraging increase during the past year by the adoption of the plan of "Systematic benevolence." The amount thus raised being double of that before given.

The church has a vigorous Young People's Society of Christian Endeavor, which holds weekly meetings. The attendance is good and the meetings are spirited. Other meetings auxillary to the work of this Society, are held during the year. There is an efficient Ladies' Benevolent Society, which does much work for the poor during the year and sends away a number of excellent "missionary boxes," also a "Ladies' Missionary Society," a "Young Ladies' Missionary Band," a "Little Girls' Band," and a "Boys' Band,"

There have been numerous seasons of marked religious interest in the congregation, the first was in 1821. Early in that year Josiah Bissell, Jr., visited Pittsfield, Mass., (the place of his nativity, when there was a revival and was converted). He returned full of ardor and zeal. He attended the evening prayer-meeting and surprised the assembly by repeating the verse in Dodridge's hymn:

> "Grace taught my soul to pray,
> And made my eyes o'erflow,
> 'Tis grace has kept me to this day
> And will not let me go."

To hear this from such a man was most deeply impressive. A revival followed resulting in the addition of 21 members to the church on confession of their faith. There was also a revival in 1827, the fruits of which added 43 members to the church on confession.

In Sept., 1830, Rev. Charles G. Finney made his first efforts in Rochester and continued here more than 6 months. For a few weeks he preached about two sermons per week in each of the First, Second and Third churches. In the evening of Oct. 1, 1830, a crowded congregation were assembled in the First Church, the building had no columns in its audience room to support its roof, the weight spread the walls so that a scantling fell over the ceiling and broke through the plastering, causing a stampede, the congregation smashed through windows and trampled down a crowd at both doors. The church was then closed till supports for the roof were set up in the middle aisle. At this time St. Paul's Church being without a rector, their vestry tendered the use of their church to the congregation of the First Church, and their pastor, Joseph Penny, D. D., preached in it till the latter part of the winter, when St. Paul's Church secured a rector. In the afternoon of Jan. 2, 1831, the First Church held their communion service in the Second Church and received 100 new members. In several other years large additions were made to the church.

This church has had at different times quite a number of students for the ministry under its care or support. Some of whom have become foreign missionaries. The following

BRICK CHURCH, ROCHESTER.

are of those who entered the ministry: James Ballantine, Henry B. Chapin, Charles R. Clark, Henry Cherry, George Dutton, T. Dwight Hunt, Mathew L. P. Hill, Everard Kempshall, Charles G. Lee, L. Merrill Miller, William N. McCoon, Gideon P. Nichols, James H. McIlvain, Jr., Henry E. Peck, Robert Proctor, Justin Gamaliel Riley, George S. Sill, Robert L. Stanton, Ferdinand DeW. Ward and Horace Winston.

CARTHAGE.

This church, containing 28 members, was received by the Presbytery of Rochester at its first meeting, April 6, 1819. No session book is found or list of names of its original members, and date of its organization. Probably it had no organized society. They worshipped in a framed building, standing on high ground, on the west side of the road, a little south of the present location of the mute asylum.

In consequence of a bridge over the Genesee river near the lower falls having fallen, and many of their members residing on the west side of the river being thereby cut off from access to their place of meeting, and many east side residents having moved away, under the advice of the Presbytery, letters of dismission were given to their remaining members, and their organization was surrendered to the Presbytery, and disbanded by them April 15, 1822.

ROCHESTER BRICK.

The Second (now Brick) Presbyterian Church of Rochester was organized November 18, 1825, by a commission of Presbytery, consisting of Rev. Asa Carpenter, Chauncy Cook, Joseph Penny and William F. Curry, and Elders Moses Chapin and Joel Baldwin.

The following 25 persons composed it: Timothy L. Bacon, Lydia Bacon, Lydia W. Blanchard, Catharine Brown, Asa Carpenter, Seth Case, Elizabeth Cherry, Lottie Cherry, Richard Gorsline, Amelia Gorsline, Silas Hawley, Sarah Hawley, George A. Hollister, Sally Hollister, Catharine S. Russell, Mary Rust, Thomas Sheldon, Jane Sheldon, Derrick Sibley, Nabby Sibley, Irene Sibley, Linus Stevens, M. D., Thankful Stevens, Delia Stevens.

Timothy L. Bacon, Linus Stevens, M. D., and Silas Hawley were elected and ordained as elders. The present elders are Seth J. Arnold, Louis Chapin, Joel G. Davis, David Dickey,* Willam H. Gorsline, Jesse W. Hatch, Truman A. Newton, George N. Storms, Charles F. Weaver, Edward Webster and Lansing G. Wetmore. Since the organization of this church there have been 29 different elders, 15 of them have died, and 3 who are now living, have resigned. Terms are not limited.

The church has had seven different deacons, all of whom resigned. Five of them are dead.

The following have been pastors or stated supplies: William James, the first pastor, was called from Clarkson, where he was stated supply, April 17, 1826, installed July 24, 1826, resigned his pastorate October 14, 1830, and was dismissed to Albany, February 4, 1831. William Wisner, D. D., was called from Ithaca, January 24, 1831, began his pastorate May 1, 1831, was installed July 24, 1831, and was dismissed to St. Louis, October 14, 1835. On the retirement of Dr. Wisner, Rev. Russell S. Cook was employed as temporary supply for some four months, until February 26, 1836. In March, following, Conway P. Wing, D. D., of Ogden, supplied the church for several months, assisted by David N. Merritt, a layman from Port Gibson, who was afterward licensed, and on the 24th of August, 1836, was engaged as

---

*David Dickey, was born September 12, 1802, united with the church on certificate, September 5, 1831; was ordained an elder September 29, 1833, and was appointed clerk of the session January 8, 1836, which office he continues to hold.

supply for one year. He continued as such more than a year and removed to Massachusetts.

Rev. George Beecher, was called from Putnam, Ohio, December, 1837, was installed June 15, 1838, and dismissed to Ripley, Ohio, October 6, 1840.

Rev. James Boylan Shaw was called from Dunkirk, November 25, 1840, installed February 16, 1841, and continued until he was retired by the Presbytery as pastor emeritus, April 10, 1888.

Rev. William Rivers Taylor, was called from the First Reformed Church, Philadelphia, Pa., Nov. 14, 1887, accepted and commenced his labors Feb, 19, 1888, and was installed April 10, 1888. He continues as the pastor. The growth of the church under the several pastorates and supplies has been as follows:

Rev. William James, 4½ years, 43 on confession, 112 by certificate.

Rev. William Wisner, D. D., 4½ years, 372 on confession, 202 by certificate.

Rev. Conway P. Wing, D. D., and David N. Merritt, 1½ years, 109 on confession, 26 by certificate.

Rev. George Beecher, 2½ years, 138 on confession, 76 on certificate.

Rev. James Boylan Shaw, 47½ years, 2,061 on confession, 1,320 on certificate.

Rev. William Rivers Taylor, 1 year, 78 on confession, 33 on certificate.

There have been received into the church on confession 2,965, and on certificates 1,763 members. The present resident membership is 1,414, besides 306 names on a non-resident list (according to Morris' Digest of 1886, Chap. VII. Sec. 49, page 640).

The Sunday school was organized on the last Sunday of November, 1825, under the superintendence of Jonathan Mann, and has been maintained without interruption. Its records show that 151 teachers and 1,638 scholars have united with the church in a little more than 62 years. Its present superintendent is Lansing G. Wetmore. It has 100 teachers, and 842 scholars. May 24, 1857, a Sunday-school was organized in what had been a tavern, on the corner of Buffalo road and York street. The tavern was bought by Aristarchus Champion, and fitted by him for Sunday school, and prayer meeting purposes. John H. Thompson, was its superintendent. George W. Mackie, a theological student, visited the section and conducted religious meetings there. The school was closed December 25, 1859, having had 426 different scholars.

A Sunday school was opened July 27, 1856, in a hall on the south side of Buffalo street, now West avenue, opposite the end of Canal street, belonging to Joel B. Bennett, under the management of teachers from the Brick and Washington street churches. This school continued till December 25, 1859, when it was united with the one from the Champion mission, and the two formed the new school in a small chapel now composing in part the Westminster Church. It remained as a union school until September 2, 1862, when a society was incorporated, called "The West Avenue Chapel." Its trustees were Joel B. Bennett, Samuel Dix, Stephen Coleman, Henry L. Churchill and Lewis H. Alling.

June 13, 1869, members of the Brick Church organized a Sunday school in District School house No. 18, on North street. In a short time the wants of the district required the occupancy of the room and the school was suspended.

July 14, 1869, the Brick Church Sunday school purchased of Hiram Davis, a lot at the corner of Hudson and Wilson streets, for $2,600, now occupied by the Memorial Church. Subscriptions to the amount of more than $7,500 were paid by members of the Brick Church congregation. Until the Memorial Church became self-sustaining, the Brick Church and its Sunday school paid $20,661, for building and supporting the Memorial Church.

At different times the Brick Church Sunday school has paid toward the education and support of 10 children in heathen lands through the American Board of Foreign Missions, to whom they gave names. Since the commencement of the Sunday school, November 25, 1825, it has contributed towards Home and Foreign Mission, Education, Church Erection, Freedmen, etc., $25,847.55.

For a few years past the school has paid to Mrs. Agnes B. Rowland $500 per annum salary, to work as a city missionary, mostly in the interests of the Brick Church and Sunday school.

The Dorcas Society, or an association of similar kind has existed more than 50 years. Its object has been to clothe poor Sunday school children. Last year they aided 135 children, furnishing to them 458 articles of clothing and 59 pairs of shoes, at a cost of $287, besides labor.

A "Girls' Missionary Society," has existed four years. They at first worked to aid Miss Emma Cochrane and a hospital in Persia. The present year's earnings and receipts have amounted to $229, which has been contributed to the Women's Board.

"Cheerful Workers," an association of about 20 young ladies, have realized $200, which has been used for Home and Foreign missions.

A few ladies hold a sewing school, called the Young Dorcas Society, which meets in the afternoon on Saturdays, and is attended on an average by 50 little girls, most of whom are from families of the poor. Such as are able, contribute one cent per week, which is used for materials.

The "Society of Christian Endeavor," has 150 members. and hold their meetings on Tuesday evenings. They have contributed $80 to missions, besides using what they needed for their own work.

A "Boys' Mission Band," of about 60 members, meets every alternate week in nine months of the year, to systematically study missions, taking up one country after another, to learn their characteristics, condition, customs, religion, needs, progress and results of mission work. They have contributed in various ways this year to missions, $45.

The "Ladies' Missionary Society" meets monthly in connection with a church sociable. They have contributed this year to mission purposes, $1,271, besides sending packages to Home missionaries valued at $289.

Plate collections have been taken for more than seventeen years, on Sundays, both at morning and evening services, for Board or benevolent purposes. They amounted in 1888, to $3,813. Collections are also taken every Sunday in the Sunday school. They amounted in 1888, to $1,854. The following persons who have been members of this church or its Sunday school, have been licensed to preach : Horace H. Allen, David Ames, Charles R. Benedict, Peter H. Burkhardt, Elisha M. Carpenter, Nathan C. Chapin, Lemuel Clark, Henry Cherry, Darwin Chichester, Hiram W. Congdon, Philos G. Cook, Henry Cooper, David Dickey, Mowatt Evarts, William C. French, John K. Fowler, Merritt Galley, Corliss B. Gardner, T. Dwight Hunt, Alanson Curtis Hall, Augustus F. Hall, Gavin L. Hamilton, Parsons C. Hastings, Alvan Ingersoll, Thomas H. Johnson, Jonathan Ketchum, George M. Mackie, Amos D. McCoy, David E. Millard, David Henry Palmer, James H. Phelps, James S. Pierpont, Augustus C. Shaw, Robert B. Stevens, John Spink, Ansley D. White, William C. Wisner, Edwin S. Wright, Worthington Wright.

Eight who have been teachers or scholars with us, have been, or now are Foreign missionaries under the appointment of the American Board : T. Dwight Hunt, to Sandwich Islands ; Edwin O. Hall, to Sandwich Islands ; Fidelia (Church) Coan, to Sandwich Islands ; Alanson Curtis Hall, to Ceylon ; Henry Cherry, to Madura ; Maria (Preston) Johnson, to Siam ; Elijah F. Webster, to Bombay, and Harriet Seymour, to Turkey.

ROCHESTER THIRD.

Residents of the east side of the Genesee river in the village of Rochester, feeling the need of a place for worship nearer to their homes than those located on the west side, decided to organize a Third Presbyterian Church and to locate on the north-east corner of Clinton and Main streets.

The Rev. Joel Parker, a graduate of Auburn Seminary, was employed to begin their services in a school house on the corner of Clinton and Mortimer streets, Dec. 31, 1826. Very soon the room was found to be too small, and they resolved to build on the north part of the lot selected for their permanent locality, a temporary house of worship, and their efficient leaders started on a Monday morning in January and had trees cut down, hewn, drawn to the site, raised, covered, floor laid, seats made, all ready for use before the next Sunday. Its size was 24 ft. by 60 ft. Later in the same year they commenced building a brick church, having a steeple and supplied with a bell, which was completed for use in 1828, on the ground now occupied by Washington Hall. The society was incorporated January 17, 1827, as the Third Presbyterian Church and Society of Rochester. Its first trustees were Obediah N. Bush, Ashbel W. Riley, Judson Booth and Isaac Waring.

By appointment of Presbytery, Feb. 4, 1827, a commission consisting of Rev. Joseph Penney, Rev. William James, Rev. George S. Sill, and elders Silas Hawley and Zolved Stevens, met on Feb. 28, 1827, and organized the Third Presbyterian Church in Rochester, containing twenty-two members, as follows: Louisa Allen, Lucy Allen, Maria Allen, Pliny Allen, Sarah Allen, Philip Allen, Henrietta Bissell, Josiah Bissell, Jr., Esther Calhoun, John T.

Calhoun, Asa Carpenter, Mary Carpenter, Elisha Ely, Hannah Ely, Harriet Moore, Harriet Parker, Hezekiah B. Pierpont, Mary Pierpont, Eliza Pratt, Persis Scofield, Salmon Scofield, and Lydia Ann Smith.

They elected Josiah Bissell, Jr., and Salmon Scofield for elders.

Rev. Joel Parker, as before stated, commenced his services for them Dec. 31, 1826; was installed over the church, June 14, 1827, and was dismissed to New York, June 17, 1830. The growth of the church under Mr. Parker's ministrations was very rapid.

In 1827, when the church occupied its temporary house of worship, the scheme of supplying every family in the county of Monroe with a copy of the Bible was proposed by Josiah Bissell, Jr., and was extensively carried out. The county was canvassed and Bibles given to all families who would receive them, or were not disposed or able to pay for them.

From Sept. 10, 1830, to March 6, 1831, Rev. Charles G. Finney, supplied their pulpit most of the time. In this period he preached ninety-eight sermons in the First, Second, and his church.

Under the preaching of Mr. Finney the church received large and influential additions. Dec. 12, 1830, there were eighty-three added to this church. Jan. 16, 1831, there were thirty-seven, and on 27th March following, thirty-nine more.

July 13, 1831, Rev. Luke Lyons was installed pastor of this church. Soon disaffection was manifested in the congregation which resulted in his dismissal, and he together with forty-six members of the Third Church were organized into the First Free Presbyterian Church in Rochester.

February 7, 1832, William C. Wisner, a licentiate, who had studied theology with his father at Ithaca, was employed. He was installed Oct. 24, 1832; he continued the charge until June 25, 1833; he resigned on account of failing health. A season of depression followed for many months.

In December, 1834, the church extended a call to Rev. William Mack, who became their fourth pastor and was installed February 3, 1835. He labored successfully till July 22, 1839, when he resigned the pastorate, and was dismissed from Presbytery, February 6, 1844, to Columbia, Tenn.

On the first of February, Rev. Albert Gallatin Hall began his labors as pastor. He was installed Nov. 10, 1840, and continued such till Sept. 10, 1871, when his spirit was called to take its place with the redeemed. His influence for good was great. He was greatly beloved by the community as well as by his own congregation. See the biographical sketch on a preceding page.

Rev. George Patton, a graduate of the University of Pennsylvania and of Newburg Theological Seminary, after ministering to the church of Seneca for fifteen years, was called and installed pastor of this church, Dec. 21, 1871. His labors have been greatly blessed, and he continues to enjoy the confidence and esteem of his people to the present time.

The elders of this church are William F. Cogswell, David Copeland, David Cory, Edward Harris, Joseph Harris, John H. Hill, Charles D. King and William S. Little. After the organization of the First Free Presbyterian Church and the death and withdrawal of influential members, the society found themselves burdened with a debt of $7,000 in 1834. They surrendered their house of worship to the newly organized Second Baptist Church, they, in consideration, assumed and paid the debts of the houseless church, which soon found shelter in the hall of the High School building at the corner of Temple and Lancaster streets. This they occupied while they were erecting a stone church on the south side of Main street, a few rods west of Stone street, in 1837. Here they found rest and prosperity until the church was destroyed by a sweeping fire, originated by a rocket on the occasion of celebrating the laying of the Atlantic telegraph cable, Aug. 17, 1858.

The church in its homeless condition next obtained shelter in "Palmer's Hall," fronting the south end of North avenue, until they bought the High School lot and erected a stone edifice and chapel costing $38,000. This was completed and dedicated for use in the fall of 1859. They occupied this place until they sold it to the Unitarian Society in 1883, and till they had erected their present chapel at the corner of East avenue and Meigs street. This property is valued at $50,000.

Twelve members of this church have entered the ministry, viz.: Samuel M. Baylis, T. Reave Chipman, Jonathan Copeland, Eugene Cheeseman, Richard DeForest, Albert G. Hall, Gavin Longmuir, Hezekiah B. Pierpont, Charles Ray, Edward Ray, Charles W. Wood, and James White.

The Ladies' Missionary Society was organized in 1876; this raised in the past year $628, and their social society, $124. The church also has an efficient working society of Young People's Christian Endeavor.

FIRST PRESBYTERIAN FREE CHURCH.

"The First Presbyterian Free Church and Society in Rochester" was organized in the school room of Franklin House, Rochester, March 28th, 1832.

On April 19, 1832, the Presbytery of Rochester, appointed a commission consisting of Rev. Alfred E. Campbell, Rev. Charles E. Firman, Rev. Silas Pratt and Elders Levi Ward, Jr., and Selah Mathews, who met in the Third Presbyterian Church in Rochester, April 25, and organized the following 46 persons into a church: Amelia Brown, John Calhoun, Rufus Colton, Henry Campbell, Francis Dana, Jr., Hannah Dana, Phineas Danforth, Nason Danforth, Ann Danforth, Mary Dobbin, Mary Ann Dobbin, Sarah Deming, Elisha Ely, Hannah Ely, Alexander L. Ely, Caroline Ely, John Gorton, Caleb K. Hobbie, Clarisa Hobbie, Maria Hobbie, Aaron Hall, Betsey Hall, Sally Ann Hall, Ruthy Hall, Nathaniel Hayward, Rachel Hayward, Adeline L. Hayward, Joanna Hammond, Lucinda T. House, Nathan Lyman, Phebe Miller, Maria McDonald, Ann Moore, Sarah Newcomb, Hosea Pratt, Lucinda Pratt, Eliza Padden, Ashbel W. Riley, William Stebbins, Jr., John Tompkins, Maria Vallette, Jane Voorhis, Manly S. Woodbury, Amelia Woodbury, Esther Willard and Sarah Willson. Caleb K. Hobbie was elected as elder.

Soon after the society was organized, a house of worship was built for their use by Ashbel W. Riley on the northeast corner of Court and Stone streets, which was dedicated Jan. 1, 1833. Rev. Gilbert Morgan preached on the occasion from the text John 8, 36. March 1, 1833, Marcus Holmes and Nathan Hayward were elected elders. On the 12th of that month, Rev. Luke Lyons was installed pastor of this church.

In the latter part of this year, a division in the Congregational Church of Brighton, resulted in 31 of their members withdrawing and uniting with this church at one time; others followed later.

July 7, 1834, the following persons were elected elders: Samuel Beckwith, Phineas A. Danforth, Asahel Fitch, John Gray, Richard B. Huntley, Ashbel W. Riley and W. G. Squires. On 20th of that month, Messrs. Fitch, Gray, Huntley and Riley were ordained, and on the 16th of Nov., Messrs. Beckwith and Squires were ordained.

Sept. 4, 1836, the Presbytery of Rochester dissolved the the pastoral relation between Rev. Luke Lyons and the First Free Presbyterian Church. On the 1st of April, 1836, the church reported to Presbytery, 425 members (which report corresponds with their session book). Soon after that a spirit of discontent prevailed, resulting in many cases of discipline and much agitation on the subjects of slavery and intemperance. At short intervals elders resigned and new ones were elected. There was a constant drawing off of members, many returning to the Third Church, and to the Brighton Church from which they had come. March 19, 1838, the session authorized elder Richard B. Huntley to give letters of dismission to all those who were known to be members in good and regular standing; and the last record made by the clerk was, that with a number of others he had given letters of dismission to elders William Shepard, Nathaniel Hayward, Samuel Beckwith, Asahel Fitch and *himself*. The church was disbanded, June 26, 1838.

The society records cannot be found. No names of trustees at the organization of the society are in the session book. In 1834, Richard B. Huntley and Ashbel W. Riley are mentioned as trustees.

Mr. Riley had given the society a deed of a lot with a framed church on the northeast corner of Court and Stone streets, which was afterward sold on the foreclosure of a prior mortgage made by Mr. Riley. The building was closed against the society, and during the latter part of their existence they met in the chamber of a wagon shop on the west side of South St. Paul street and south of Court street.

ROCHESTER CENTRAL.

The Bethel Free Church was organized August 4, 1836, with 39 members, who presented certificates from the First Church. It was organized on the following basis: "A Missionary Church established upon the principles of

Christian consecration and devotedness." " A free church, embracing also a Bethel interest." " Open for discussion on all moral topics, such as temperance, slavery, etc." " The control of the church in its secular as well as its spiritual relations to be vested in the church exclusively."

The names of the original members were as follows: George A. Avery, Frances Avery, Thomas Adams, Cornelia S. Adams, Michael B. Bateham, John Priden, Jr., William S. Bishop, John F. Bush, William Cook, Lydia Cook, Mary M. Cook, Spencer Davis, Eliza Davis, Joseph Farley, Walter S. Griffith, Elizabeth S. Griffith, Henry D. Griffith, Theodore B. Hamilton, Julia M Hamilton, Lydia Hatch, Fanny E. Hatch, Ebenezer Knapp, Polly Knapp, Apollos Luce, Josiah Newell, Mary Newell, Mary Jane Porter, Preston Smith, Eliza N. Smith, William P. Smith, Eunice Smith, Henry F. Smith, John Still, Louisa Still, Newell A. Stone, Joseph Stone, Nancy Stone, Richard P. Wilkins and Mary P. Wilkins. The first elders ordained were George A. Avery, Walter S. Griffith and Preston Smith.

The present elders are Lewis H. Alling, William Alling, Henry Churchill, Darius L. Covill, Frank M. Ellery, Heman Glass, John N. Harder, William A. Hubbard, William A. Hubbard, Jr., Alonzo L. Mabbett, Samuel Sloan and Henry Wray.

The first pastor was Rev. George S. Boardman, who began his labors, 7th of May, 1837, was installed Oct. 19, 1837, was dismissed June 28, 1842; under his charge the church grew to a membership of 239 on Jan. 1, 1842.

June 28, 1843, the church withdrew from the Presbytery and became independent. June 3, 1844, it voted to return to Presbytery, and was received July 20, 1844.

From July, 1842, until Feb. 1, 1845, the church was supplied by Rev. Messrs. John T. Avery, George W. Bassitt, George R. H. Shumway, Frederick W. Graves and Parsons C. Hastings.

The second pastor, Rev. Milo J. Hickok, began his labors Feb. 1, 1845, was installed Feb. 25, 1845, and continued until March 15, 1854.

The third pastor, Rev. Frank F. Ellinwood, began his work Nov. 4, 1854, was installed Jan. 9, 1856, and continued until Jan. 24, 1866.

The fourth pastor, Samuel M. Campbell, D. D., began his labors March 1, 1866, was installed June 14, 1866, and was dismissed April 11, 1881.

Rev. Theodore W. Hopkins was elected pastor Sept. 5, 1881, and labored as such until June 12, 1887, when he withdrew. From that date till the 1st of March, 1888, the pulpit was supplied mainly by Professor James S. Riggs of Auburn Theological Seminary. March 11, 1888, Henry H. Stebbins, D. D., began his labors, and was installed April 17, 1888.

The Sunday school of 18 scholars was organized in the Crane school house on Sophia street on the first meeting of the church, Aug. 12, 1836, and has continued in vigorous existence. It has supplied to the church a majority of those who have united with it on confession. Its first superintendent was Walter S. Griffith. Its present one is Joseph T. Alling. The present membership is 750.

In the spring of 1856, a Sunday school was organized by William S. Bishop in a hall on the south side of Buffalo street (now West avenue), fronting Canal street, in a block owned by Joel B. Bennett. It was manned by teachers from several churches, but mostly from this church. Dec. 25, 1859, this school was discontinued to unite with a school from the Champion district in forming the school organized Jan. 8, 1860, in a brick chapel, which is now a part of Westminster church. Sept. 2, 1862, a society was incorporated called "The West Avenue Chapel." Its trustees were Joel B. Bennett, Samuel Dix, Stephen Coleman, Henry L. Churchill and Lewis H. Alling.

In 1869, a Mission Sunday school was organized in District No. 7 school house on Lake avenue. William A. Hubbard was its first superintendent. A chapel was built by the members of Central Church, at the corner of Fulton avenue and Locust street, at a cost of $7,000. It was dedicated Aug. 11, 1874. It was in this chapel that the North Church was organized Feb. 12, 1884.

A Woman's Missionary Society of the Central Church was organized Sept. 30, 1872, which has contributed annually from $300 to $700 for Home and Foreign Missions.

The "Jenny Lush Missionary Society," organized in Feb., 1876, was organized for the special purpose of supporting her while a missionary in Africa.

The "Do What You Can Mission Band," a children's society, organized Dec., 1884, contributes to mission work generally.

The Society of Christian Endeavor was organized in March, 1882, and has grown into great influence and usefulness. It has a membership of 256. Its contribution to benevolence in 1888 was $885. It also has a branch of "King's Daughters."

In the winter and spring of 1842, Rev. Charles G. Finney, in connection with the pastor, Rev. George S. Boardman, conducted a series of revival meetings resulting in large acquisitions to the church. In the winter and spring of 1857, this church united with the Brick and Plymouth churches in revival meetings under Mr. Finney's preaching, which were also greatly blessed. In the spring of 1860, special efforts, under the pastorate of Rev. Frank F. Ellinwood, were greatly blessed, resulting in the addition of 63 at the April communion and a total of 91 in the year, mostly from the Sunday school.

In April, 1863, Rev. Edward P. Hammond engaged in a special effort in connection with this and the Brick Church.

It resulted in an addition to this church at the June communion of 136 on confession. Again in 1869, a similar effort under Mr. Hammond resulted in an addition of 65 new members. In the spring of 1886, this church engaged in a union effort with the First and Brick churches under the ministrations of Rev. Edgar E. Davidson, of Newtonville, Mass. He preached daily in each of the three churches, two weeks. As a result 110 new members were added to this church. A similar effort was made in the spring of 1887. It terminated suddenly on account of Mr. Davidson being called home by sickness in his family. As the fruit of this effort 58 new members were added.

"The Trustees of the Bethel Free Presbyterian Church and Society" was organized, Aug. 29, 1836. Its trustees were Michael B. Bateham, John Biden, Jr., John F. Bush, Theodore B. Hamilton and Samuel D. Porter. April 23, 1845, the society was reconstructed under the name of "The Trustees of the Washington Street Church in Rochester." Its trustees were Carlton M. Avery, William W. Brewster, Winthrop A. Parker, Samuel B. Stoddard and Edward Terry. March 30, 1858, the Legislature of the State of New York changed the name of the church to "The Central Presbyterian Church of the City of Rochester." Its present trustees are H. Austin Brewster, Isaac H. Dewey, John W. Goss, Charles S. Hastings, Horace McGuire, Samuel Sloan, Henry F. Smith, Charles A. Vickery and Louis L. Williams.

The Bethel Church was built of stone in 1837, on the west side of Washington street, north of the Erie canal at a cost of $15,000. In 1844, it was repaired and improved at a cost of $3,500. This building was set fire to in the steeple by an incendiary in the night and burned, Nov. 22, 1861. The lot is now a coal yard.

The Central Church building was begun July 21, 1856, and was dedicated April 8, 1858. Its size is 68 by 145 feet. The total cost was $40,000.

The following members of this church have entered the ministry: George S. Bishop, Frederick Campbell, Willis Clark Gaylord, Dullis D. Hamilton, Simon J. Humphrey, Frederick J. Jackson, Robert McLean, Simon J. McPherson, Daniel F. Stewart, Charles W. Torrey and Theodore B. Williams.

The following persons have gone from this church as Foreign Missionaries: Miss Isabella Atwater to China, 1847; Miss Carrie E. Bush to Eastern Turkey, May 28, 1870; Miss Jennie M. Lush to Western Africa, Oct. 12, 1873; Miss Fannie M. Nelson to South Africa, Nov., 1846, and Miss Hattie Seymour to Eastern Turkey, 1865.

The present membership is 990. The church is united and harmonious, and under the able leadership of its newly settled pastor, Henry H. Stebbins, D. D., is well equipped for the Master's service.

THE FIFTH PRESBYTERIAN CHURCH OF ROCHESTER.

February, 1838, the Presbytery of Rochester appointed a commission consisting of Rev. Tryon Edwards, Rev. George S. Boardman, Rev. Richard De Forest and elder Benjamin Campbell, to organize the "Fifth Presbyterian Church in the city of Rochester." On the 15th of that month all the commissioners met in the house of Benjamin Herrick and organized the following twelve persons into a church: Caleb K. Hobbie, Benjamin Herrick, Cynthia Herrick, Relief Thorpe, Mary Earle, Ann Palmer, Richard H. Lee, Sarah P. Lee, Almedia Conkey, Sarah Hutchins, Rachel Janes Chatterton and Elizabeth Doe. The new church then elected and ordained as their elders Caleb K. Hobbie and Richard H. Lee. On May 12, 1840, Reuben Hill was ordained an elder.

The name of this church was changed Feb. 6, 1844, to the "Fourth Presbyterian Church of Rochester."

Rev. Richard De Forest began his labors with these people before their organization, Jan. 9, 1837, and continued with them till May 12, 1840. Rev. Jacob Burbank moderated the session June 4, 1843, and on the last time Jan. 5, 1845. Rev. David L. Hunn was employed as supply, Dec. 7, 1845, continuing only a short time. During the church's existence 33 members were received on confession and 16 on certificate, but removals to a distance resulted in such a depletion of the church, that Feb. 1, 1848, the Presbytery of Rochester disbanded their remaining 9 members.

In the latter days of the church the Presbytery criticised the "*cession*" for "*incorrect spelling.*" No entries were made on their session book after Jan. 7, 1846. The book was examined by Presbytery the last time, Feb. 3, 1847.

On the same day the church was organized, Feb. 15, 1838, the congregation organized a society, called the Fifth Presbyterian Church of Rochester, and elected as trustees Caleb K. Hobbie, Elias Gates and Joseph Gates.

The society built a framed house of worship on the east side of the road a few rods south of Norton street. After the church was disbanded their house of worship was sold and removed to the corner, then of Atwater, now Central avenue, and Leopold street; where it was for many years occupied by a "Holland Dutch" church; it has since been used for livery stable, the congregation having removed to a building on Oregon street.

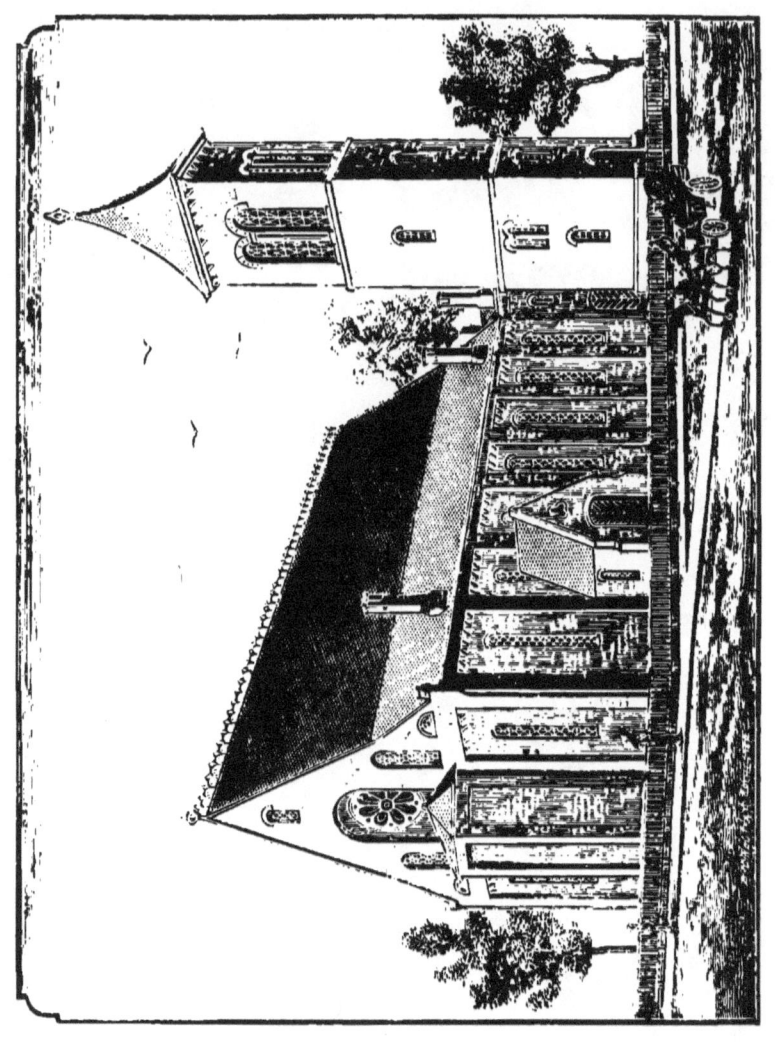

ST. PETER'S PRESBYTERIAN CHURCH, ROCHESTER.

Dissolved June 1923

ROCHESTER ST. PETER'S.

This church originated in the thought and benevolence of Hon. Levi A. Ward. The corner-stone was laid June 7, 1852, and the edifice completed at a cost of $32,500, was dedicated Oct. 25, 1853. Soon after a chime of nine bells was hung in the tower of the church by Mr. Ward. The first regular Sabbath service was held in the church Oct. 3, 1853, and the first celebration of the holy communion, May 14, 1854.

On the 12th day of December, 1853, a special meeting of the Presbytery of Rochester City was held in the chapel of the church, at which meeting the following twenty-eight persons were constituted by the Presbytery, the " St. Peter's Presbyterian Church of the City of Rochester:"

Lowel Butler, Mrs. Chloe Butler, Mrs. Emily R. Beckwith, Jane Bradbury, Mrs. Emily Chumasero, John S. Dean, Mrs. Chloe Dean, Mrs. Caroline B. Dwinell, Lorenzo D. Ely, Mrs. Caroline C. Ely, Mrs. Mary A. Holyland, Ellen M. Kemp, James Murray, Mrs. Pesinah Murray, Ann E. Murray, Mrs. Caroline E. McAlpine, Mrs. Betsey L. Oothout, Edward A. Raymond, Mrs. Eugenia C. Raymond, Samuel B. Raymond, Mrs. Harriet M. Raymond, Mrs. Susan M. Selden, Levi A. Ward, Mrs. Harriet Ward, Mary E. Ward, William H. Ward, John F. Whitbeck and Mrs. Elizabeth A. Whitbeck.

In connection with this meeting, Edward A. Raymond and Levi A. Ward were elected elders, and they were ordained as such on the first day of January, 1854. Four years later the session was enlarged by the election of Hiram Banker and William Slocum.

The present session is as follows: Harvey W. Brown, Henry C. Clark, Ira C. Goodridge, Edwin S. Hayward, Sidney A. Newman, Jonathan E. Pierpont, Richard E. White.

Originally the elders were chosen to serve for life, but at present the term of active service is three years.

Deacons were first elected Nov. 10, 1858, but none were ordained till April 24, 1864, when Joseph B. Ward, and Marcus K. Woodbury were set apart to this office, since which time others have been chosen as needed.

The first stated supplies of their pulpit were Rev. T. Coit and Rev. Leonard W. Bacon. Rev. Richard H. Richardson was installed May 4, 1856, and dismissed Dec. 3, 1857; Rev. Joseph H. Towne was installed May, 1858, and dismissed March 7, 1860; Rev. John T. Coit was installed June 1, 1860, and died when on a visit at Albion, Jan. 23, 1863; Rev. Edwin Dorr Yeomans was installed June 7, 1863, resigned April 28, 1867, and was dismissed May 1, 1867. He died at Orange, N. J., Aug. 27, 1868. John M. Crowell, D. D., was installed May 16, 1869, and dismissed Dec. 4, 1870; Rev. Asa S. Fiske was installed Jan. 1, 1872, and dismissed Sept. 12, 1875; Rev. Herman C. Riggs, D. D., was installed April 2, 1876, and dismissed Sept. 24, 1885; Rev. Alfred J. Hutton, the present pastor, began his labors, Oct. 16, 1887, and was installed on the following 15th day of November.

Several seasons of special religious awakening have been enjoyed by the church, the most marked being in the pastorates of the Rev. Drs. Yeomans and Riggs. The main growth of St. Peter's Church has been, however, rather by smaller and more frequent accessions. The whole number received during the thirty-five years is 925, of whom, 420 were received on confession, and 505 by certificate. The present membership is 486.

The St. Peter's Church Congregation was incorporated Nov. 7, 1853, at which time the following persons were chosen trustees: Josiah W. Bissell, Charles H. Clarke, Lorenzo D. Ely, Charles A. Jones, Belden R. McAlpine, Samuel B. Raymond, Samuel L. Selden, Jerome B. Stillson and Charles P. Smith.

The present board is as follows: Frederick P. Allen, Henry C. Brewster, James G. Cutler, William H. Farrand, Alexander E. Hayden, William S. Kimball, William H. Ward, Howard L. Smith.

On the 4th day of June, 1860, Mr. Levi A. Ward conveyed the church property by a duly executed deed to the board of trustees for the nominal sum of $20,000, donating the remaining $12,500 personally to the society. On the 8th of March, 1868, the building so conveyed was destroyed by fire, and ten months later it was replaced by the present building, at a cost of $49,000. Not long after the original chime of bells was also replaced by a larger one, of twelve bells, at a cost of $4,000.

The Sunday school was organized contemporaneously with the church. Mr. Edward A. Raymond was its first superintendent. The school, though never so large as some others of the city, has always been prosperous in the best sense of the word, and never was more so than now, under its present superintendent, Mr. Sidney A. Newman.

A Ladies' Benevolent Society has also existed almost from the beginning.

A Young Ladies' Society was formed in 1876.

On the 2d Oct., 1877, the Woman's Missionary Society was organized with fifteen members, and under the presidency of Mrs. Sarah R. A. Dolley, M. D., this society has held regular monthly meetings and has greatly increased the missionary activity of the church. Mrs. Dolley is still its efficient and accomplished president.

As a complete record of the finances from the beginning does not exist, the statement must be approximate. The aggregate of society congregational expenses for the thirty-five years is very nearly $290,000, and that of benevolence, about $40,650.

NORTH STATE STREET CHURCH.

"The Trustees of the Lower Falls Presbyterian Society" were organized, Dec. 6, 1852. Their first trustees were Adam Aldrich, Gideon Leavenworth, Robert Roberts, Oliver Brooks and C. C. Vancanon. Rev. Archibald Furgerson was active in canvassing for funds for the erection of a house of worship, and R. Graham King donated a lot for the same, located on the east side of State street a few rods north of Phelps avenue, conditioned that if for the term of two consecutive years it should cease to be used for a Presbyterian church it should revert to the donor or his heirs. This resulted in the erection of a small framed building with a steeple. For about one year, Mr. Furgerson was the stated supply of the church. After that the Rev. James Harkness supplied them about three years.

At a meeting of Presbytery held in Brockport, April 27, 1854, Rev. Messrs. Joshua H. McIlvain, Albert G. Hall and Archibald Furgerson were appointed a commission to organize a church at Lower Falls if the way be open." On the 4th of Oct., 1854, "Said commission reported the organization of the North State Street Church."

Efforts were made in 1875 to find society or session records; none were found or heard of; nor do the records of Presbytery show any dissolution of the church.

In the General Assembly minutes of 1855, the name of the church is published without its statistics. In 1856, the church is reported with 75 members; in 1857, as having 42 members; in 1858, as having 53 members, and in 1859, as having only 15 members and vacant. The name of the church was dropped from the roll in 1862.

The number and names of the original members are not known. Samuel Benton was ordained their first elder.

Mr. Harkness being discouraged, discontinued supplying the church, while a Sunday school was continued in it. He preached for a time to an unorganized congregation in the small brick church that stood on west side of State street a few rods south of Brown street, that had been built for the North Congregational Church under the pastorate of Rev. Henry Peck. The building is now occupied as a store house.

In the night of July 24, 1864, the church of the Lower Falls society took fire in the steeple from burning shingles blown from the burning coopers shop of the Western House of Refuge.

In due time the lot reverted to the King estate according to the terms of the original deed.

ROCHESTER CALVARY.

Rochester Calvary was organized June 15, 1856, with the following sixteen members: James S. Badger, Catherine Badger, Eliza A. Barrett, James Barton, Charles Barton, Elizabeth Blunn, William T. Cushing, Mrs. Arabella Cushing, Henrietta Dempsey, Mrs. Olive Howes, Helen M. Howes, Mrs Mary Ingraham, William Stebbins, Mrs. Eliza B. Stebbins, Mrs. Hannah Ray and Mrs. Jane G. Stolhoff.

The first elders were William Stebbins and William T. Cushing. The present elders are Thomas Oliver, Franklin S. Stebbins and Franklin T. Skinner. All were elected without limit as to term. The church has never had deacons.

The first pastor installed immediately after the organization of the church, July 30, 1856, was Rev. Charles Ray, who was dismissed Aug. 15, 1858. Rev. James Nichols was soon after employed as supply until April 7, 1861, when Rev. Belville Roberts was elected and installed pastor. He was dismissed June 25, 1865. Rev. Alfred Yeomans succeeded him, and was dismissed in April, 1867. Rev. Herbert W. Morris, D. D., who succeeded him, was installed June 11, 1867, and remained until May 3, 1877. Soon after that, Rev. Edward P. Gardner took charge of the pulpit until the next December, when he accepted a call from Portland, Maine. On Jan. 1, 1878, Rev. Edward Bristol commenced his labors as pastor elect. He was not installed, but continued to supply the pulpit till the close of 1889.

The Sunday school was organized early in 1856, and has continued until the present time. At first the attendance was small, but it has steadily advanced until it now numbers more than 200 scholars. It is well organized under earnest and competent teachers. In the fall of 1874, for the accommodation of the school and meetings for social worship, it was resolved to build a chapel in close proximity to the church. The work was commenced the last of November and completed by the first of February. This was accomplished mainly by donated materials and gratuitous labor solicited by the pastor. The balance of the whole expense, $1,200, was raised by the Sabbath school. The school has furnished to the church many active and earnest members.

The Ladies' Missionary Society is an efficient body. They are now educating a girl in Alaska, and a boy who bears the name of Edward Bristol, the pastor of this church.

The Young People's Society of Christian Endeavor is connected with the general organization of that name in the city. Its meetings are well attended, and they are doing their share in the good work.

There have been several seasons of special religious interest in the history of this church. The first notable one was in January, 1874, when 22 were admitted to membership on confession of their faith; in April following 19; in February, 1876, 7 ; in December of same year 16, and in September, 1883, 9.

At the commencement of Calvary Church in 1856, the society took the building formerly occupied by and belonging to the St. Paul Street Congregational Church. It was considerably in debt. During the pastorate of Rev. Belville Roberts, he succeeded in raising sufficient money to pay it off, but as the building was old and unsuitable for the growing necessities of the church and community, Rev. Dr. Morris took the great labor upon himself of raising sufficient money to re-model and re-build the church, which he accomplished, and the present neat and handsome structure stands as the gratifying result of enterprise, activity and faith. Dr. Morris, not content with his great success in rebuilding the church, built also, as above stated, a chapel on the lot in the rear (south) of the church, raising for both objects something over $9,000.

This chapel was used by the church for nearly fourteen years, when it was torn down to make room for the larger and more commodious building now connected with the church, which was started and carried to completion by the Sunday school at a cost of about $4,800. The dimensions of the lot are 74 by 165 feet, covered entirely by the church and chapel except a small space in front. The church stands on the corner of South avenue and Hamilton place in the most desirable part of the Twelfth ward. This part of the city is increasing in population and wealth.

ROCHESTER WESTMINSTER.

On June 29, 1856, a union Sunday school called the Buffalo Street Mission was organized in a hall belonging to Joel B. Bennett, on the south side of Buffalo street, fronting the south end of Canal street. August 10, 1858, the

Westminster Presbyterian Chapel was incorporated. The trustees were Albert Aldrich, James Rugs and William Charles. Its teachers were mostly from the Brick and Central churches. William S. Bishop was its first superintendent. The school continued its sessions until Dec. 25, 1859. May 24, 1857, a Sunday school called the Bull's Head Mission was organized in a building that had been a tavern standing at the southwest corner of Buffalo and York streets. The tavern had been bought by Aristarchus Champion and altered to adapt it so far as possible to the wants of a Sunday school. John H. Thompson was its superintendent. Its teachers were mostly from the Brick Church. George W. Mackie, a student in theology, was employed part of the time to visit in the neighborhood and to conduct religious meetings in the house. The school was closed Dec. 25, 1859. During its continuance it had 426 different scholars.

Jan. 8, 1860, a large portion of the above mentioned two schools assembled in a chapel which had recently been completed and is a part of the present Westminster Church. The school was first superintended by George W. Parsons and later by Henry L. Churchill. The school varied in attendance but had a roll of more than 500 members. In May, 1861, Mr. Champion employed Rev. Anson Gleason for one year to officiate as supply and local missionary.

Sept. 29, 1859, the West Avenue Chapel was organized. Its incorporation was recorded Oct. 6, 1859. Its trustees were Joel B. Bennett, Samuel Dix, Stephen Coleman, Henry L. Churchill and Lewis H. Alling.

July 12, 1875, the society name was changed, by order of court, to the Westminster Church.

After Mr. Gleason closed his labors, continuous services were held with good results. For six months just preceding the organization of the Westminster Church, Mrs. L. A. Shepard, of Utica, visited in the vicinity and held prayer meetings which resulted in many conversions.

On Sunday evening, April 5, 1868, in the Central Church 82 of their members were dismissed and constituted the Westminster Church, under the care of Rev. Henry M. Morey, late of Pittsford. The new organization held its first meeting in their place of worship on the following 12th of April, 1868. Their first elders were George N. Mitchell and Truman A. Clark.

Mr. Morey was called to the pastorate April 5, 1871, and installed on the 27th of the same month. He resigned Oct. 2, 1874, and was dismissed on the 20th of the same month.

Rev. Corlis B. Gardner was called from Cuba, N. Y., Nov. 30, 1874; began his services Jan. 3, 1875, and was installed Feb. 4, 1875, and continues its pastor.

The elders now are John M. Cheeseman, James L. Tarrant, Harvey B. Graves, William F. Parry, Benjamin H. Hill and Jeremiah B. Whitbeck.

The lot on which West Avenue Chapel was built, 66 by 165 feet, was valued at $800 and was the joint gift of Aristarchus Champion and Joel B. Benett. The chapel, of brick, 40 by 60 feet, was built at a cost of $1,700 and was dedicated Jan. 1, 1860. In 1867 the chapel was improved and refurnished at an expense of $1,000. In the summer and fall of 1870 it was rebuilt and enlarged into a church audience room and chapel, each 40 by 70 feet, at a cost of $10,174. The new edifice was dedicated Jan. 26, 1871. The property is now valued at $16,000. The present trustees are George P. Bortle, Eber R. Clark, Warren B. Huther, Charles K. Newbury, William F. Parry, Julius H. Reinhard and James F. Parry.

The church doubled its membership in the first year, having received 65 on confession and 18 on certificates. In the fall of 1873 Rev. Orson Parker performed evangelistic work which resulted in receiving 40 members on confession.

In the winter of 1883-4 a revival occurred under the

labors of the pastor resulting in the further addition of 40 on confession. There were 31 new members received in 1886. The present number of communicants is 270.

Missionary and other organizations have from the beginning had liberal aid, and the monthly concert has always been observed. The church has a Woman's Missionary Society which was organized in the spring of 1884. The Mission Band was organized in 1876; the Young People's Society of Christian Endeavor, Oct. 7, 1883.

Miss Jane M. Lusk, a member of this church, sailed as a missionary to Africa in Oct., 1873. She died in Rochester, March 28, 1884. Rev. John Q. Adams, now pastor of Westminster Church in San Francisco, was a member of this church when pursuing his studies.

The Sunday school at organization of the church had 455 members with average attendance of 250. It now has 400 enrolled and an average attendance of 260.

The Eighth ward, in which this church is located, was erected in 1845, and probably had in 1856, when the Buffalo Street Mission was begun, a population of about 4,000 with no Protestant Sunday school or church within its bounds. It is now supposed to have 12,000 population and has 2 Presbyterian, 2 Baptist, 1 Episcopal and 1 Methodist churches, notwithstanding the six largest leading churches of the city are in near proximity to this ward.

ROCHESTER MEMORIAL.

In 1869, members of the Brick Church resolved to make an effort in the direction of church extension, and after visiting various localities decided on making a plant in the Thirteenth ward. The first act was to open a Sunday school in the unfinished district school-house No. 18 on

MEMORIAL PRESBYTERIAN CHURCH, ROCHESTER.

North and Draper streets, June 13, 1869, under the superintendence of one of their elders, Truman A. Newton. The pressing needs to use the whole building for school purposes necessitated the vacating of the room occupied by the Sunday school and it was disbanded.

Soon after this the Brick Church Sunday school authorized Louis Chapin and Edwin T. Huntington to purchase of Hiram Davis the lot at the corner of Hudson and Wilson streets for the purposes of a chapel at a cost of $2,600.

During this year the General Assemblies of the "old" and "new school" had at their May meetings in New York arranged preliminaries for their reunion, which was consummated at Pittsburgh, Pa., Nov. 12, 1869.

Profoundly grateful to Almighty God for the restoration and return to union of the two bodies, the Brick Church resolved on making a memorial offering, in pursuance of which they, in the early part of 1870, raised by subscription a little more than $7,500 to erect a chapel on the lot bought by their Sunday school the fall before. The corner-stone of the chapel was laid by appropriate ceremonies June 20, 1870, and the edifice was dedicated Nov. 20, 1870, the lot and building having cost about $11,000.

Nov. 27, 1870, the Sunday school was reorganized under the superintendence of Dwight H. Wetmore. On account of Mr. Wetmore's failing health his brother, Lansing G. Wetmore, succeeded him as superintendent in the fall of 1871.

Jan. 1, 1871, the Rev. Gavin L. Hamilton (who had been stated supply over the Presbyterian Church at Pittsford) commenced his ministration in this chapel.

Jan. 19, 1872, a commission appointed by Presbytery organized the Memorial Church, consisting of the following 54 members: James Critchell, Mrs. Ann Critchell, Isaac De Ridder, Mrs. Maria De Ridder, Mrs. Kate Ellwanger, James Fraser, Mrs. Justina Fraser, Hanna Fraser, Charlotte

Elizabeth Fraser, Mrs. Jannette L. O. Harrison, Edward Lockley, Mrs. Winnefred Lockley, John Manley, Mrs. Catharine Manley, Catharine Margaret Manley, Mary Jane Manley, Mrs. Alice Moore, Abraham Orange, Mrs. Susanna Orange, Mrs. Maria Vanderberg, Mrs. Charlotte Vanvechten, Ida R. Vanvechten, Josiah Warren, Mrs. Elizabeth M. Warren, Ann Wright, George G. Becker, David Ely, M. D., Mrs. Angeline Ely, Mrs. Catharine A. Hamilton, Mrs. Lasena Owens, David Rudman, Mrs. Eliza Rudman, Mrs. Jane Southgate, Maria A. Southgate, Jennie Southgate, Clara Southgate, Mary Williams, being received by letter, and Cornelius Brown, Mrs. Joanna Brown, Mrs. Ellen S. Dickinson, Anna Jane Hartley, Gertrude H. Hiddrink, Mrs. Mary Jane Loebs, Mrs. Margaret A. McCauley, Geo. Nicholson, Mrs. Mary Nicholson, Jacob Orange, Nathan Picot, Mrs. Anna Picot, Sarah J. Picot, Henry G. Picot, Jessie Simpson, Sarah S. Waker and John C. Van De Walle being received by confession.

George H. Nicholson and Abram Orange were elected ruling elders.

Rev. Gavin L. Hamilton acted as stated supply of the church, closing his labors December, 1874.

For nearly two years the church was without pastor or stated supply, though preaching services were held every Sunday. The shepherdless flock became scattered and discouraged. Some of the city pastors and friends of the enterprise thought it so difficult a field to cultivate as not to warrant its continuance as a church organization, but advised that it disband and maintain only a preaching station and Sunday school. Some members took letters, others moved away until they had hardly fifty members remaining.

Oct. 26, 1875, the society voted to extend a call to the Rev. Charles P. Coit, then laboring in Baltimore, Md., to become their pastor. Mr. Coit responded to the call and began his labors on Sunday, Nov. 21, 1875. The Presbytery approved of the act and installed him as pastor Jan. 2, 1876. James B. Shaw, D. D., preached the sermon, Rev. Corlis B. Gardner gave the charge to the pastor, Pres. Martin B. Anderson, LL. D., gave the charge to the people, Herbert W. Morris, D. D., offered the installing prayer and Rev. Charles E. Furman presided as moderator. Mr. Coit continues to be pastor.

Dec. 27, 1876, the society elected their first board of trustees, consisting of Henry H. Babcock, Aaron P. Lawrence, Albert C. Irving, Henry J. Tailler [Taillie], George H. Rudman and Charles Barnes.

Jan. 1, 1879, the session voted that thereafter the hour for their Sunday school to assemble should be changed from 3 o'clock p. m. to 12 at noon.

July 22, 1881, the trustees of the Brick Church deeded the chapel and its lot to the trustees of the Memorial Church. During this year the church in the exercise of great faith in God, in the exercise of unusual self-denial, by the aid of outside friends mostly of the Brick Church, enlarged the chapel to a church. Its new corner-stone was laid July 26, 1881, and the enlarged edifice was re-dedicated free of debt Dec. 18, 1881. The cost of the enlargement was about $9,500. Its main audience-room, shaped like an Egyptian cross, has 106 pews with a seating capacity of 500 persons. The prayer-room back of the pulpit can be opened by sliding doors and add room for seating 250 more.

The church became self-supporting in Nov., 1882. In the spring of 1885 a pipe-organ was purchased and put in the church. In the fall of 1888 a choir loft was built in its north transept.

The present elders are Edward W. Warner, Geo. H. Rudman, David C. Rudman, William F. Smith and Gottleib W. Hauert. They adhere to the rotation plan.

The present trustees are Chas. R. Barber, Wm. Magrain, Albert E. May, David C. Rudman, Geo. H. Rudman, Wilber F. Smith and Nelson A. Weigand. The following organizations exist in the church: A Woman's Missionary Society, a Ladies' Parish Aid Society, Temperance Society and Young People's Society of Christian Endeavor, all in vigorous condition. The society depends solely on voluntary offerings of its members for financial support, discarding fairs, festivals, suppers and the like. The services of Evangelists are never sought. Special nightly meetings are held each year beginning with the week of prayer and continued two or three weeks. The present membership of the church, Dec. 1, 1888, is 334, that of the Sunday school is 510.

ROCHESTER NORTH.

The North Presbyterian Church is an outgrowth of the North Mission Sunday school, which was organized in Number 7 Schoolhouse, April 18, 1869, with William A. Hubbard as its superintendent. It was held in this schoolhouse about five years. A chapel was built by the Central Church at the corner of Fulton avenue and Locust street, which was dedicated Aug. 23, 1874. Addresses were made on the occasion by Samuel M. Campbell, D. D., Rev. J. Lovejoy Robertson, Rev. George Patton, and elders George W. Parsons and William A. Hubbard.

The school continued as a mission until the time seemed to be ripe for a church organization. Accordingly in the fall of 1883, Rev. Peter Lindsay, of Seneca Falls, was employed to work up the field. He began his labors Dec. 16, 1883, and God's blessing followed his efforts so that on the 12th of February, 1884, the North Church was organized with seventy members, thirty-one of which were on the confession of their faith, and thirty-nine on certificates. Their names are as follows: Lina E. Aldrich, Isaac Bower, Sophia Bower, Theodore D. Beckwith, Aramenta Beckwith,

Cora M. Beckwith, Robert H. Byers, Kate Byers, Mathew T. Byers, Margaret Byers, Charlotte Blackwell, Sarah Blackwell, Harriet L. Blackwell, Ellen E. Blackwell, Altha M. Benton, Adelia M. Brady, William J. Boyce, Julia C. Brown, Emma L. Butler, Frederick W. Clark, Elizabeth Clark, Edgar Clark, Jennie Clark, Anna M. Craig, Margaret Craig, William J. Craig, Ida E. Craig, Maggie Craig, Frank H. Clement, Louisa S. Clement, Flora Ann Chapman, George C. Cross, George W. Davidson, Lizzie Davidson, Harriet M. Davidson, Clara Daningburg, Phebe Fuller, Mary A. Griffing, Charles T. Griffing, Mrs. M. L. Harrison, Hiram T. Jones, Andrew Jamison, Ida Kincade, Cornelia R. Lindsay, Katie A. Luitweller, Georgianna Martin, Eliza Martin, Sarah Martin, Frances Martin, James B. McLelland, Margaret McLelland, Mary B. McLelland, Lizzie McLelland, Alfred Marsh, Esther A. Marsh, James Mets, Alfred Porter, Carrie Porter, E. Stanley Race, Jennie Race, Degarmo G. Robbins, Frank J. Shields, Marion Shields, Carrie Spear, Ida A. Sanford, Frederick R. Taylor, Josephine Taylor, Amy Taylor, Daniel Weeks, Frederick W. Zoller.

The following elders were elected and ordained: Isaac Bower, Frank H. Clement and George W. Davidson. On this occasion the Presbytery of Rochester donated to this society the bell that had come into their possession by the dissolving of the Penfield Presbyterian society.

This mission was under the care of the Central Church, which gave through the Board of Home Missions, $400 towards its support. But such was its growth in numbers and wealth that it has been self-supporting since its organization. The present elders are Frank H. Clement, Frank J. Shields, George W. Davidson and Hiram T. Jones.

"The North Presbyterian Church Society," was organized Jan. 4, 1884, and David C. Rumsey, William A.

Hubbard, George W. Davidson, Mathew T. Byers, Frank J. Shields and Levi S. Sherwood were elected trustees.

Oct. 9, 1886, the trustees of the Central Church deeded the chapel and lot to the North Presbyterian Church. The names of the present trustees are Irving Rouse, William B. Jones, M. D., John A. Seel, Mathew T. Byers, E. Stanley Race and Albert Bennett.

The corner stone of the new church was laid Sept. 10, 1888. Addresses were made by the following ministers: Rev. Corliss B. Gardner, Rev. Charles P. Coit, Rev. Edward Bristol, Rev. William R. Taylor, Rev. George E. Soper, Rev. Alfred J. Hutton and Rev. James S. Root. Henry H. Stebbins, D. D., laid the corner stone and offered prayer. All money necessary for the completion of the church has been pledged and it is expected that the church will be dedicated free of debt about the first of next May.

The present and only pastor was installed May 14, 1885. Rev. Edward Bristol, moderator of Presbytery, presided. The exercises were: opening prayer by Rev. Corliss B. Gardner; sermon by Rev. Charles E. Robinson, D. D.; charge to the people by Rev. J. Edward Close; charge to the pastor by Rev. Theodore W. Hopkins; installation prayer by Rev. George Patton.

The young people have a Society of Christian Endeavor, organized in March, 1884. The boys and girls have a Mission Band, organized in Oct., 1885. The Woman's Missionary Society was organized April —, 1886.

During the five years existence of the church it has received in all, 398 members, 203 on confession, and 195 on certificates. The present membership is 322. The church has observed 31 communion seasons, and at each has received additions both by confession and certificates. The Sunday school membership is about 450.

ROCHESTER EMMANUEL.

Emmanuel Presbyterian Church was organized May 2, 1887, with the following persons as members: Thurlow W. Abell, Mrs. Mary L. Abell, David H. Abell, Richard S. Abell, Mrs. Charlotte W. Abell, Arthur Y. Alling, Thomas Ashton, Mrs. Margaret Ashton, Herbert W. Brower, Mrs. Maggie L. Bradley, Eva L. Bradley, Mrs. Hattie A. Birdsell, Mrs. Alice W. Durgin, Mrs. Harriet DeFries, Lottie DeFries, Mrs. Addie W. Evans, Minnie Emery, Estella M. Forward, James Glasgow, Mrs. Margaret Ann Glasgow, Alice Hall, James P. Henry, Mrs. Eliza Henry, Mary Henry, Eliza M. Henry, John W. Hertel, Mrs. Elizabeth Hertel, Anna Henderson, Mary Jane Henderson, Mrs. Harriet Hogg, Anna W. Harris, Florence E. Hanvey, Mrs. Marion Hixon, Lillian Johnston, Henry Kingdon, Mrs. Sophronia Kingdon, Mrs. Pauline Keily, George Lockwood, Mrs. Eliza Ann Lockwood, Leon D. Lewis, Dora Miller, Lillian Mallory, Francis Noye, Mrs. Mary E. Noye, Myrtie S. Noye, Mrs. Mary J. Patterson, Homer P. Reed, Mrs. Sarah L. Reed, Maie Reed, George Reed, Mrs. Mary A. Rogers, Edwin F. Shutt, Mrs. Elizabeth A. Shutt, George A. Skinner, Mrs. Jessie Skinner, William H. Shewman, Mrs. Elizabeth Shewman, George H. Shewman, Mrs. Hattie Shewman, Mrs. Barbara Shewman, Lillie Shewman, Mrs. Isabel T. Simpson, Mrs. Fanny M. Taylor, George A. Tanner, Mrs. Catharine C. T. Tanner, Mrs. Violetta B. White and Minnie Webb.

Francis Noye and Edwin E. Shutt were then elected elders of the church, and were ordained by the moderator of Presbytery, Rev. Peter Lindsay.

The present Elders are, Francis Noye, Edwin E. Shutt, Henry Kingdon,[*] George Lockwood, Frank F. Dow, M. D., and George A. Tanner.

[*]Died Jan., 1889.

The present deacons are Arthur Y. Alling, and John W. Hertel. Elders and deacons are elected for limited terms.

The first and present pastor, Rev. James S. Root, was called May 24, 1887; began his ministrations to them July 10, 1887, and was installed June 26, 1888.

The following statement gives some of the facts that preceded the organization of this church:

At the call of the Presbyterian Alliance of Rochester (now unfortunately extinct) a few persons, principally from the First Presbyterian Church, assembled at the house of Ezra Taylor, corner of Plymouth avenue and Strong street, on the afternoon of Sunday, June 8, 1873, for the purpose of organizing a Sunday school. Rev. J. Lovejoy Robertson presided and George E. Boardman was elected superintendent. More than forty adults and thirty children were present. Nine of the adults engaged at once as teachers. A committee was appointed to secure a room to meet in, and visit the neighborhood and invite the attendance of such children as were not connected with other Sunday schools. On the next Sunday the committee reported that they had secured the basement of a lager beer saloon on the corner of Plymouth and Frost avenues. It was small, damp, and badly ventilated. To this place "Bethany Sunday School" adjourned for its first session. Sixty-nine scholars being present were organized into thirteen classes. Collections were made at the first meeting. In that year a book case and library were furnished. Thirty-six testaments were distributed as reward for attendance and lessons.

From this place the school moved to the Friends' meeting house on Hubbell Park. Here also it prospered. It being necessary to have more permanent provision made, Oscar Craig, Esq., secured funds to erect a building on the site now occupied by Emmanuel Church, Mr. Edwin A. Frost having donated one-half the value of the site. In the last days of 1874, 15 officers and teachers, and 169 scholars took possession of and dedicated the new building, which was 70 feet long by 36 feet wide, under the name "Emmanuel Mission Sunday School," as suggested by Mrs. Oscar Craig.

For the next thirteen years the school continued to grow till their roll of scholars exceeded 500, and the attendance at times 450. With such prosperity it was apparent that an advance movement must be made. Preaching services began in 1886. The school had outgrown the room and through the liberality of friends, mostly of the First Church, a large annex, 40 ft. long and 36 ft. wide, was erected on the east side of the original building, at a cost of $3000.

Rev. Thomas Morey Hodgman was engaged by the Session of the First Church for the preaching services, and under the Session's direction, through Elder David M. Hough, the superintendent, and Arthur Y. Alling, the assistant superintendent, aided by preacher Hodgman, steps were taken to organize a church.

It should also be added here, that had not this the "mother church" carefully cared for the interests of this Sunday school, Emmanuel Church would never have had an existence.

A Woman's Missionary Society, auxiliary to the Woman's Presbyterial Society of Rochester Presbytery, was organized Sept. 11, 1887. The first year's offerings for Home and Foreign Missions amounted to $25. They continue to hold monthly meetings.

The Emmanuel Aid Society was organized Nov. 1, 1887.

The Young Peoples' Society of Christian Endeavor was organized February 16, 1888.

Previous to July, 1888, the Sunday school was held at 3 o'clock. It was therefore largely a union school. At the change to 12 o'clock there was a membership of 162, which has now increased to nearly 300.

The Emmanuel Church Society of Rochester was organized May 27, 1887. Its first trustees were Arthur Y. Alling,

Homer B. Reed, George A. Skinner, William H. Shewman, George H. Hixon and Charles E. White. The present trustees are Arthur Y. Alling, William H. Shewman, George A. Skinner, Homer B. Reed, George H. Hixon and George W. Merick.

Since the organization of the church eighty-eight have been added to it. New members have been received at every communion service. Its present membership is 140.

When "Bethany Sunday School" was opened in 1873, a large portion of the 8th ward was uncultivated land. Its population was about 7,000 with but three churches. Now the population exceeds 15,000 and there are eight churches in the ward, and its growth is still rapid. In the near future this church is likely to be not only self-sustaining, but a contributor to the support of others.

RUSH.

The first religious society in Rush was formed by a colony of Baptists about 1804. The origin and date of the Presbyterian Church at Rush are among the faded memories of the past. I have been unable to find any printed data of such, and the records of the church were lost by fire about 1843.

This church is referred to in the minutes of Ontario Presbytery, as early as June 16, 1818, and continued to be represented in their meetings until August 26, 1828, nearly five years after being set off to Rochester Presbytery. The first mention of the church in the Rochester minutes is, February 5, 1829, with twelve members. After that, it was represented in the meetings of the Presbytery as late as 1840, when a committee was appointed to visit the church and try to arouse it to more efficiency. Their number became diminished by removals to other towns, until the last of them were finally received to the Presbyterian Church at Honeoye Falls, March 5, 1843. The records of this latter church bearing said date, read as follows. "Session met. All the members present. Opened with prayer. The following persons from the 'Presbyterian Church of Rush' made application for admission to the church: Luther Campbell, Eunice Campbell, Simeon Rowley, Lucy Rowley. They were without letters, and gave as a reason that the church had no officers, except a clerk, Mr. Campbell, one of the applicants, and that even the church records were lost, having recently perished in the flames which consumed the house of Mr. Campbell. They requested to be received on our knowledge of their having long been members of the Presbyterian Church of Rush, or upon their mutual testimony to the fact of membership." "They were accordingly received." This is definite as to the end of the Rush church.

In 1831, the church consisted of 11 members; in 1823, of 23 members. It appears that Rev. Messrs. Eric Prince, Abner Benedict, Chauncey Cook and Conrad Ten Eyck, have been stated supplies to the church, under the patronage of the American Home Missionary Society, and also, that in 1829, Rev. George G. Sill, preached one-third of his time at Rush, and two-thirds at Honeoye Falls, under the General Assembly's Board of Home Missions.*

---

*Compiled from "Half Century of the Presbytery of Rochester"; Hotchkin's History of Western New York, and Honeoye Falls Church records.

THE UNITED CONGREGATION OF DANSVILLE AND SPARTA.

The origin of Presbyterianism in the town of Sparta is involved in considerable obscurity on account of the loss by fire of all the papers which could have given information on the subject.

Its existence, however, may be safely dated to the time when the first settlers entered this township, which then included what is known as the towns of Sparta, West Sparta, Groveland, Dansville and part of Mount Morris.

The first settlement appears to have been at a place called Williamsburgh, now in the town of Groveland, where certain Presbyterian families made choice of a home about the year 1795.

They were supplied with sermons occasionally by the Rev. Daniel Thatcher, the Rev. John Lindsley and others, the persons named being missionaries under the care of the General Assembly.

There is no record of any church having been organized in Williamsburgh, but the names of certain elders are given as having been connected with the worship of God in that place, and the Lord's supper must have been dispensed among the settlers, who had previously been in the Presbyterian connection, as early as the year 1800.

The settlement at Williamsburgh having been broken up, its component elements afterward constituted the churches of Groveland and Sparta.

Not far from the time that Williamsburgh was occupied, a settlement was also formed near to the place, where the Second Church of Sparta now stands.

The settlers having been principally members of the Church of Christ in Pennsylvania, from whence they emigrated, and many of them being of Scotch or Scotch-Irish origin, their first concern appears to have been, after choosing their location, to have the ordinances of religion regularly dispensed.

Various persons are spoken of as having occasionally preached to them, but for many years, they had no settled ministry.

The Rev. Andrew Gray of the Dutch Reformed church, who moved to Alleghany in 1795, took charge of the churches of Almond, Angelica and Dansville, all in connection with that denomination.

His call was dated November, 1803, and was sustained by the classis of New Brunswick in September of the same year. He continued his labors in that connection till the year 1807.

The Church of Dansville bore the name of The United Congregation of Dansville and Sparta (or Ontario and Steuben) at that time, and included the town of Sparta, which covered ground within the counties of Steuben and Ontario; as Livingston county had not then been formed.

. About the year 1804–05, the above United Congregation of Dansville and Sparta received valuable additions from the settlement at Williamsburgh, which had been discontinued; and as a consequence the church appears to have formed a connection with the Presbyterian denomination.

This is supposed to have been in the year 1806, but no record of the exact date is extant.

In the year 1807, June 18th, there is a call extant addressed to the Rev. Andrew Gray from the above society, which states that " they having changed their situation from under the direction of the Dutch Reformed Body, and having cast themselves under the jurisdiction of the General

Assembly of Divines, they had chosen themselves a body of trustees according to law, etc."

This call stipulates that Mr. Gray shall leave the Dutch Reformed body, and connect himself with the Presbyterian church.

Mr. Gray did not accept this call, having been appointed about the close of this year, or the beginning of 1808, by a Missionary Society in New York City, to become a missionary among the Tuscarora Indians.

From this time the "United Congregation," as it was called, appears to have depended on Missionaries of the General Assembly and stated supplies for the ordinances of religion for a number of years.

They gave an invitation to a young man of the name of Wm. Glasgow, who had preached to their great acceptance to become their pastor, but were again disappointed.

The Rev. Andrew Gray returned from the Lines in 1814, having been burned out by the British during the war, and many of his former friends wished him to resume his ministerial labors among them, which he accordingly did.

But at that time the Rev. Silas Pratt was officiating as a stated supply, and the consequence was that the church became divided.

The latter principally occupied the field where the Second Church now stands and the village of Dansville; while the former preached at Haven's Corners where the First Church of Sparta now stands, and at the Gully schoolhouse in the town of Groveland.

The present church edifice of Second Sparta was built about the year 1810, but was afterwards renovated and greatly improved in 1850.

The united congregation decided where its location should be fixed by casting lots.

But as Dansville began to increase in population the members of the church residing in and around that village decided to have a separate organization.

This took place in the year 1825, when the Rev. Silas Pratt was the officiating minister. The separate existence of Dansville church appears to have interfered with the prosperity of the congregation in Sparta to such a degree, that measures were taken to change the site to Haven's Corners, and forming a union with those worshipping there, and those worshipping at the Gully schoolhouse. A meeting to effect this object took place April 28th, 1827, which stated that on account of the weakened state of the church by the departure of some of the members to Dansville, and considering that it would be highly injurious to join the church there they resolved in the future to meet at "Haven's Corners."

SPARTA FIRST.

The organization of the first church at that place, which is now known as the First Church of Sparta, took place January 19th, 1828. Its ecclesiastical origin in connection with the General Assembly, however, must be assigned to a period prior to the date of the call to Mr. Gray, and probably took place in 1806. As already stated, measures were then taken to build the present house of worship, and a deed of the ground on which it stands was obtained, bearing date Feb. 19th, 1829.

A substantial and commodious building was erected in the course of the year, and William W. McNair, Richard W. Parkinson, William D. McNair, Samuel M. Mann, James McNair and John Wood were elected by the congregation its first board of trustees.

Messrs. William W. McNair, William D. McNair, Isaac Bean and James Scott were its first elders.

The result of this measure was the amalgamation of the two parties known as those who adhered to Mr. Gray and Mr. Pratt.

This was consummated at a meeting of the Presbytery of Ontario, held in Sparta, April 10th, 1830.

The Rev. Silas Pratt continued to sign the minutes of session till Jan. 24th, 1829.

The Rev. F. S. Gaylord then became stated supply, and was succeeded by the Rev. Amos P. Brown, who signed the first minutes of session, Sept. 11th, 1830.

He was installed pastor, Aug. 24th, 1831, and during his ministry the church appears to have had a time of great awakening, and many were added to the roll of communicants.

He was dismissed Jan. 22nd, 1834, "on account of ill-health," and was succeeded by the Rev. Lemuel Hall, in 1837.

March the 5th, the Rev. William H. Snyder is spoken of in the record as pastor, but is believed to have been only stated supply for a number of months.

During his ministry the church resolved to join the O. S. General Assembly. The meeting at which this was determined bears date, August 20th, 1837.

The Ontario Presbytery met at Union Corners, Aug. 23rd, 1837, and in reviewing the session's minutes, took exception to them on four grounds, and especially for this resolution to become "O. S."

The fourth exception states that "the Presbytery feel bound to express their disapprobation, regarding as they do the leading measures of the Assembly, as being unconstitutional, unrighteous, and consequently null and void."

The Rev. Alfred White signs as "Moderator of Session," Feb. 18th, 1838, at which meeting it was resolved to apply for admission to the Presbytery of Susquehanna. to meet at Bath, Steuben Co., Feb. 20th. 1838.

Mr. White officiated as stated supply for about six months, when the congregation invited, first, the Rev. George Morris, and afterwards, the Rev. Dr. Hugh Mair to become their pastor, but neither of them accepted the invitation. The Rev. Thomas Aitken was then called April 23rd, 1839, and was installed pastor, Aug. 15th, 1840, his installation having been deferred to that date on account of the Assembly's rule respecting foreign ministers.

In April, 1855, by action of Presbytery the two congregations of First and Second Sparta were united, not as one church, but as two separate organizations under the pastoral care of the Rev. Thomas Aitken, which relation was sustained until Sept. 18th, 1882, when, at his own request it was annulled, and he was made "Pastor Emeritus" of these two churches, and was succeeded in May, 1883, by Rev. Evan R. Evans, who served the two organizations as stated supply until January, 1886.

In May of the same year, Robert K. Wick, a licentiate of the Presbytery of New York, began a service with the First and Second churches of Sparta as stated supply, and served in that capacity until Sept. 30th of the same year, when he was ordained and installed pastor of the two organizations.

A Sabbath school has been connected with the church from its earliest years.

A Ladies' organization is also connected with the church, the germs of which began in 1874; now called the "Society for Church Work," and as such was organized June 24th, 1887.

The church has its representatives in the foreign field, two of its members, the Rev. Frank P. Gilman, and his wife, Marion McNair Gilman, who are engaged in missionary work among the people of Hainan.

It elects its elders for life; and at present Mr. James S. Gilman, Chas. B. McNair and Edward L. McFetridge compose its session, while Messrs. James S. Gilman, Edward

L. McFetridge, Samuel Wambold, Edward W. Mann, John Logan and William Henry Havens comprise its board of trustees.

SPARTA SECOND.

The Second Presbyterian Church of Sparta was organized on the fourth day of May, 1848, by a committee appointed by the Presbytery of Steuben, composed of Rev. Jesse Edwards, Rev. Richard Kay and Elder Peter Titsworth.

The following persons presented letters of dismission from the First Presbyterian Church of Sparta: James McNair, Joseph Knappenburgh, David McNair, Hugh T. McNair, Phoebe Jane McNair, Samuel McNair, Margaret K. McNair, William D. McNair, Jane McNair, Mrs. Jane McNair, Jacob Knappenburgh, John W. McNair, Catharine Knappenburgh, Nancy Culbertson, Anne McNair, Frances McNair and Ann Shafer.

Also letters of dismission from the First Presbyterian Church of Dansville were presented by James Sturgeon, Samuel Sturgeon, Mary Ann Sturgeon and Margaret McNair.

James McNair and William D. McNair, who had held office as ruling elders in the First Presbyterian Church of Sparta, Samuel Sturgeon, who had held the same office in the First Presbyterian Church of Dansville, and Hugh T. McNair were duly elected and ordained as elders.

Rev. Jesse Edwards, by appointment of Presbytery, became stated supply of the new church and continued in that relation for the two following years.

In the autumn of 1850, Rev. James E. Miller was elected and installed as pastor, which office he held until April, 1854. One year later Rev. Thomas Aitken, upon the invitation of the church and with the consent of the Presbytery, assumed the pastorate in connection with that of the First Church of Sparta. During the long period of 27 years thereafter he served the Master in that capacity with great fidelity and acceptance until, through the increasing infirmities of age, he was obliged to relinquish the trust, and by the action of Presbytery, in September, 1882, was honorably retired and his name placed upon the list of pastors emeritus. Two years later he was called to his reward on high.

Rev. Evan R. Evans occupied the pulpits of the two churches, as stated supply from May, 1883, to January, 1886. Considerable accessions to the membership took place under his ministry.

In May of the same year the services of Robert K. Wick, a licentiate of the Presbytery of New York, were secured, and in August following, by a vote of the two congregations, he was elected pastor, and a month later was ordained and installed. He has very acceptably and with gratifying results continued his labors to the present time. The elders now in office are Hugh T. McNair, David McNair and Samuel Alexander. The office is permanent in this church.

A Sabbath school, with little intermission, has been in operation since the date of the organization of the church.

A Woman's Missionary Society was organized in 1872, and has been successfully sustained, as has also a Children's Mission Band organized at a later date. These societies have paid into the treasuries of the Mission Boards of the church or sent directly in the form of supplies to Home Missionaries an aggregate of $2,179.86.

The church building, which came by inheritance, as it were, to the church at the time of its organization, was erected in 1809, and was said to have been the second church structure put up in the state west of Cayuga bridge, which (latter) was an old time land mark.

It was hoary with age and much dilapidated, but greatly prized on account of the hallowed memories of former years, and the people entered heartily into the work of renovation. An outlay of about one thousand dollars transformed it from a place fit only for the owls and the bats into a decent and commodious sanctuary and as such it was duly dedicated to the worship of Almighty God in the autumn of 1852.

The following persons composed the first Board of Trustees: John Culbertson, Hugh T. McNair, Samuel Sturgeon, John W. McNair, Jacob Knappenburgh and David McNair.

The members of the board now holding office are J. A. Knappenburgh, C. F. McNair, Warren M. McNair, J. A. Culbertson, William G. Carney and William Driesbach.

The church is situated in a rural district, about three miles north of Dansville, and has suffered in past years from the depleting effects of change of inhabitants, which is so common in all the older parts of the country. The present membership is sixty-three.

Not a few of those who have gone out from it are usefully engaged in the Lord's work elsewhere. One of these, Rev. Theodore M. McNair, is now a missionary in the Empire of Japan.

The ordinances of the Gospel have been maintained with an encouraging degree of success, and with results which clearly indicate the approval of the Master and give promise of richer fruitage in the years to come.

SPRINGWATER.

This church, originally Congregational, was organized by Rev. Lyman Barrett, of Naples, Feb. 10, 1821, who preached from Matt. 5:16. The church was formed with twelve members, viz: Alpheus Phelps, Alfred Phelps, Jotham Dyre, Daniel Ward, Nathaniel Adams, Lucinda Ford, Esther

Flanders, Mercy Adams, Clarissa Phelps, Nancy Brown, Malinda Goot and Mary Whalen.

The number who have belonged to the church up to the present time (1889) is 200. The largest number at any one time was 46. This was 1844.

The church had no regular preaching for nine years after its organization, but was supplied occasionally by Rev. Lyman Barrett, Rev. Warren Day and other neighboring ministers.

In 1830 Rev. James Cohoon was engaged as stated supply and remained about three years. Rev. E. Brunson followed and supplied the pulpit during part of the year 1834. Rev. S. Thompson was stated supply from January, 1836, until March, 1839.

The first settled pastor, Rev. Daniel B. Woods, was ordained and installed Sept. 19, 1839. The sermon was preached by his venerable father, Rev. Dr. Woods, of Andover. His pastorate continued a little less than two years.

Rev. William Hunter, a graduate of Auburn Seminary, commenced labors as stated supply in October, 1841. He was ordained and installed pastor Sept. 25, 1844. The sermon was preached by Rev. R. Hill, of East Bloomfield. Mr. Hunter's health being feeble he resigned his charge in 1865, but preached occasionally as his strength permitted. Having recovered health he complied with a unanimous request of the church and resumed labors as pastor in October, 1868. If the above interim be included he has now (1889) been pastor for over forty-seven years.

Daniel Ward, the first and only deacon, was chosen to that office April 9, 1830, and served the church faithfully.

Nov. 10, 1827, the church voted to change the form of government from Congregational to Presbyterian, and at the same time elected four elders, viz: Jotham Dyre, Daniel Ward, John Slack and Benjamin Boyd. The church was received under the care of Ontario Presbytery, Jan. 16, 1829.

Ten years afterwards, owing to death and removals, the eldership had become extinct. From 1837 to 1870 business was again transacted according to the Congregational form, the church still remaining under the care of Presbytery.

May 8, 1870, Charles Brewer, Christopher Osgood, William Rosenkrans and Samuel A. Howe were ordained as elders, the pastor being assisted in the services by Rev. J. R. Page. Dr. T. D. Conner and Frank S. Grover were set apart to the office of elder, Aug. 5, 1888. Up to the present time the church has had only ten elders. Messrs. Howe, Grover and Conner constitute the present session, T. D. Conner being clerk.

For twenty years the church worshiped in school houses and private dwellings. In 1840 Mr. Jonathan Bassett donated a lot of land for a meeting-house and parsonage. A convenient house of worship, 50 by 36 feet, was built the same year and dedicated Dec. 31.

In 1872 the building was thoroughly repaired at an expense of $2,000. It was re-dedicated Feb. 20, 1872. Rev. Dr. Shaw, of Rochester, preached the sermon, and addresses were made by Dr. I. N. Sprague and Rev. Messrs. Dobbin, Burghart, Hibbard, DuBoys, Weed, Page and Jessup. The services were successful in the raising of $1,500 of the $2,000, so that the entire amount was provided. The parsonage was built in 1843.

The first Sabbath school was organized in 1840 by the pastor, Rev. Daniel B. Woods. For several years it was the only school in the town. The school at the church has been continued ever since. Two or three others were kept up at different times in school houses. The one at the "Bell school house" was very prosperous. Most of the large scholars, during a revival, became Christians. In the school now held at the church there are about 60 scholars and seven teachers. Dr. T. D. Conner is superintendent.

When the present pastor commenced his labors in 1841,

there were seven "taverns" in town. Drunkenness was common, but the friends of temperance were united and persevering, and at last through the Divine blessing gained the victory. In the spring of 1875 the town voted "No License" by a majority of 127. The same vote has been repeated every year since, and now for fourteen years there has been no liquor sold in town. The increased prosperity of the place in consequence of the change has been wonderful.

The most general and powerful revival was in 1843. In the early months of that year there was a general awakening in all the churches. The pastor had help from Rev. Charles Morgan, of Geneseo, and Rev. D. M. Merritt, of Dansville. As fruit of the revival twenty-five united with the church.

In 1856 there was another general religious awakening throughout the town. Union meetings were held and fourteen members were added to the church.

Union meetings were again held in the winter of 1869–1870. A large number professed conversion but the additions to the churches were small. Only eight joined this church. Other seasons of religious interest have been enjoyed at different times.

This church has never had more than a "little strength." It commenced with few members and little wealth, and has never been other than one of the "feeble" churches. But through the divine blessing it has held on its way, and survived unrecorded trials that threatened its very existence. It has been the dear religious home of many who have gone to the "home above," and of some who are still serving the Master in connection with other churches. It is not known that more than one of its members entered the ministry—the Rev. Levi G. March, now the able and beloved pastor of the Presbyterian church of Lewiston, N. Y.

SWEDEN.

What is now the Presbyterian Church of Sweden was organized Sept. 5, 1816, under the name and title of "The First Congregational Society of Sweden." There were present, as executive council, Rev. Comfort Williams, of Rochester; Rev. Alanson Darwin, of Riga; Rev. Henry Smith and Rev. Elam Clark, home missionaries; Deacon Levi Ward, of Bergen, and Deacon Davis, Justus Brown and Asahel Finch, of Parma.

The following persons presented themselves for the purpose of being formed into a church, viz: Theda Clark, Abigail Smith, Lydia Lee, Sally Hollister, Lucretia Bennett, Abigail Beedle, Daniel Avery, Elisha Smith, Samuel Blair, Joseph Langdon, Rebecca Cone, Anna Brown, Artemas Lyman, Sarah Stickney, Rosanna Avery, Diodate Lord, Silas Judson—total 17.

Daniel Avery was elected the first clerk of the church, Artemas Lyman the first standing moderator, and Diodate Lord and Samuel Castle the first deacons.

The first board of trustees was elected Jan. 26, 1819, and was composed of the following persons, viz: Silas Judson, Silas Parker, Artemas Lyman, Oliver Spencer, Abel Root and John Reed. The original certificate of incorporation was recorded in the county clerk's office of Genesee (Sweden being then in Genesee) on Feb. 4, 1819, in Liber I of Miscellaneous Records, page 293.

For seventeen years from the date of its organization the church was managed on what was known as the "accommodation plan." But in May, 1833, at a regular meeting of the church, it was duly resolved to become a Presbyterian church. Accordingly, Abel Page, Chauncey Staples, Sisson Taylor, Joseph Staples, Samuel V. Way and Daniel J. Avery were elected ruling elders, and Elias D. Wilcox and Oliver Spencer were chosen to serve as deacons, all of whom were ordained to their sacred offices by Rev. Samuel Marsh, on June 9, 1833.

The church, as nearly as can now be ascertained, was served by the following ministers during the years set opposite their names:

Rev. Abraham Foreman, from 1822 to ——.
Rev. David Page, from 1826 to 1829.
Revs. P. Kimball and —— Myers from 1829 to 1830.
Rev. Josiah Pierson, from 1830 to 1833.
Rev. Samuel Marsh, from 1833 to 1834.
Rev. David Johnson, from 1834 to 1839.
Rev. W. M. Benedict, from 1839 to 1841.
Rev. Moses Gillett, from 1841 to 1845.
Rev. Truman C. Hill, from 1845 to 1849.
Rev. William R. Platt, from 1849 to 1855.
Rev. J. L Jones, from 1855 to 1858.
Rev. William Dewey, from 1858 to 1861.
Rev. John C. Taylor, from 1861 to 1865.
Rev. John Cunningham, from 1865 to 1876.
Rev. James Robertson, from 1876 to 1879.
Rev. Emerson G. Wickes, from 1879 to 1884.
Rev. John Mitchell, from 1884 to 1888.

This church has been favored with repeated revivals, of which the following were the most marked: In the winter of 1835-6, under the ministry of Rev. D. Johnson, 35 persons joined on profession of faith. In the spring of 1867, under the ministry of Rev. John Cunningham, and with the assistance of Rev. O. Parker, Evangelist, 41 persons joined, of whom 15 were heads of families. Other similar refreshings, resulting in good fruits, have been repeatedly enjoyed.

Very early in the history of the church, a Sabbath school was established in connection with it, which has been maintained ever since. For many years the church has also had its "Ladies' Missionary Society," which has supported some missionaries and helped to support others. It has likewise two or three Young People's Societies, aiming respectively at some good work.

When the first house of worship was put up is not recorded, but the present church edifice was built in 1845, repaired and remodeled in 1861, and repaired again, after a fire, in 1881. The parsonage was built in 1835, and repaired and improved in 1881.

The ruling elders serve for a term of five years each, and those in office at the present time are Beman B. Roberts, George H. Way, James Mershon, Charles J. White and A. M. White, elders Way and Mershon acting as deacons.

Owing to the gradual extinction of the purely American families and the influx of foreigners in this region of country, the numbers and strength of the congregation have declined accordingly. But faithful and earnest souls still remain in it, and by these the belief is fondly cherished, that this church which has been the object of so much self-denial, fervent zeal, and prayerful interest on the part of those now gone to their reward, will not cease to exist, not at least during the present generation.

TUSCARORA.

This church was first organized in 1839, by Rev. Israel Hammond, as Reformed Dutch.

In the year 1846, it was re-organized as the Second Presbyterian Church of Mount Morris, now Tuscarora, having the following members: Wm. H. Cownover, Jacob Petrie, Peter Van Nest, Garrett Cownover, John Michael, Geo. S. Kershaw, Isaac Van Deventer, William Post, Charity Van Deventer, Juliana Dodge, Susan Kershaw, Permela Powers, Margaret C. Howell, Ida Post, Ann Conklin, Jane Birch,

Elizabeth Van Nest, Catharine Cownover, Ann Van Orsdall, Sarah Van Auker, Mary Milholen, Sarah H. Cownover, Sarah Ann Lashels, Eleanor Howell, Frances I. Howell, Ketura Davis, Catharine C. Michael.

The following persons were ordained, elders and deacons:

Elders. Aaron Cownover, Wm. Howell, James Conklin, Stephen Birch.

Deacons. Wm. N. Hall, Wm. Van Deventer, Aaron Davis.

The church was received under the care of the Presbytery of Ontario, June 2d, 1846.

From the time of the formation of the church till October, 1851, it was under the care and ministrations of the Rev. Peter S. Van Nest, who labors were abundantly blessed, in the edification of the church and the salvation of souls.

During the ministrations of the Rev. Peter S. Van Nest, the relationship of the church was changed from Ontario Presbytery new school, to Wyoming Presbytery old school.

September 2d, 1852, the church issued a call to the Rev. Thomas L. Dewing to become its pastor, and he having accepted the call was duly installed Oct. 20th, 1852, by a Commission of Wyoming Presbytery, Rev. Thomas Aitken preaching the sermon, Rev. Isaac Oakes charging the pastor, and Rev. Mr. Young, the people. He remained one year.

In the year 1852, the church changed its name from the Second Presbyterian Church of Mount Morris to the Presbyterian Church of Tuscarora.

In November, 1833, Rev. Washington D. McKinley commenced his labors with the church as S. S., and remained about eleven years.

During his ministrations, the church enjoyed a fair degree of prosperity, yet no marked awakening characterized its history. Rev. Mr. McKinley resigned his charge in August, 1864, and was succeeded by Rev. Robert W. McCormick in January, 1865, as pastor. He remained with the church till September, 1869, when the pastoral relation was dissolved.

In May, 1870, the church of Tuscarora formed a union with the Presbyterian Church of Union Corners, called the United Church of Tuscarora and Union Corners. Rev. William E. Jones was called to the pastorate of the united church and commenced his labors June 26th, 1870. He ministered to the united church for three years.

In the interim of vacancies, the church has had various supplies for a brief period and in several instances has experienced revivals of more or less interest, and of salutary results.

In 1875, the church severed its connection with the Union Corners church, and called to its pastorate the Rev. Silas McKinney, who ministered to the church about three years, and was succeeded by Rev. John Mitchell, January, 1880, who also ministered for the term of three years, both of them S. S. During Mr. Mitchell's term of service, G. C. Conklin and E. Marsh Petrie were ordained elders.

In 1883, the church extended a call to the Rev. William F. Millikan to become its pastor, and he having accepted the call was installed March 20th, 1883, by a commission of Rochester Presbytery. Rev. J. E. Kittredge, D. D., presided and offered the prayer of installation. Rev. Levi Parsons, D. D., preached the sermon. Rev, J. R. Page, D. D., charged the pastor, and Rev. John Mitchell, the people. Mr. Millikan ministered to the church during two years, when the pastoral relation was dissolved.

October 18th, 1885, an invitation was extended to Rev. T. H. Quigley to minister to the church. The invitation was accepted, and he is at present its stated supply.

Its present board of elders consists of Garret C. Conklin, E. Marsh Petrie, Andrew Johnson and William N. Hall.

For the past few years, the church has suffered by deaths and removals so that its numbers are depleted and its financial resources crippled, yet it has steadily maintained its standing.

All or nearly all its pastors and stated supplies have been instrumental in leading greater or less numbers to Christ. They have without exception rightly divided the word of truth.

The church has long maintained a flourishing Sabbath school.

The house of worship was erected in 1844, and has subsequently been thoroughly repaired and remodelled about the year 1870.

Adjoining the church lot, the society owns a commodious parsonage.

The Sabbath school was organized in February, 1846. Its present superintendent is Mr. Charles Whitenack. The present trustees of the society are Garrett C. Conklin, Charles Whitenack and E. R. Creveling.

UNION CORNERS.

The Presbyterian Church of Union Corners was organized Aug. 21, 1825, by Rev. Elihu Mason with the following nine members: Garret VanWagnen and Mary, his wife, Mrs. Catharine Bogart, Mrs. Catharine Thompson, Abraham Thompson, James O'Brien and Nellie, his wife, James J. Amerman, and Jacob Van Middlesworth. The elders who were then ordained were Garret Van Wagnen, James J. Amerman and Dea. Jacob Van Middlesworth.

The present three elders are Jacob Bergen, Andrew Sedan and Jacob Knappenberg. Jacob Bergen is the only deacon, and these officers are not elected for limited terms.

After the organization no further record appears until

August 6th, 1828, when the Rev. Norris Bull received Catharine Thompson, Archibald Ten Eyck and Eliza, his wife, Philip Thompson and Hannah, his wife, and Hannah G. Thompson.

Sept. 17th, 1828, Rev. N. W. Fisher, moderator, Philip Thompson and Archibald T. Ten Eyck were elected elders.

April 19, 1832, the following elders were elected to the session: Obed Cravath, Calvin E. Clark, Jacob Bergen and Samuel Comstock.

March 5, 1834, the following were chosen as the first trustees: Jabez Hungerford, Stephen Trowbridge, Samuel T. Comstock, Jacob Bergen, Abraham T. Thompson and Gilbert Bogart.

The following is a list of the ministers who have labored with this church:

Rev. Amos P. Brown, 1829–1830.
Rev. Ludovicus Robbins, 1831–1832.
Rev. Leonard Rodgers, 1833–36.
Rev. Leveret Hull, 1837–40.
Rev. Samuel A. Rawson, 1841–42.
Rev. Horatio Norton, 1843–44.
Rev. William Bridgeman, 1844–45.
Rev. William Fithian, 1846–53.
Rev. Norris Barton, 1855–56.
Rev. Timothy Darling, 1857–59.
Rev. Robert W. McCormick, 1865–66.
Rev. Peter S. VanNest, 1867.
Rev. Willis Clark Gaylord, 1868–70.
Rev. William E. Jones, 1870–73.
Rev. James M. Harlow, 1874–75.
Rev. Silas McKinney, 1876–77.
Rev. Burton A. Partridge, 1878–79.
Rev. John Mitchell, 1879–81.
Rev. William F. Millikan, 1882–84.
Rev. Wilmer McNair, 1885.
Rev. Timothy H. Quigley, 1886.

Of the above ministers the Rev. Willis Clark Gaylord was ordained and installed as pastor, Oct. 6, 1868, the Rev. S. M. Campbell, D. D., of Rochester preaching the sermon, from which relation he was released April 1st, 1870, in order that the church might be united with the church in Tuscarora in the choice of a pastor.

Rev. William F. Millikan was installed pastor, March 20, 1883, Rev. Edward Bristol, of Rochester, preaching the sermon, from which relation he was released Jan. 1st, 1885.

The church enjoyed extensive revivals during the ministries of Rev. L. Hull, Rev. W. C. Gaylord and Rev. B. A. Partridge. The latter, being a Methodist minister was instrumental in connection with the revival, in forming a Methodist church about 1879, which movement very much weakened the Presbyterian.

The present house of worship was built in 1835, but was never dedicated until 1880, at which time it was very thoroughly repaired.

The present trustees are Jacob Knappenberg, William J. Slaight and Sherman Strivings.

Jacob Bergen was born Jan. 11, 1803, united with this church, April 5, 1832, elected elder, April 19, 1832, and is the only one living, June, 1888, who contributed of his substance for the erection of said church.

Mrs. Cynthia Sedam, a sister of Jacob Bergen, was born June 17, 1798, and united with this church, April 4, 1830. She is still living and attends church occasionally.

The church has been closed for about two years with but little prospect that services will be resumed.

It was received under the care of Presbytery of Ontario, Aug. 23, 1825, and followed the same in its union with the present Presbytery of Rochester, reporting in 1888, twenty-eight members. This church is located in the town of West Sparta, only a few rods from the boundary line between it and Mount Morris, and only two miles from Tuscarora.

VICTOR.

The First Presbyterian Church of Victor was originally a Congregational church, organized by Rev. Reuben Parmele, who had previously been settled in Hinesburg, Vermont, and came to Victor in 1798. The society was incorporated Sept. 13, 1798, under the title, "The North Congregational Society in Bloomfield," and the trustees named in the act of incorporation were Jared Boughton (the original purchaser of the town of Victor), Joseph Brace, Jr., and Thomas Hawley. Subsequently, in 1811, the corporate title was changed to "The Northeast Congregational Society in Bloomfield." Victor was set off from the town of Bloomfield in 1812, but the corporate title of the church was not changed thereafter until 1888, when it became "The First Presbyterian Church in Victor." The church was duly constituted, and its first pastor, Mr. Parmele, was installed Feb. 13 and 14, 1799. Nine persons united by letter to form the church, under the authority of an ecclesiastical council of which Rev. Seth Williston was a member. The Victor church is the fifth oldest church organization extant west of Seneca Lake.

Palmyra church organized 1793.
Lima church (Presbyterian) 1795.
Lakeville church (Presbyterian) 1795.
East Bloomfield church (Congregational) 1796.
Victor church (Presbyterian) Sept. 13, 1798.

The first church building in Victor was erected by this society in 1805-6, and was located on the hill north of the center of the village, near the ground where De Nonville repulsed the Senecas in the battle of July 13, 1687. The present church building was erected on ground near the ambuscade, and was dedicated Thursday, Jan. 24, 1833. The building has since been enlarged and improved, while

VICTOR PRESBYTERIAN CHURCH.

adjoining the church on the east is a good parsonage and pleasant grounds.

This church was connected with the "Ontario Association" until that body was merged in the Geneva Presbytery, May 5, 1813. Subsequently, about 1818, it became connected with the "Genesee Consociation." Feb. 8, 1827, the church decided to become Presbyterian, and the minority withdrew and remained a Congregational church. The Presbyterian branch joined the "Ontario Presbytery" at its meeting in Geneseo, Jan. 16, 1828. A compromise and reunion were effected between the two branches, Sept. 20, 1832, and subsequently the church again became Congregational. March 8, 1858, the church finally became Presbyterian, and since then has been known as the "First Presbyterian Church in Victor."

The church, as thus constituted, united with the Rochester Presbytery April 7, 1858. In 1871 it was transferred to the Presbytery of Geneva; but in 1874, upon its own application and the concurrence of the Rochester Presbytery, it was restored to its connection with that body. The Sabbath school was organized by a single class as early as 1814. The Ladies' Missionary Society (Home and Foreign) was organized in April, 1874, previous to which time a Ladies' Aid Society occupied the field.

The children's "Lend a Hand" band was organized in 1885, and the "Sabbath School Missionary Band" in 1888.

The Young People's Sunday Evening Prayer-meeting was re-organized in 1885, and "The Young People's Society of Christian Endeavor" was organized Feb. 21, 1887.

The membership roll of the church since organization aggregates about one thousand. For many years the church has been compelled to fight its way against the blighting influence in the community of a Universalist organization, which has, religiously, been hardly more than a rallying center for infidelity and anti-Christ, with their attendant evils. The peculiar history and condition of this church could never be understood, nor estimated without the above statement. But in all its peculiar trials God has been with His church. The great revival of 1799, which swept over the churches in this region, included Victor. Again in 1816, when 36 were added to its communion, and in 1830-31, 49; in 1833-34, 54 members; in 1837, 39; in 1839, 48; in 1843, 65; in 1853, 26; in 1868, 57; in 1885-87, 134. These were all seasons of precious awakening and large additions to the membership. The church at present has a membership of over 200.

From this church and Sabbath school have gone out into the ministry and missionary work a number of earnest workers, among whom may be mentioned Miss Emeline Dryer, of Chicago, and Miss Marietta Rawson (Mrs. Webster), Bombay, India; Miss Mary Moore, Rev. Dr. D. Henry Palmer, Rev. Frederick W. Palmer, Rev. Clark B. Gillette, Rev. A. S. Bacon, Rev. George F. Swezey and Miss Abbie E. Parks.

Roll of Pastors: Rev. Reuben Parmele, Feb. 14, 1799, to May 5, 1812; Rev. Philander Parmele, 1812-14; Rev. Ebenezer Raymond, 1819-25; Rev. Jabez Spicer, 1826-27; Rev. Daniel Johnson, 1828-31; Rev. Richard Kay, 1832-35; Rev. Jairus Wilcox, 1936-38; Rev. Charles E. Furman, 1838-46; Rev. Charles Merwin, 1846-49; Rev. C. Van H. Powell, 1850-51; Rev. Calvin Waterbury, 1851-55; Rev. Charles C. Carr, 1856; Rev. Job Pierson, D. D., 1856-63; Rev. William H. Webb, D. D., 1863-65; Rev. Gideon P. Nichols, D. D., 1866-69; Rev. Henry T. Miller, 1871-73; Rev. Wm. B. Marsh, 1873-75; Rev. Robert Ennis, 1876-77; Rev. Thomas E. Babb, 1878-83; Rev. Clarence W. Backus, 1884, present incumbent.

Isaac Root was the first deacon.

Elders in 1889: Albert Simonds, D. Henry Osborne,

Stephen J. Tallmadge, Stafford S. Lusk, William A. Higinbotham and C. Lewis Simonds.

Deacons in 1889: Albert Simonds, D. Henry Osborne and James F. Draper, M. D. The office of elder and deacon is permanent.

Board of Trustees in 1889: Marvin A. Wilbur, Orrin S. Bacon, Willis D. Newton, William B. Osborne and John Van Vechten.

WEBSTER.

"The town of Webster was taken from the town of Penfield."

"The settlement of the town must have commenced about the year 1800." The church was originally known as the church of North Penfield and Ontario, and sometimes "Penfield Second Church," and "North Penfield." It was organized August 25, 1825, by Rev. Asa Carpenter then preaching in the Penfield church. Eleven members, taken wholly or in part from the Penfield church, constituted the church at its organization. being Nathaniel Abbott and Hephzibah, his wife; Benjamin Ford, and wife; Stephen Sherman, and wife; John Atwood and Betsey, his wife; Mrs. Naomi Hughes, and two others. The church was received by the Rochester Presbytery, September 20, 1825. In 1826, it reported 16 members; in 1831, 109; in 1834, 143; and in 1847, 128. The first elders were Benjamin Ford and John Atwood, the term of office being permanent. At first worship was held in a schoolhouse or private dwelling. The church struggled hard for an existence and made little progress until 1829. In the early part of this year, Rev. Richard Dunning began his ministry here, and was ordained and installed June 3, 1830. A revival followed, long remembered as the barn revival, because held in a barn. August 5, 1829, the first board of trustees was elected, being William Middleton, William Hicks, Nathaniel Abbott, George Mandeville, Robert Gregg and Samuel Preston. The church was greatly strengthened and encouraged during this year. Mr. Dunning was dismissed February 5, 1835. Under his labors the Holy Spirit was poured out, and as many as 75 or 80 united with the church upon confession. In support of Mr. Dunning the church were aided by the American Home Missionary Society. Rev. Richard DeForest succeeded Mr. Dunning and remained two years. The first church building erected in 1834, was occupied about 30 years. December 8, 1840, the name of the church was changed to the First Presbyterian Church of Webster. After Mr. DeForest the church employed stated supplies until near the end of 1840, when Rev. Lemuel Brooks was called, and having accepted was installed January 5, 1841, and continued in charge, with a brief interruption on account of ill health, for seven years. His first year was marked by a precious revival and 43 were added to the church, 31 on confession. In 1848, and during the ministry of Rev. Joseph R. Mann, a revival added 22 on confession. January 22, 1850, the church voted to join the Presbytery of Buffalo City, and was received by that body the 13th of February following. Rev. Chester Holcomb was in charge of the pulpit in 1854, and a revival followed his labors, 24 being added on confession. Rev. George McCartney supplied the church from 1864-70, and his labors were blessed and the membership increased. Rev. Jonathan Copeland the present incumbent has ministered to this church since January, 1876. While there have been yearly accessions, in 1883, there was an interesting revival and 26 were added on confession ; 11 were received at the April communion in 1888. The church is at present in better condition than at any other period of its history.

During the present pastorate the building has been greatly improved, furnished, and a good lecture room fitted up. A Sabbath school is regularly maintained, the date of its organization being unknown. There is also an active Ladies' Aid Society. Within the last two years have been organized a Ladies' Missionary Society, and a Young People's Missionary Band, and a Children's "Earnest Workers" Missionary Society, all of which are doing excellent work. The present church building was erected in 1853, and cost about $3,000. In 1854, the society purchased a parsonage, which in 1877, was remodeled and improved. There have gone out from this church as ministers, Rev. Horatio Abbott, Rev. Henry McCartney, Rev. Chester Holcomb (a Missionary to India); Rev. William S. Holt (Portland, Oregon) found his wife in this church, and they spent the first years of their married life as missionaries in China.

The following ministers have served this church in the order named: Rev. Asa Carpenter, Rev. Jabez Spicer, Rev. Richard Dunning, 1829-31; Rev. Richard DeForest, two years; Rev. Lemuel Brooks, 1840-47; Rev. James McFadden, 1847; Rev. Joseph R. Mann, 1848; Rev. Augustus Hall, 1850-53; Rev. Chester Holcomb, 1854-57; Rev. Thomas Bellamy, 1857-59; Rev. Robert McMath, 1861; Rev. George McCartney, 1864-70; Rev. William F. Hayward, 1873-75; Rev. Jonathan Copeland, 1876-89, and still in charge.

WHEATLAND.

The early population of the town of Wheatland, like that of the western part of the state generally, was a mixture of New Englanders, Scotts and English. For several years, no house of worship of any kind existed among them; but more or less preaching was had in school-houses and private dwellings. Of the several denominations represented, the first to take steps to organize a religious society were the Presbyterians. These called a public meeting for this end, and on the 30th of December, 1822, a church was duly organized, under the name and title of "The First Presbyterian Society of Wheatland." The organization was effected by a commission from the Presbytery of Rochester, and three months later the infant church was placed under the care of that body.

Those who were thus originally constituted into the church of Wheatland were previously members of the churches of Caledonia, Riga and Chili, their number was eleven, and their names, so far as preserved, are the following: Clark Hall, Betsey Parker Hall, Samuel B. Graves, Betsy Graves, Fayette Cross, Mary Brinsmaid, Truman Smith, Mrs. McIntyre, and three names lost. Total 11.

The first deacon named in the records was Mr. Clark Hall.

The first board of trustees was composed of the following persons: Clark Hall, Abraham Hanford, Isaac J. Lewis, Stephen Warren and Ebenezer Skinner.

The first stated minister was Rev. John Mulligan, whose labors extended over a period of three years; the second was Rev. William F. Carry, who preached about a year; the third, Rev. Abiel Parmele, who remained for two years; and the fourth, Rev. Jacob Hart. The church at this early period, as a matter of course, was weak, and to support these supplies received aid from the Home Missionary Society.

After due consideration, on the 30th of May, 1831, the congregation unanimously decided to build for themselves a house of worship. A suitable lot was selected in the village of Scottsville, for which the sum of $200 was paid. The work of building was at once commenced, and before the setting in of the following winter the house was completed and dedicated to the service of God.

The next year witnessed another advancing step. The society was organized upon what was called the "Plan of Union," but in the year 1832, it became fully equipped, as a Presbyterian church by the election of five ruling elders; these were Isaac J. Lewis, Freeman Edson, Daniel Van Antwerp, John Colt and Philip Garbutt. These were ordained for their sacred office by Rev. Lewis Cheesman, who was at this time the pastor of the church.

Mr. Cheesman began his labors with this church in 1831, but was not installed as pastor till the year 1834, and two years later he resigned. He was an earnest and successful preacher, and won many souls to Christ. As the result of a protracted meeting held during his ministry, more than one hundred were added to the church on profession of faith.

Towards the close of Mr. Cheesman's ministry differences and dissentions arose among the members; and while the church was in this disturbed condition, their difficulties were brought to a crisis by the passing of the "Exscinding Act," by the General Assembly at Philadelphia. In December of that year, 1837, some fifty members, including three ruling elders, withdrew from the church, and formed themselves into a separate church under the name of "The First Presbyterian Church of Scottsville," and attached themselves to the Presbytery of Wyoming. When this new congregation had completed for themselves a house of worship, the

Rev. Mr. Cheesman was called to be their pastor, who labored among them with zeal and success till the year 1842, when he resigned. He was successively followed in the pulpit by Rev. Richard Kay, Rev. H. L. Doolittle and Rev. J. Jones, whose united ministries reached down to the year 1859, when, after a separation of nearly 22 years, the two churches, by mutual concessions became one again.

Returning now to 1837, the year of the unhappy division, we find the pulpit of the First Church of Wheatland occupied by Rev. Eli S. Hunter, D. D., whose pastorate though of but two years' duration, served to add a goodly number to the membership. For the next fifteen months the pulpit was supplied by Rev. Selden Haynes.

In the spring of 1841, Rev. Linus W. Billington became the pastor. His faithful and conciliatory ministration had a happy effect in uniting and strengthening the church. During his third year a quiet work of grace resulted in the hopeful conversion of 23 souls; and during his entire pastorate of seven years, 60 were added to the roll of communicants.

Immediately on the retirement of Mr. Billington, in 1848, Rev. Milton Buttolph took charge of the church. His labors in their very beginning were attended with a gracious refreshing from the presence of the Lord, 33 souls being gathered into the fold in the course of a few weeks, and these mostly from among the young. During his whole ministry of four years, there were received into the church 40 on profession of faith, and 16 by letter.

In the spring of 1853, the church extended a call to the Rev. Dugald D. McColl, which he accepted on condition that they transferred their ecclesiastical relation to the " Presbytery of Rochester City " (old school). His ordination and installation took place, June 21, 1853; and the next year, the congregation built him a substantial parsonage, at an expense of $2,700. Mr McColl was a sound and impressive preacher; in the course of his ministry the church was favored with repeated revivals; and during his entire pastorate, which embraced a period of 17 years, there were added to the church 153 on profession of faith, and 19 by certificate.

In the winter of 1856, this church suffered a great loss, their house of worship together with its organ and all its furniture being destroyed by fire. But the congregation, nothing discouraged, immediately took steps to rebuild, and in less than fifteen months had another and a better house all completed. This cost them about $6,000, and was dedicated, May 7, 1857.

Mr. McColl was dismissed in the spring of 1870, and was succeeded in the fall of the same year by Rev. Thomas A. Weed, who served the church acceptably for nearly twelve years; during which period there were added to the church 82 on profession of faith, and 37 by letters from other churches.

The next pastor of the Wheatland church was Rev. David H. Laverty, who began his labors in January, 1883 and closed them in February, 1885. The ministry of Mr. Laverty was not without its good fruits, but he left the church in somewhat of a divided state, and a number of the congregation about that time withdrew and helped to establish an Episcopal church in the village.

After the dismissal of Mr. Laverty, the pulpit for about six months was supplied by candidates or such preachers as could be obtained for the day. Then came the present incumbent, Rev. G. B. F. Hallock, who began to preach in August, 1885, and was ordained and installed the following October. He soon after had the gratification of welcoming to the communion of the church a large number of converts. The first year of his pastorate, there were added 52 on confession of faith; in the second year, 17; and in the third, 11. And the good work continued to prosper in his hands, till he resigned his charge, which took place Dec. 30, 1889.

A Sabbath school was organized in connection with this church at an early day, but the precise date cannot be given. The present attendance is about 110. The "Mission Band" was formed in 1883; the "Willing Workers," in 1884; and the "Society of Christian Endeavor," in 1885.

The present elders are D. C. McPherson, Myron Miller, Wilson R. Ballentine and George V. Hahn.

The present board of trustees is composed of Thomas Stoke, John C. McVean, Myron Miller and George O. Cox.

INDEX.

	Page.
Aitken, Rev. Thomas,	51, 71, 94, 289, 290
Allen, Rev. Solomon,	33, 135, 193
Association, Ontario,	5
Associations, Presbyterial,	62
Auburn Seminary,	20
Avon,	128
" Central,	134
" Free Church,	76, 131
" Springs Church,	59, 133
Baker, Rev. John E.,	99
Barnard, Rev. John, D. D.,	19, 76, 178, 199
Billington, Rev. Linus W.,	312
Bissel, Josiah, Jr., his conversion,	244
Bonney, Rev. Elijah,	91
Brighton,	59, 135
Brockport,	138
Brodt, Rev. J. H.,	80, 162
Brooks, Rev. Lemuel,	30, 89, 151, 153, 154, 308
Bull, Rev. Norris, D. D.,	13, 34, 156, 177
Bush, Rev. Charles P., D. D.,	29, 33
Bushnell's Basin,	141
Buttolph, Rev. Milton,	87, 312
Caledonia,	143
Candidates,	58, 116
Carthage,	245
Catalogues,	35, 109
Catechetical instruction,	30
Chapin, Louis,	29
Charlotte,	146
Chili,	149
Churches of former Presbytery of Rochester,	29
" " Genesee River Presbytery,	57
" " Ontario Association,	7
" " " Presbytery,	12, 13
" " Rochester City Presbytery,	48
" present Catalogue of,	119

	Page.
Churchville,	152
Clarkson,	155
Clerks,	118
Coit, Rev. J. T.,	46
Concepcion Church, Chili, S. A.,	60
Colleges, graduates from,	71
Conklin, Rev. Luther,	77, 107
" " Oliver P.,	107
Copeland, Rev. Jonathan,	93
Corliss, Rev. A. H.,	73
Curry, Rev. Wm. F.,	34
Dansville,	157
Dansville and Sparta, United Congregation of,	284
Davidson, Rev. E. E.,	63, 189, 260
Deaths, list of,	69–70
DeNoon, Rev. Alexander,	12, 143
Douglass, Rev. Alexander,	82
Dunning, Rev. Richard,	79, 308
Durfee, Rev. Charles S.,	60, 100, 185
Eddy, Rev. D. R.,	86
Education, Ministerial,	19
Elders, Ruling, present Catalogue of,	122
Endeavor, Societies of Christian,	68
Excision, Act of,	31
Finney, Rev. Charles G.,	23, 64, 136, 244, 259
Fitch, Rev. Ebenezer, D. D,	12, 176
Fowlerville,	60, 163
Freeman, Rev. Samuel A., D. D.,	100, 105
Free Masonry,	30
Furman, Rev. Charles E., D. D.,	29, 74, 75, 85
Gardner, Rev. Corliss B.,	104
Gates,	167
Genesco, Churches of,	4, 60, 173–189
Gillette, Rev. Charles,	99
Groveland,	190
Hall, Rev. Albert G., D. D.,	34, 43, 74, 253
Hastings, Dr. Thomas,	27
Henrietta,	193
History of Ontario Presbytery,	22
Histories of Churches,	128
Honeoye Falls,	195
Hotchkin, Rev. James H.,	7, 157, 166
Hough, Rev. Justus,	77

	Page.
Hoyt, Rev. Alexander S.,	104
Hunn, Rev. David L.,	102
Hunter, Rev. Wm.,	71, 293
Incorporation of Presbytery,	68
Indians at Squakie Hill,	20, 208–209
Installation, the first,	5
James, Rev. Wm., D. D.,	34
Kittridge, Rev. Charles,	86
Lane, Rev. Joshua D.,	78
Licensures,	49, 115
Lima,	4, 198
Livonia,	201–4
Lowrie, Rev. Isaac N.,	73
Mason, Rev. Elihu,	301, 208, 211, 220
McCartney, Rev. George,	93
McLaren, Rev. Malcolm N., D. D.,	29, 34, 97, 143
McMath, Rev. Robert,	74
McNeil, Rev. Benjamin,	98
Mendon,	204–7
Millham, Rev. Wm. H.,	105
Ministers present Catalogue of,	119
Missionary Society, A. B. C. F. M.,	27
" " Genesee,	27
" " Presbyterial,	21
" " Woman's,	27, 28, 65
Missionaries, Foreign,	32, 55, 58, 66, 210, 214, 250, 261, 292, 309
" Visits of,	4, 5
Moscow,	208
Mount Morris First,	211–215
" " Second,	215, 298
Newspaper, first in Livingston Co.,	208
Nichols, Rev. James,	45
Nunda,	59, 216
Oakes, Rev. Isaac,	83
Oakland,	59, 220
Ogden,	222
Ordinations by Ontario Presbytery	12–13
" " Rochester "	44
" " " City Presbytery,	57–58
Ossian,	224
Page, Rev. Joseph R., D. D.,	24, 29, 79, 92, 95, 137
Parker, Rev. Joel, D. D.,	34, 204, 251
Parma Centre,	226

	Page.
Patton, Rev. George,	102
Pease, Rev. Calvin, D. D.,	47
Penfield,	49, 61, 229
Penny, Rev. Joseph, D. D.,	33
Pierpont, Rev. Hezekiah B.,	75
Pierson, Rev. Josiah,	33
Piffard,	61, 233
Pittsford,	236
Popular meetings,	63
Presbytery of Albany,	9
" " Bath,	10
" " Genesee River,	50, 57
" " Geneva,	11
" " Niagara,	10
" " Oneida,	9
" " Ontario,	11, 55
" " Rochester,	54
" " Rochester (former),	28, 55
" " " City,	43, 56
Revivals,	63
Robinson, Rev. Charles E., D. D.,	84
Rochester Brick Church,	245
" Calvary "	267
" Central "	256
" Emmanuel "	279
" Fifth "	261
" First "	240
" Free "	254
" Memorial "	272
" North "	276
" North State Street Church,	266
" Third Church,	251
" Westminster Church,	269
Rush,	282
Sabbath Schools,	32, 67
Semi-Centennial at Mount Morris,	24
" " " Rochester,	29
Seminaries, Theol., graduates of,	71
Shaw, Rev. James B., D. D.,	30, 34, 71
Slavery,	23–24
Societies, Voluntary,	25, 30
Sparta First Church,	287
" Second "	290

	Page.
Springwater,	292
Statistics,	31, 64, 66
Stewart, David F.,	84, 144
Stockton, Rev. Benjamin B.,	43, 139, 179
Sweden,	296
Temperance,	22, 23, 67, 196
Thatcher, Rev. Daniel,	4
Treasurers,	118
Trustees of Presbytery,	117
Tuscarora,	59, 298
Union Corners,	59, 301
Victor,	59, 304
Ward, Rev. Ferdinand DeW., D. D.,	29, 83, 97, 179, 183
" " George K.,	81
" Hon Levi A.,	203
Webster,	307
Weed, Rev. Thomas A.,	92
Western New York, early history of,	3
West Greece,	49
Wheatland,	310
Wickes, Rev. Henry,	91
Williams, Rev. Comfort,	28, 33, 296
Wisner, Rev. Wm., D. D.,	34, 246
Woman's Christian Temperance Union,	67

www.ingramcontent.com/pod-product-compliance
Lightning Source LLC
Chambersburg PA
CBHW030313240426

43673CB00040B/1152